DATE DUE

GAYLO

D1115437

the
happy
medium

About the Author

Jodi Livon has worked as a psychic medium since 1980, helping individuals learn how to move forward in life by tuning in to and trusting their own intuitive wisdom. Her business, The Intuitive Coach LLC, serves clients ranging from corporate executives seeking new ways to incorporate personal insight in moving to the next level to individuals wanting to connect with lost loved ones.

As well as offering individual consultations, Livon also holds workshops and seminars that help attendees build their own intuitive bank of knowledge about the other side. Her work is based in the faith that to act on an intuitive impulse is to celebrate one of the most joyful aspects of life on this planet. Livon resides in Minneapolis, Minnesota with her husband and three children.

JODI LIVON

the

happy
medium

awakening to your
natural intuition

Llewellyn Publications
Woodbury, Minnesota

First Edition
First Printing, 2009

Cover art: sky background © 2009 by Image Source/Jupiter Images
          Photo of Jodi Livon © Jason Brown
Cover design by Kevin R. Brown

Llewellyn is a registered trademark of Llewellyn Worldwide, Ltd.

Library of Congress Cataloging-in-Publication Data
Livon, Jodi, 1962–
  The happy medium : awakening to your natural intuition / Jodi Livon.
—1st ed.
    p. cm.
  Includes bibliographical references.
  ISBN 978-0-7387-1463-9
  1. Spiritualism. 2. Intuition—Miscellanea. I. Title.
  BF1286.L58 2009
  133.9'1—dc22
                              2009009896

Llewellyn Worldwide does not participate in, endorse, or have any authority or responsibility concerning private business transactions between our authors and the public.

All mail addressed to the author is forwarded but the publisher cannot, unless specifically instructed by the author, give out an address or phone number.

Any Internet references contained in this work are current at publication time, but the publisher cannot guarantee that a specific location will continue to be maintained. Please refer to the publisher's website for links to authors' websites and other sources.

Note: In the depictions of psychic readings in this book, names and other non-essential information have often been altered to protect privacy.

Llewellyn Publications
A Division of Llewellyn Worldwide, Ltd.
2143 Wooddale Drive, Dept. 978-0-7387-1463-9
Woodbury, Minnesota 55125-2989, U.S.A.
www.llewellyn.com

Printed in the United States of America

In loving memory of my father, Marshall Livon
June 10, 1934 – March 4, 2008

CONTENTS

INTRODUCTION XI

1. Intuition Illuminated 1

2. The Groundwork of Grounding 55

3. Your Space or Mine? 87

4. Small Mediums 121

5. Love and Intuition 141

6. The Universal Code of Ethics 173

7. Intuition and the Workplace 205

8. Death and Grieving 219

9. Mourning and the Other Side 247

CONCLUSION 275

ACKNOWLEDGMENTS 283

BIBLIOGRAPHY 285

FAYE LIVON
January 9, 1906 – February 6, 1985

INTRODUCTION

Fey:
Having or displaying an otherworldly, magical,
or fairylike aspect or quality.
Having visionary power; clairvoyant.
The American Heritage College Dictionary

A Flourishing Medium

My paternal grandmother, Faye Livon, influenced me deeply. When she was alive, she taught me how to love. When she died, she taught me how to be a medium. Her presence gave me the security to discover who I was and why I felt everything with such intensity. She believed in me, and delighted in my unique personality and spark for life. Most of all, she offered maternal love and affection that wrapped itself around my soul and stayed. Though she did not give me my life, she surely saved it.

I would not have trusted anyone other than my grandmother to teach me to become a flourishing medium. She was the one soul I knew could never deliberately hurt me. It was from her love that I eventually overcame my fear of ghosts—when she became one and began to visit me from the other side, I was able to look beyond the veil without fear. It was with this new perspective that I moved forward as a medium and became truly receptive. My Grandma Faye was the most instrumental force in my ability to decipher my own intuitive code and learn to speak the language of intuition.

My name is Jodi Livon. I grew up in the suburbs of Minneapolis, Minnesota, in a conservative, middle-class Jewish home. We were not allowed to swear, use the word "hate," be late, or talk about the dead. Back in the day, when the word "psychic" was considered dirty and the word "medium" referred more to a shirt size than a person who communicated with the dead, I was a teenager struggling with a bizarre and uncanny sixth sense. That is what it was referred to in the 1980s—a sixth sense. It was not considered to be worth much, not even six cents.

As a young child, I first discovered the art of seeing the invisible. I could perceive how other people felt, what their futures might be, and the energy of those who had crossed over. This really got in the way of, say, dreaming I'd be invited to prom. Either I just plain sensed I wouldn't be asked, or some disembodied spirit would whisper in my ear, giving me a well-meaning heads-up that I shouldn't get my hopes up. And there were countless times when lights, TVs, and radios would turn on by themselves. My bed would shake me awake in the middle of the night, or I'd hear a tapping noise on the outside of my second-floor window. Sound spooky? I used to think so. Back then, I was unmistakably afraid of ghosts.

Yet these experiences proved to be the beginning of a life-long practice, which eventually turned into a profession. As early as my teenage years, I was acting as a professional psychic medium. Had I known then what I know now, I still would follow the same path, of course minus one or two bumps in the road. Perhaps sharing my experiences in *The Happy Medium* will help pave a smoother path for those who are just now learning the language of intuition.

As a psychic medium, I am able to interface with those who have crossed over. Think of me as a long-distance carrier—really long-distance. I'm a conduit between worlds. The journey to becoming a happy medium has been long, difficult, gratifying, and challenging. I learned the hard way; either I would have my intuition, or it would have me. The key is balance. It is important to have a healthy perspective, to take information with a grain of salt, and to find a happy medium. My personal mantra is "trust your gut, follow your heart, and use your head."

My name has rarely, if ever, shared a sentence with the term "mainstream." That is, until recently. My uncanny ability to identify solutions that prove to be significantly useful in the business world has made me highly sought-after as an intuitive coach. My database includes Fortune 500 members as well as members of the PTA. Overall, the work of psychic mediums is much more accepted now than it used to be, in part because scores of people from all walks of life are learning to draw on their own inner voice or senses, reclaiming what has been theirs all along. It is all about perspective. When things don't add up, intuition helps you do the math.

Each one of us is born with our instinct intact. Over time, life and fear may have hammered it down, but now it is time to recoup it. *The Happy Medium* is filled with true stories about people like you, who have lost loved ones and wish to reconnect with them. It is brimming with sensible, hands-on tools and techniques aimed at igniting your natural intuitive insight, which is your birthright. Psychic intuition has a place in love as well as in loss. *The Happy Medium* helps you find that place in your own life while you build your sense of soul.

Early in my career, I met some individuals who seemed larger than life and could do some amazing things with their intuitive abilities. A few were able to somehow move furniture in the living room while standing in the kitchen. Others could actually levitate and/or effortlessly and painlessly walk on hot coals. While I had the utmost respect for the skill it took to do such things, I had no desire to do the same.

In my development as a medium, the first thing I wanted to do was learn to control how out-of-control I felt when I was psychically overloaded. Two of my deepest wishes were to stop feeling everyone else's emotions, and to help people deal with their own. I needed desperately to build psychic boundaries. Though I searched thoroughly, there were, at the time, no professionals in the industry who were specializing in the area of psychic protection and boundary building. Most wanted to teach what I already knew—how to conduct readings. Accurately reading people has never been an issue for me. Learning to *not* read them has.

There are a number of components to the intuitive process. Imparting psychic information, which is one, is so effortless for me that I did not understand for a long time what made my work so distinct. Nor did I understand why on several occasions of having a reading myself, I was told there was a strong probability of my becoming prominently recognized and respected for the particular type of psychic work I would do. The information troubled me because all I profoundly wished for was to be emotionally healthy, and to feel safe and normal. Obviously I was too young to know there is no such thing as "normal." But

I wanted to help people without being so publicly *out there*. Yet out there I was, unguarded and unsuspecting as a result.

At eighteen, I found myself connected to one or two nationally known psychics who were nearly twice my age. I worked briefly with a few of them, in conjunction with authorities, on solving a particular national crime. It proved too much for me, emotionally speaking. The impact reverberates within me profoundly to this day. I was not anchored or mature enough to handle psychically seeing the faces of beautiful young children before they were murdered. Not being able to save them, yet seeing them clearly with my inner eye, eradicated my desire to work as a psychic for many moons.

Those who had crossed over did not really care that I had placed a "closed, no longer in business" sign on my door. I wasn't closed and they knew it, so they just continued whispering in my ear and moving me forward. Since I had tried to shut my inner eye, my inner ear was doing double-time. The words I heard were gentle and precise. I found that not being able to help those adorable little children broke my heart, not my spirit. Since I have looked in the face of the dead and of the dying, neither scares me now.

What did terrify me was the threat of living this life locked in a place of fear about who I am, and allowing what other people thought to prevent me from stepping up to the plate and doing what it is I came here to do. If boundaries were what I needed to protect myself, and achieve my goals, I was determined to find a way to grow them.

As a medium, I interface with those who have crossed over. It is an element of my vocation. Another element is illuminating the barriers that block the path of the soul. My job is to connect with people like you, and let you know that you are not alone. It is more than acceptable to stand up and be exactly who you are. It is, incidentally, what we all came here to do. When you follow your instincts, you are giving voice to your soul.

Inner Voice, Outer World

This book was written for everyone who has ever been told that they are too sensitive, deep, odd, unique, weird, strange, not enough, or too much. It is for everyone who has had a significant insightful moment and wanted to celebrate it, yet felt they had to conceal or apologize for it instead. The list could go on, and often does in our hearts and minds. It can continue until some inner form of acceptance and understanding quiets your self doubt, leaving a form of peace in its wake. The song of inner knowing is now free to make its happy sounds.

I chose the book title *The Happy Medium* because it has taken me so long to become one. People often ask me, "When did you realize that you were a psychic medium?" It happened when I began to understand that most people aren't. It had never occurred to me that other people are not as frequently overwhelmed by strange emotions, or know precisely why someone hurts or who is at the door before the bell rings, or sense a presence essentially undetectable. Having the ability to feel the energy of those who have died was not considered nonsense back then—it wasn't considered at all. Perhaps that is part of why I was so tuned in to the unseen. I understood what it was like to feel invisible.

Being Sensitive

For the most part, I am self-taught. The foundation of my work is based on a deep belief that my talent and abilities were given to me to help others, not to exploit them. The most important components of my growth as a person and as a medium include a strong connection with a higher power; therapy, which helped me to establish boundaries and understand where my space ends and another person's begins; reading scores of books about metaphysics; and accepting who I am, no matter what the cost.

Coming to terms with, and accepting, who I am as a person and a medium has given me the confidence to come out of the proverbial psychic closet. I did all this before being a medium became what it is today. I am grateful to the brave mediums who, in some cases, had to insist on being heard. The great psychics and mediums who have written about their experiences have paved the way for other "sensitive" people to move forward more unreservedly. Their work provides a blueprint of sorts, and substantiates the unspoken. Most recently, two of those mediums are Allison Dubois and John Edward. Their hard work has put mediums on a new map.

That quiet inner voice that guides and calms is naturally part of all of us and deserves to be honored. Understanding its signals, allowing it to be our guide, and knowing the difference between fear, desire, and intuition are all key tools in the navigation process. It is with this in mind that I wrote *The Happy Medium*. Being deaf to intuition does not have to be a prerequisite to getting along in the world. If more of us were alive to our senses, the world would make more sense.

Recognizing Your Intuitive Voice

Young people experience spontaneous insights with ease, and are naturally great, for instance, at knowing truth from lies. They have not yet learned to stifle their inner voices, so they live by them. Those inner voices are the soul speaking. When it is not acknowledged, it becomes suppressed. When it is acknowledged, it blooms.

While the intuitive voice can be discreet, it can also be loud and bold. Do you often sense that a particular person is going to call right before the phone rings? Or perhaps when the phone does ring, you know who it is without checking your caller ID? When someone is suddenly on your mind, do you find yourself bumping into him or her spontaneously?

Do your gut feelings about people repeatedly come true? Do you find that you unconsciously respond to future events prior to your knowledge of them? Have you, for no apparent reason or on a hunch, taken an unusual route while driving home, only to find later that a serious accident had occurred on your usual course?

Make no mistake about it—intuition is your inheritance. Innate, spontaneous, and beautiful insights arise from within and are a natural part of being human. Your intuitive voice is the voice of instinct and reason.

Dreams foretelling future events are sure signals from your intuitive self. An example might be a dream about your grandfather saying goodbye to you days before he actually died. Another example might be a dream depicting your sister pregnant months before she even conceives. It does not matter if your intuitive voice is soft and knowing or noisy and persistent; all insights are born from truth. If you honor these insights, they most certainly will grow.

Intuition and You

So how does all this relate to you? You may consider yourself sensitive or not so sensitive, yet you picked up this book at exactly this moment in your day, mood, and life. Your intuition is asking to be heard. It helps guide you in making decisions about whom to date, which house to purchase, which name to choose for your child, which car to drive, which pizza to eat, and what career to pursue. It is a partner in the creative force that helps you magnetize that which you most desire.

Tapping into the universal bank of information does not require a club membership. It requires only that you understand how to connect with your inner sense of knowing. I am writing this book in hopes of shedding some light on your fears, and of guiding you in, perhaps, tapping into your own intuition and spiritual mastery. Intuition is a gift from God. It is your birthright. What you do with it is your gift back.

1

Intuition Illuminated

When you trust your gut, follow your heart,
and use your head, magic happens!
—The Happy Medium

Psychic versus Psychic Medium

During the early stages of writing *The Happy Medium*, my publisher asked me whether I am more of a medium or more of a psychic. The two are so intertwined that they are often difficult to distinguish. One is the vehicle, the other the road.

In other words, all mediums are psychic. However, not all psychics are mediums (although I do believe everyone has some mediumistic capabilities). A medium is a mediator between the spirit world and the physical world. Mediums have a telepathic connection with souls in both worlds. Psychics have a telepathic connection with people in this world, and are able to sense what was, what is, and what will be. They are able to ascertain these things in varying ways. If psychics are considered radios, then universal information is the radio wave. The way in which they connect with the knowledge, and interpret it, takes both capability and skill.

The Psychic Freeway

There are psychics with abilities that can be compared to a two-lane freeway, with information coming in at a two-lane speed. There are also psychics who work as a ten- or twenty-lane freeway. When I was in my teens and still struggling to control the flow of information that was constantly pouring through me, I met someone who had once worked with the government of a foreign country. He was aware of the professional use, and the testing, of psychics. He told me that I was overloading because I was more like a twenty-lane freeway. Psychic information was pouring in at a torrential rate of speed.

As a psychic medium, I am an interpreter of sorts. I live with my body in one world, while my soul dances in between two worlds. It is also one of the greatest honors in my life to help people in both worlds connect once again, and consciously pass love from one side to the other.

The Psychic Skeleton

To better illustrate the working foundation of a psychic, I use the term "psychic skeleton." Included in this psychic skeleton is the well-recognized term "clairvoyance." Clairvoyance is a French word that transliterates as "clear seeing." Clairvoyance breaks down into five basic categories, which I refer to as "the Five Clairs": clairvoyance (clear seeing, which is associated with the third eye), clairaudience (clear hearing), clairsentience (clear sensing or feeling), clairallience (clear smelling), and clairgustance (clear tasting). Yes, some psychics actually taste things intuitively.

When I conduct a reading, I tap into all five clairvoyant attributes. The picture I hold in my mind is of five wise women, all with the first name of Clair, each offering differing intuitive traits. They allow me to work with them and through them. I see, hear, feel, smell, and taste what is happening, has happened, or may potentially happen to my clients on this side and the other. The manner in which intuition is tapped is as individual as the person tapping the information.

Types of Mediums

There are various genres of mediums. All are able to communicate with souls on the other side. The array of popular descriptions used to define the genres starts with the simple and goes to the sublime. The three most recognized types of mediums are physical mediums, trance mediums, and mental mediums.

A physical medium's energy is used to manifest paranormal activity, such as the physical materialization of objects connected with a spirit from the other side. A trance medium, also referred to by some as a channeler, is able to go into a trance and allow spirits from the other world to use their bodies to communicate. Mental mediums communicate with spirits through telepathy. They are able to hear, see, feel, and even smell messages from those on the other side.

As a teen, part of my self-prescribed curriculum for study of the sixth sense was to watch other psychics at work. While at a psychic fair, I was told by a well-respected medium that I was a trance medium who could allow spirits from the other world to use my body to communicate. I was supposed to step out during a trance state, and the spirit would step in. I wanted no part of that scenario.

Had the medium been tuned in to my fear, she might have explained that as a medium, I had choices. It was not necessary for me to leave my body and allow another spirit to take over in order to do my work; there are other modes of communication between worlds. That explanation would have made sense, because I had always been able to communicate with spirits through telepathy.

Dead people talking to me and/or attempting to literally enter my body held no attraction. As a kid, I would not listen to ghost stories, and could not watch any movie with one in it. A TV show called The Ghost and Mrs. Muir, about the love between a deceased sea captain and a live woman, was as close as I would get to viewing horror films.

Empaths

All of us have empathetic experiences, since it is part of being human. It is also a component of being sensitive. Intuitive empaths are people who absorb other people's feelings, both physical and emotional. Simply being around people in groups for long periods of time is exhausting for them. When someone standing near them has a headache or is depressed, they feel the pain and depression as if it were their own. Empaths need time alone to rejuvenate. They are hypersensitive to smells, sounds, and commotion in general. A common trait found in intuitive empaths is a strong dislike of being in a crowd. For them, the likelihood of becoming overstimulated is exceptionally high. As a result, many find it more comfortable to be with only a small number of people, or alone.

In the same way that everyone is a little psychic, everyone experiences involuntary empathy. Feeling compassionate and sympathetic is not the same as being a full empath, however.

Likewise, occasionally feeling drained by friends and family is only slightly similar to the experience of an empath.

Personally, I adore attending parties and delight in watching the bright colors in people's souls. Unfortunately, after only a few hours at best, I become completely exhausted from feeling everyone's emotions and physical ailments. As a psychic sponge, which is a variation of empathy, I absorb what is not mine and become thoroughly saturated. Once I learned to retain my own energy and not give it away, however, I became an empowered and more conscious medium.

One of the more creative ways I stop absorbing emotions that are not my own is by imagining myself as saturated with white light. If a sponge is saturated, it can no longer absorb. White light is like an all-purpose stain remover. It gets anything out!

While empathy continues to play an active role in my life, it does not perpetually rule it. Decent boundaries protect me from energy that is not my own.

Going Retro and Seeing Ahead

The process of learning how to work with creative and intuitive abilities, yet not be worked by them, may be lifelong. The manner in which people tap into their higher selves and intuitive code varies. Learning styles differ as much as personalties do. In sum, whatever opens the door to intuition and brings you heightened consciousness is working.

During my workshops, I discovered that coining terms for areas of the intuitive process (such as "Going Retro" or "the Five Clairs of clairvoyance") is useful. Some people find the terminology helpful in defining their own unusual experiences. In *The Happy Medium*, I include such terms in order to expand understanding, not limit it. As with everything you read, take what works and disregard the rest. There is no quiz at the end of this book! Okay, there is, but it's just for fun.

The terms "retrocognition" (also known as "postcognition") and "precognition" refer to a knowledge of events of the past or future, respectively, which could not be known by ordinary means. "Retro" is from the Latin word "backward." "Cognition" means "knowing." Retrocognition often happens spontaneously. In some cases it can be accomplished deliberately. There are accounts of trained psychics who, seeking information about proceedings of the past, are able to tap into events. The psychics report that these visions are complete with sounds and smells.

Toward the end of my senior year in high school, I had a powerful experience relating to a past life. My friends and I were at a senior party, doing a dance together called "The Time Warp" from the movie *The Rocky Horror Picture Show*. Our junior and senior year Friday nights were spent in uptown Minneapolis, joyfully watching that movie (though it had a plot none of us understood). During the dance that night, I felt myself shift to a scene from the early 1900s. Everything in the scene felt strangely familiar. I was sitting at a long, formal dining table along with two or three of my high school friends, one of whom was a major player in my current life. He was the person sitting at the head of the table, and was most definitely in control of the group. We were all in our late twenties or early thirties, and were dressed in austere, dark colors.

Though none of us looked exactly like we did in our current lives, there could be no mistaking who was who. It was as if our current faces were superimposed on the early 1900s faces. But as quickly as I'd dropped into that picture, I snapped out. The scene must have lasted only seconds. During that time, something clicked in my head and I understood why my relationship with at least two friends felt familiar. I knew, without anyone telling me, that I had had the privilege of glimpsing one of my own past lives.

This retrocognitive experience helped me move forward in a way that I had not previously been able to do. I was tremendously grateful for the incident, though I had not consciously sought it. It was spontaneous, as all my retrocognitive exposures have been.

If you have had a possible past-life encounter, take the knowledge you gained and use it to help you move forward in your current life. A critic may say it was all in your imagination, but it does not matter where it came from. The significance is in what you do with it. Make it a thing of wisdom and you cannot lose.

Explaining the sensations of an intuitive experience is similar to explaining love. You cannot see love; you can see its expression, however. You cannot see wind, only the effects it has as it whirls and dances, changing the atmosphere and perhaps moving what stands in its way. The same is true of an encounter a medium has during a reading. You may not be able to see a spirit, though the sensation of feeling one nearby is as encompassing as the wind, and can be as moving as love.

"Precognition" is from the Latin word *prae*, which means "prior to." Again, "cognition" means "knowing." Precognition is a detailed knowledge of events that will take place in the future through extrasensory means. It is far more common than retrocognition, and usually occurs in dreams. Precognitive events may also present themselves as a strong sense of knowing, impromptu waking visions, and rapid, clear flashing thoughts popping in and out of the mind. I refer to these as "drop-in insights." Precognitive knowledge may also be gained through trance, channeling, and divination.

Precognition is a tool used by the higher self. The higher part of ourselves sends messages to our future selves in an effort to help prepare us for future events. People who experience pre-cognition often comment on dreams or visions that took place prior to a life-cycle event such as the birth of a child or death of a loved one. Especially when the life-cycle event is a sad one, shock alters the senses and opens people up psychically, making it easier to remember the precognitive dream that outlined the upcoming event.

Our higher selves recurrently deliver precognitive dreams prior to life-altering events. The dream may be forgotten until the situation actually transpires. For instance, a detailed dream about a car accident may slip your mind until after the accident occurs.

The dream is not necessarily sent to change the course of events. Rather, precognitive dreams help prepare us for what is to come. So it is not necessary to berate yourself if you did not act on a dream or remember it until much later in time. Precognitive dreams pave a smoother path for the rough emotions ahead. If, indeed, you are meant to change an upcoming experience, another sign would manifest. Trust in your higher self. Be open, and maintain a healthy perspective by moderating between your hopes and your fears. Dreams dwell in whatever level of consciousness benefits you most.

Some precognitive visions, thoughts, or dreams are sent to us to use as tools for transformation. Much depends on how the intuitive self is built. In other words, the goal is to raise your consciousness. This, in turn, benefits your soul. If you are trying to choose between two breeds of dogs and continue to dream about only one of them, your higher self is likely sending you a furry message. Further research about that pooch is in order. The dog in your dreams may be the dog of your dreams. Watch for patterns.

If, in hindsight, you see a clear pattern leading up to an important event, your recognition of the pattern will help sharpen your intuitive senses. Seeing someone who looks like your best friend from high school several times in one week may not just be your mind playing tricks on you. If something happens soon after that is related to high school or your friend, you can be sure that it is a sign.

Intuitive Keys

My great-grandfather escaped the pogroms of nineteenth-century Russia, fleeing first to Canada and then to the United States. Historically, Jews have long been the targets of such venomous, baseless attacks. A wise man, my great-grandfather must have seen the writing on the wall and followed his instincts. He gathered his wife and five young children, leaving all their belongings behind, and managed to escape certain death. Most of those who chose to stay, or who could not escape Russia, were killed during the pogroms or the Holocaust.

My Grandpa Max told us this story frequently. It is his story, and the story of how his father, John, used his wits to survive and thrive. While some people are merely entertained by their intuitive instincts, others, like my great-grandfather, know that these instincts are key, and revere and live by them.

Maintaining one's integrity is another character trait that can unlock the door to the intuitive process. My Grandpa Max had a majestic aura and was well recognized in the community for his powerful wisdom. People were constantly drawn to him and to the astute advice he bestowed. Shortly before he died, we had one of the most meaningful conversations of my life. He told me he had always known that I was wise in a way far beyond my years. For the first time, he confided that he had come to support the choices I'd made, even though they went against convention and tradition. He then began to relay a series of life events that were clear proof of his own intuitive capabilities. I hadn't had any idea that my grandfather had detailed dreams outlining a recipe for success in a number of personal and professional ventures.

I did know that my grandpa's wife, Faye, came from spiritually advanced lineage. She was a direct descendent of a world-famous Italian rabbi by the name of Meir Katzenellenbogen (aka Meir of Padua). Throughout her life, Faye operated from a place of higher consciousness. She responded to others with an elevated awareness and enduringly showed an astonishing capacity and willingness to love and forgive, whatever the circumstances. Love and intuition are closely related, and the combination of love and wisdom is a powerful one—love understands the wisdom in forgiveness, while wisdom understands the brilliance of love.

If it is true that psychic intuition is passed down from generation to generation, it was from Max that I inherited an element of mine. But it was from Faye and her unusual capacity for love that I grew brave enough to understand what lay before me. I remain honored to have received such an inheritance.

The key to growing your intuition is knowing how you feel and who you are. You can do this with far greater ease when you know that you are protected and loved. Love, after all, is the fingerprint of the soul.

When Faye died, death took on new meaning for me. In time, I learned to differentiate between missing my grandmother and feeling her presence. Before her death, visits from those on the other side had often frightened me. But I had no feelings of alarm when Faye dropped in, because she was still, after all, my grandma. She was a rare soul, and continued to comfort me in her magical way, even from the other side.

The Music of Soul

When we mature and allow ourselves to broaden, our psychic potential naturally increases. Loving and accepting ourselves is central to this end. Healthy self-expression is hearty self-love. Loving ourselves is directly connected to the health of our bodies, minds, and spirits. Remember, we are allowed only the love we heap upon ourselves.

When you enter a state of higher awareness, an understanding of who you are, your soul, and its purpose are illuminated. Of the multitude of roads available to reaching a higher state of consciousness, music is a favorite for scores of people. Music speaks to us through the emotion it evokes from within. As it rocks us, it melts barriers and opens us up. When we are unlocked, we are in a place of receiving. When we are unbound, we are closer to comprehending what we already have and what we need. Expression through music and all artistic endeavors is simply a way to illustrate the colors in our soul. Every soul has its own musical code and vibrational frequency. Certain sounds unlock the doors we erect, revealing our own melodic notes.

Specific kinds of music appeal to each of us because the melodic notes match the particular vibration of our soul. They mirror our own heart's song at that moment. We respond to that which is hidden deeply within and longing to be recognized. The musician's vibration, too, plays a part in how the music invites us in. It is not unusual for close friends to be attracted to similar music. Where souls are drawn together, harmony is found.

As a young mystic, music saved me. It was my drug of choice and I was willingly addicted. Music helped elevate my own vibration. It was and is the vehicle I use to transcend this plane and find solace in another. Certain types of melodies would put me into a trancelike state in a matter of moments. Though I love words and how they dance together to invoke peaceful images, thoughts, and feelings, it has always been the rhythmic, repetitive part of music that has sent me elsewhere.

Chanting is a universal portal that has been long used by religions around the world. It is employed as a way to connect with the divine. When done well, chanting alters consciousness and raises psychic energy. Differing rhythmic, repetitive chants are composed of syllables, words, and names. The name of God is almost universally considered to make for the strongest chants. This was true among Hebrew mystics who used the secret names of God, such as Elohim, Yahweh, and Adonai.

A type of Hasidic (Jewish religious movement) music thought of as a wordless tune is called a *nigun*. It is a form of chanting. Hasidim treasure the human voice. They find great value in singing and telling stories. Among Hasidic Jews, singing a wordless song is thought of as a way to elevate the soul to God by moving the singer beyond the sensual and rational toward the mystic. It is considered particularly effective when done in accord with others.

Native Americans are well recognized for their beautiful use of chanting in ceremonies such as powwows, where souls speak in harmony with God. The Dakota refer to chanting as *ceye*, which means "to pray." Chanting is done in preparation for ceremonies such as weddings, funerals, initiations, healing, hunting, and battles. Mantras and chants are also revered greatly in shamanism. An assortment of chants in Buddhism and Hinduism use the popular Om sound. Regardless of being Theravada or Mahayana, nearly every Buddhist school has some variation of chanting associated with it. Musical chanting is powerful. It places the singer in neutral and is a beautiful and useful way to alter our states of consciousness.

Music, yoga, meditation, contemplation, and prayer are disciplines or vehicles used to reach mystical union, a place where there is connection to all that is, a knowing comprehension that we are all one. Our perception of the world goes beyond intellect and belongings. It is an understanding that we all belong, because we are all connected in this Universe as one.

It is from this peaceful space of mindful acceptance that we understand who we are and how we externalize that vision. In other words, we understand how exactly we project ourselves into the world and, most importantly, to those close to us. We understand what the higher part of us has been working toward and now can more easily magnetize it to us. When it comes to love, maintaining or even touching mindful acceptance and/or a oneness with all that is, often acts as a beacon. If it is love that we seek, the path leading to it and us is illuminated. We glow.

You had something special planned by and for your own soul when you arrived on this earth wearing the name you wear today. Trust in the Universe. Be open, welcoming, and receptive. Have confidence in yourself. Know that you have the experience to deal with whatever comes your way. Remember, this is your life and you are here to shine.

Religion and the Afterlife

Modern religion has played a strong role in our general view about what happens following death. A range of religions speak to the subject of hell and how to avoid it. Many address heaven and hell, karma, dharma, or reincarnation. Some routinely include prayers of remembrance for the dead. Various organized faiths consider taking care of the souls of dead ancestors a primary component of religious responsibility. Interestingly, prayers for and in acknowledgment of the soul have an impact on those on both sides of the veil.

When one compares some of the major religions of the world, a surprising amount of commonalities are evident about the subject of death. For example, the belief that once the body dies, the soul separates from it and moves into another world is not uncommon. It is to that world, or rather to those who reside in it, that mediums such as myself naturally respond.

After losing someone dear, people are often more open to the possibility of the ongoing life of a soul. This, for some, is due in part to a sense of their loved one being near. For others, it is a hope made from love, and a deep sense of loss and grief.

A newly broken heart can open a closed mind. Once the shock of losing someone close recedes and a little balance is found, people reach for what they intuitively know is the truth— that humans are more than skin, blood, and bones. "Ashes to ashes, dust to dust" are words we recite when someone dies. But "ashes to ashes, dust to dust" does not mean the end. We are more than our bodies. We are our souls.

Soul Accountability

A growing number of books have been published on the subject of past lives and life between lives. I have found a good deal of them to be utterly fascinating and worth the read. One of the original doctors to investigate the past life of a patient in therapy is Brian Weiss. In the 1980s, his *Many Lives, Many Masters* broke ground by opening minds to the possibility of life after life. Michael Newton has written a number of fascinating books pertaining to life between lives including *Journey of Souls, Destiny of Souls*, and *Life Between Lives*.

When something I have read is similar to something I have learned from a spirit on the other side, my stomach fills with butterflies. Those butterflies act as a sign that the information has a legitimate base. It is a solid confirmation.

When you read something about mysticism, be aware of how your body and intuitive self react. Your response is a key to your intuitive self. Everyone will eventually know firsthand what their journey entails. Until then, exploring the possibilities heightens the senses.

The only way to grow intuitively is to seek information. Remember, you get to choose what works for you. Increasing your knowledge base about a subject of interest expands your mind and nourishes your soul. Advancing your perception in matters of the spirit is not an either/or state of affairs. Some of the greatest religions of our time have significant tenets in common. Your religious footing is not shaken when you explore the possibilities, because there is no obligation to trade one understanding for the other.

My own client base is made up of people from various religious backgrounds. Some of them grew up in an environment that forbade talking about any religion or spiritual belief that differed from their own. Their willingness as adults to explore the possibilities is evidence of their own sparkling spiritual journey. Isocrates wrote, "The noblest worship is to make yourself as good and as just as you can."

There is a difference between the study of religion and the study of spirituality. One is the lyrics, the other the music. Given the opportunity, each can complement the other. It is not necessary, however, to hold any certain religious or spiritual belief in order to be a medium or psychic. For some it adds a dimension; for others it does not.

I believe my soul automatically understands particular matters of spirit. This life is merely a reminder and test of what I naturally recollect from lives past. My soul responds to the words of the Torah. Still, I am far from an expert on religion, my own or any other. The area in which I most excel is living my spiritual wisdom. When a message comes from my heart and soul, I have learned to take serious note.

Fear is a fake teacher, and a defective teacher as well. Allowing it to rule the mind does not help you expand in wisdom. Fear stops the intuitive process in its tracks. If something frightens you, learn more about it from a distance that feels comfortable. If something intrigues you, do the same. Knowledge is power.

Stepping out into the unknown is wise when you know how to measure the information fairly and perhaps take it with a grain of salt. Go to a bookstore or library and allow your instincts to help you choose a book. What subject or section gives you a sense of vivacity? Do you feel inspired? An upwelling of positive energy is a sign from the inner you that you are onto something good.

Before I clearly understood how to protect myself from wandering earthbound spirits, I felt uneasy during discussions about "ghosts." I would read books about everything from Greek mythology to reincarnation—any publication I could get my hands on about spiritual practices celebrated throughout the world, past and present, was quickly explored. Yet I could not even touch nonfiction books about haunted houses. Watching the news when a murder story was covered proved unsafe for me. I felt as though the energy of the murdered spirit had found me and sprinkled my world with a dark vibe. It was difficult to ascertain whether the discomfort I felt was the spirit's or my own. As a young medium, I was not a happy one.

It has been a long time since I was that vulnerable. Study of the afterlife of the soul through my practice as a medium has been instrumental in calming my fears. If I am in danger or feel fearful now, a protective block arises. From this place of calm, I am able to make straightforward decisions, read anything I want, and live more peacefully.

The number of clients who worry that their loved one may not be in a safe place following death is significant. When I am able to validate unusual personal facts about my client's friend or family member who has crossed over, worry slides off my client's face and relief floods the room. Messages from those who have crossed over are not ones laden with fear, repercussion, or anger. The roles they once had and the issues they played out when they were incarnated on earth have no place on the other side.

A crossed-over loved one is characteristically communicating out of love. The desire to help is evident in the messages. It has long seemed to me that the one pervasive sense of anything related to sadness in the messages has been due to the love the spirit did not demonstrate during their time on this side of the veil. Over the past several decades, the spirit energies I have encountered during readings generally have all come back to help, in love.

Spending time reflecting on lessons learned is time well spent. Those on the other side are powerful teachers. When my life is over, I want to be like the spirits I have met in my travels as a medium—spirits who are filled with joy, and choosing love instead of fear.

Science and Psychics

Cynicism and skepticism are like sisters. When faced with something new, both take a step back. The difference is, only one will choose to move forward. While cynicism believes in nothing, so has naught, skepticism is open to the possibilities and recognizes the plausible—so it has much.

I am a bit of a skeptic myself. If I did not personally experience what I do every day, intuitively speaking, I would require some sort of reputable substantiation to further open my mind. And my objective is to open my mind.

As an intuitive business coach, I work with companies that are owned and operated by people with varying religious and spiritual beliefs. It is not uncommon for an initial consultation with a company to include at least one partner or manager who is not 100 percent on board with the whole "intuitive thing." It is at those times that I refer to a well-known physicist and author by the name of Russell Targ, a pioneer in the development and advancement of the laser and laser applications. Along with his colleague Harold E. Puthoff, Targ co-founded a twenty-three-year, twenty-five-million-dollar research program that looked into psychic abilities and the operational use of these abilities in the U.S. intelligence community. In his 1998 book, co-authored with Jane Katra and titled *Miracles of Mind: Exploring Nonlocal Consciousness and Spiritual Healing*, Targ cited numerous examples about how the United States Army Intelligence community, including the Defense Intelligence Agency, CIA, and Army Intelligence, utilized unambiguous psychic abilities which Targ refers to as "remote viewing": the ability of a person to gather information on a remote target, hidden from the physical perception of the viewer and typically separated from the viewer by some distance. Remote viewing is, in other words, a form of extrasensory perception. Targ and Puthoff had first introduced this term in 1974.

Targ is the co-author of five books pertaining to the scientific investigation of psychic abilities. He received two National Aeronautics and Space Administration awards. Before retirement, Targ was employed by Lockheed Martin Missiles & Space Co. as a senior staff scientist. He developed airborne laser systems for the detection of wind shear.

With the help of people like Targ and Puthoff, assumptions about what it means to be psychic begin to fall away. The U.S. government is learning to utilize a source that other countries' leaders have tapped into for decades. Quantum physics, metaphysics, and extrasensory perception are three of the countless thresholds into the world of possibilities. It does not matter which door one enters by, as long as one enters.

Energy and Attraction

What spooked me as a child was not so much my ability to feel the presence of someone after they had died, but the common message from society that they were completely "gone" and that what I sensed was wrong. There are so many ways to view death, however. Religion and science aside, each one of us eventually will find our own truth. As a student of both this side and the other, I wholly believe that when people cross over, they continue to exist. They have merely changed form.

There are those who find comfort in understanding life after death through the eye of quantum physics. Quantum physics presents a scientific view to what has long been considered a spiritual truth. It is related to quantum theory, also known as quantum mechanics. It is considered a physical science centered in part on matter and energy. It pertains to matter, and how it interacts with other matter. It is all about energy, and the Universe is pure energy!

Everything in the Universe—clothing, cars, animals, plants, and people—is made of pure energy. Energy itself is made up of atoms. Those who are well versed in science might indicate that energy is neither created nor destroyed, but transformed. It's transferred as atoms, particles, electrons, waves, heat, and light, for example. When we die, the twirling atoms and molecules that we are change form. It is a metamorphosis. We cross from this side over to the other, our spinning energy increasing rapidly in speed without a body to slow us down.

The popular notion of like attracts like, or the law of attraction, has long been linked to quantum physics. The concept is not a new one. It can be found in a number of ancient teachings, such as in Hinduism and Buddhism. In the past decade, movies, documentaries, and books pertaining to the law of attraction, such as *What the BLEEP* and *The Secret*, have greatly captured public interest.

Understanding the law of attraction can help us more consciously create our future. When we set our focus—our energy—on something, this causes that something to grow. Our feelings and thoughts create an actual vibration! That vibration magnetizes (to us) experiences that mirror our thoughts. That is why it is imperative that we have true conscious control of our minds. Otherwise, we create by default.

Representative of this truth are words of the wise, written long before the term "new age" was ever popular. Marcus Aurelius said, "Your mind will be like its habitual thoughts; for the soul becomes dyed with the color of its thoughts ... " Ken Keyes Jr. said, "You should always be aware that your head creates your world." Furthermore, as stated in the Jewish Book of Proverbs, 23:7, "As a man thinketh in his heart so he is."

When speaking about death to my children, I explain that nothing vanishes—it simply changes shape. I compare people to monarch butterflies bursting from the cocooned state. The caterpillars move from one form of themselves into another.

Most importantly, I reiterate that all souls infinitely maintain the love they receive, and love never dies. Like monarch butterflies moving from one form of themselves to another, we change structures when we cross over. Our soul, and the love that is part of it, remains the same.

Restoring Personal Power

Life offers us so many challenges. One of my greatest challenges is finding appropriate outlets for all of my energy and abilities. In order to do well in my work, I not only had to find myself but had to believe in myself. The vibration of those who have crossed over is subtle; it takes a certain amount of self-assurance and trust to step out and verbalize these invisible sounds.

Yet, even in the face of no one understanding me as a child, I found my confidence. I restored my personal power when I relinquished hope of always being accepted. In other words, when I lost hope of being "suitable," I established a new level of self-confidence. A psychological lost and found! The uncanny abilities I was born with have truly been a blessing, and my work as a medium has been freeing. To be discouraged from acknowledging something as natural and loving as the wise voice from within is nonsense—not the other way around!

When you stop asking for approval, your need for it decreases. It is one way to quiet the noise inside. The subtle nuances of the intuitive language are then more able to surface. Remember, everything you place your attention on grows. Acknowledge moments of insight. They will bloom and so will you! Put careful attention where your attention is drawn, and a new form of insight is sure to follow.

A Home Built on Trust

One great example of how intuition works is the story of how my husband Jason and I purchased our first home together. It is a story of instincts and trust. When we first met, I owned a charming house in south Minneapolis that had been home to many loved domestic animals, including cats. Jason was renting an apartment in a new development on the other side of town. Because of his severe allergies to animals, most seriously to cats, he could not spend time at my house, let alone live in it. After we became engaged, I put my house on the market and together we searched for our new home. My house in south Minneapolis was shown over and over again. It seemed to show well. No negative comments from potential buyers or real estate agents ensued. But there weren't any offers, either.

Six months into our adventures in real estate, we happened upon a beautiful brick house with a warmth unequaled by any other we had seen. We agreed it was what we hoped for and wanted to put an offer on the house. It had been empty and on the market for over a year with no offers, past or present. At the time, we had not had one offer on the house in south Minneapolis. My husband was only comfortable signing an agreement that was contingent upon the sale of my house. I told him that he had to trust me, and that we had to make a noncontingent offer.

Jason is in finance as a profession, so you might guess that my suggestion went over like a lead balloon. I intuitively sensed that another couple was about to make an offer on the brick house of our dreams, and that the current owners would quickly accept. I saw the other couple's van and heard their voices. More importantly, I felt an urgent need to make an offer, and a feeling of peace once we did. I've always been good with money, no matter how little I had, and taking ineffectual risks was never part of my makeup. But I recognized that persistent voice within me, and nodded in agreement to my higher self.

I remember standing in what is now our living room, knowing that this was a pivotal moment in my relationship with my husband. Looking into his sweet blue eyes, I told him exactly what I sensed. To my delight and surprise, Jason agreed. We made a noncontingent offer. And that night, a purchase agreement was submitted on my house in south Minneapolis! The next day, as I had warned, a competing offer was made on the home we hoped to purchase. After some negotiating, one house was sold and another was purchased. Score one for intuition, trust, and love.

Calling Cards from the Other Side

At one time or another, everyone has felt the frustration of not being able to communicate what they need to say. Imagine how you might feel if you dropped into a room filled with those you love and found them weeping over your death. Although you are standing next to them, they cannot see or hear you. You are aware that when you died, you simply altered forms. You still feel like you! But your loved ones think you have ceased to exist.

It is, of course, not quite possible to know exactly how a spirit might feel following their own death. I only know what has been shared with me by souls on the other side, who have a deep desire to assure loved ones that they are safe and peaceful. They send signs—calling cards, if you will—meant to comfort us.

But time after time, sign after sign is ignored. When something happens that is perhaps an indication of the presence of a loved one in spirit, fear stands in the way of acknowledging such an encounter, even to ourselves. As souls still encased in bodies, we experience the world through glasses colored with our particular level of consciousness. We forget that another form of existence endures after the body dies. Though our loved ones are gone from our everyday lives, they are not lost.

Signs from the other side are numerous in form. The spirits sending them aspire to communicate a message or simply be acknowledged. A sign may be exclusively meant for one person, or more neutral in nature. Some people connect the scent of cigarettes to a deceased loved one who smoked, or recognize the particular aroma of a favored food that a loved one prepared regularly. Such defined scents, suddenly in the air, are a common way for spirit to say, "Hello, I'm still here!" Another sign is a rare and favored song played repeatedly on the radio, especially on an anniversary date or a birthday. Music is a compelling way to connect.

If hearing a song on the radio provides comfort, take it. If a favorite 1970s movie that you once watched with your crossed-over someone all of a sudden is played continually on cable and is unexpectedly a subject of conversation at work and at the coffee shop you frequent, it may be a sign from the other side. If newly replaced light bulbs burn out in lamps all around the house and your electrical system is healthy, a loved one in spirit may be calling.

As a general rule, there is no such thing as coincidence. If you find yourself reading too far into something, take a moment and pause. You will know if you are onto something when you receive the sign from the other side effortlessly. As in an "aha" moment, your own intuition will highlight the sign. You do not have to try too hard to notice a calling card from a crossed-over loved one; just remain open minded and pragmatic at the same time.

Other popular calling cards from those on the other side include a tapping felt on a person's back, tapping sounds on the window, and tapping sounds on the floor. Further examples include lights turning off of their own accord, children's battery-operated toys, radios, and TVs going on in the middle of the night, and VCRs or DVD players recording without previously being programmed (now that is enlightenment!).

Photographs seem to be easily altered at the film developing shop in the sky. For example, an unexplained light or orb visible only after a photo is developed may be your loved one showing up in spirit. Add to the list an exceptionally vivid, peaceful dream with a loved one featured as the star. A ringing sound in the ears is also a general form of contact. (There are medical conditions that cause a ringing in the ear, such as tinnitus, which of course are not related to spirit contact.) Movement seen peripherally is yet another potential calling card, one that children in particular are privy to.

More signs include wildlife, such as birds or butterflies, appearing at poignant moments; drapes moving on a windless day; the sound of something stirring in an empty room. Coins appearing often and in odd, unexpected places is a familiar sign from the other side—one that ordinarily evokes a smile out of the receiver.

Last on my inventory of the more common indicators from the other side is my personal favorite (lots of sarcasm here)—the shaking bed. This does not happen to me as routinely as it once did. Since my husband might be a bit startled, spirits only use it as a last resort to get my attention. (When I first broached the subject of a "shaking bed" to Jason, the bed moving when we were both asleep was not what he had in mind!) I felt much like Samantha Stevens on *Bewitched* when I told my then boyfriend, now husband, about my intuitive gift (I pull the word "gift" out when it will help explain my abilities in a less intimidating way). Jason was about to learn an entirely new language, so I felt the need to ease him in!

There are the times, of course, when contact with the spirit world may be frightening rather than comforting. Hairs standing up on the back of your neck or arms is a well-recognized indicator of this. Keep in mind that this also could be a response to a spirit visit in general, but a growing comprehension of all that the Universe offers brings the fear level down. When you feed fear the cold hard facts, it will starve!

An unexplained feeling of warmth on the cheek of a grieving friend or relative is a touching way for spirit to say, "I am here, and I love you." Spirits know how much we grieve, and signs can be a beautiful way to send the most meaningful and powerful message on either side of the veil: love.

It is not necessary to hire a medium to speak with your loved one in spirit. Your voice is definitely heard. The distinction is that a trained medium is able to hear the voice of those on the other side. As you become familiar with signs, your intuitive ear will open further, as will your mind, thus increasing the chances that you will perceive the messages and feel the affection meant for you in the first place.

Finding Your Guides

Spirits and spirituality were not hot topics during my childhood. Not at school, and certainly not at home. Religion was deeply important and celebrated with family and friends, yet the spiritual end of life was left to the imagination. Since I could hear people's thoughts and speak of things most adults felt uneasy about, my odd questions were received with fear and irritation. It was not always what was said to me in response to my inquiry that hurt, but how I sensed people felt about what I'd said that made me stay silent and shamed.

As a young medium sprouting legs, I needed reinforcement. Information was my strongest ally. There were negative circumstances and energies around that were foreign and dark and made me feel ice cold inside. But within me, there was a calm, soothing, and familiar voice that provided welcomed reassurance. I often experienced it out of nowhere. It seemed to originate from somewhere in my own head or heart. I recognized that this inner guidance was extremely helpful and never harmed anyone or anything. I could depend on it, though I was totally unclear at the time about what it was.

What I did recognize was that the inner guidance was something caring, so I imagined it was God. What I now understand is that the guiding voice I have long trusted has been the combined energies of what most people refer to as "guides." I have forever thought of them as my inner parents.

The idea of inner parents held immense comfort for me. During my childhood, my mother and father were characteristically unavailable for various reasons. My dad was loving and warm but I rarely saw him. He was, as I can affectionately say now, a workaholic. My relationship with my mother was always terribly difficult, and remains so today. Thankfully, my faith in a higher power pointed me in the direction and to the protection of my guides.

Each of us has one senior guide who has been with us throughout many lifetimes. Guides are multifaceted. They stand beside us in all that we do, giving us the space to learn and earn a higher place of consciousness. Our spirit guides have paid their karmic debt in full before they are appointed to us. A guide's core job is to alight our paths.

As we move through our years, junior guides emerge based on our life choices. Though they too have paid their karmic debt, they are not as advanced as senior guides. A junior guide may be a specialist in an area that we have chosen to move toward.

If you were going to move to a foreign country and did not speak the language, who might best prepare you for the move? Wouldn't you want someone, an expert who was born and raised in that particular country, to teach you the language and about the culture? Junior guides all have an area of expertise. Once you become self-sufficient and adept in that area, that particular junior guide moves on. It's not uncommon to be working on multiple areas in life and have the help of several junior guides simultaneously.

Believe it or not, your senior guide's vibration is already familiar to you. You may think that this steady inner voice is simply your own. Here is a clue to assist you in learning to differentiate between your guides and your fears. The voices will sound the same, but your guide will always be assuring and never deliver an unconstructive message. Your fear will.

Think back to a time when you made a significant decision and soon after, felt uneasy about it. The edgy feeling persisted for days. Your guides were doing some nudging, trying to encourage you to rethink your choice. Soon after, you learned that your selection had far-reaching negative ramifications. You were, of course, not yet familiar with the tried-and-true recommendation from the Happy Medium: trust your gut, follow your heart, and use your head. Now, however, you know that intuition leads and guides guide!

When you are in a peaceful place and making unusually outstanding choices that greatly impact your life, generally your guide is guiding you. It is of course true that you deserve praise for responding well to such guidance and using your best judgment. As a result, everything flows with increased ease. It's a team effort.

Art or Science?

I have a profound trust in, and love for, my guides. They work for a higher power, the highest of powers. There are innumerable names used to identify this beautiful Almighty Creator or Power such as the Universe, Jehovah, and God. Though I often use the term "Universe," the name means less than the force itself. From somewhere deep inside, I have always believed that God is everywhere, both within and beyond, before and after, this or any universe. God is loving, forgiving, and all knowing, and lives in the heart and soul of each one of us. This is what connects our souls to one another.

The foundation of my work is based on this deep belief and also that my talent and abilities were given to me to help others, not to exploit them. Intuition is a gift from the Universe. What I do with it is my gift back. Conducting readings is a fitting venue for such work. I extend that gift by doing what I am guided to do, which is help amplify the voice of the soul. This in turn helps illuminate the soul's chosen path.

A reading is more of an art than a science. I have learned to take everything with a grain of salt, to trust my gut, follow my heart, and use my head. In doing so, I am able to find the middle ground and have become a happy medium.

Deciphering the Psychic Code

Spirits must slow down their vibrations in order to communicate with those on this side of the veil. At the same time, mediums must increase their personal vibrations significantly. The medium's spirit guide (a senior guide) can help the medium receive messages from those on the other side, acting as an escort to the information being transmitted. There is a difference, of course, between the energy of those who have crossed over and the consistent vibration of a spirit guide, and a medium must be able to recognize the subtle vibratory differences each being emanates.

During the first few minutes of a reading, my own guides make a connection with my client's guides. I refer to this as the download process. While my client's guides highlight relevant topics to be covered, my own guides help organize the arrangement. When I have hit on something particularly germane, I feel a sense of weightlessness in my solar plexus. If the client denies its importance, either a loved one in spirit or a guide confirms the information and encourages me to persist. Though the players in a reading may be on differing sides of the veil, everyone is on the same team! We are all present and supportive of the one receiving the reading.

Learning how to communicate with those on the other side is a process. Time and experience have been first-rate teachers for me, as has Faye. Because my desire to communicate with her was bigger than my fear, I became more available to the communication process. The intuitive language—or psychic code—involved in deciphering messages from the other side is unique to every medium. As I develop my skills, the language becomes simpler to understand, and the codes easier to decipher.

I have discovered that spirits use my life experiences, especially the ones that have the most meaning for me, to illustrate their messages. For instance, if a picture of a wedding is dropped onto the screen in my head, I know that the spirit wants me to reference a large, joy-filled family celebration. If I have a flash of what I looked like at twelve, I know that somehow my client is or was dealing with someone who is in a fight with her hormones.

If someone's deceased paternal great-aunt wants a word with her grand-niece, I am able to precisely describe the deceased's energy. It is relatively simple; the feelings I had when near my own great-aunt on my father's side felt a certain way to me. My client's great-aunt, as a way of communicating exactly who she is, projects those same distinct sensations into me. My relationships and life events are used as tools to help me be an astute medium.

For years, I've wondered what mode of communication spirits use to identify each medium's individual intuitive code. In other words, how do they crack the code and learn how to get the optimum use out of us? Well, while in a meditative state once, I was shown a picture of an original, old-fashioned, fully lit telephone switchboard. Every light represented a medium's unique intuitive code. In order to communicate, spirits needed to match the same color wire and light. Once the connection was made, communication could ensue.

The first thing I am shown by my guides, or by a visiting spirit, during a reading is often a major component in my client's life. If, for instance, I see her standing behind a white fence, this indicates a childhood scene. Whatever is happening in the scene holds a long-standing relevance. If I sense someone from the other side and see them on the screen in my head, I look up and to the right. This indicates that the spirit is dropping in for a visit and may have other spirits in tow. When they stand behind my client's shoulder, I know the spirit is recurrently nearby his or her loved one.

All memories are somehow filed away in our minds. Mine are part of the makeup of my own intuitive code. When a spirit wishes to highlight an event in their loved one's life, they simply reference something similar in mine. Use of my life-events file cabinet helps those on the other side place pictures and sensations inside of me that are relevant to their own life, or that of their friend's, on this side of the veil. This is how those on the other side are able to help me help them convey their information. It is an effective way through which I can validate spirit communication.

During a reading, I am totally focused on my client and the information flowing into me. When a disembodied spirit is trying to get my attention, I occasionally may not notice immediately because the spotlight is on my client. But those on the other side are able to find effective and humorous ways to catch my eye—or sometimes, my nose. For a while, I suspected I might have an allergy to something in my office. Out of nowhere, my nose would begin to itch furiously. I soon noticed a pattern: my nose would become irritated only when I was conducting a reading. There was no polite way of explaining my itchy nose to clients, of course. The whole situation reminded me of one of my favorite shows as a child, Bewitched (which I liked because it made me feel less odd to see the characters in the show do things not everyone else did). But now I was the one with an unrelenting itching sensation in my nose. Nice. I felt like such a lady as I dove for a Kleenex.

I do not get to choose the information I perceive. It zips onto the screen in my mind and is then replaced by an emotion that is placed in my heart. Then it turns into words whispered in my ear. All of it is relevant to my client's life—past, present, or future. When spirits from the other side make themselves known, I just roll with it. I know my hit ratio is good because I recognize when I hit home. A sense of absolute peace washes over me.

If a client wishes only to speak with their dearly departed during a reading, and not receive any other information, I decline their patronage because it does not work that way. I am not able to "dial in" in response to the whim or even wish of a client. Rather, I dial in to help people learn what their soul has to say.

We are all reacting, over and over throughout our lives, to someone or something that deeply affected our developing souls. When we ignore that pinpointed pain, a pattern of fear sets in and creates a hole in our ability to love. A seemingly small trauma might be ignored, or a large incident is over-analyzed and under-understood. As Carl Jung said, "Until you make the unconscious conscious, it will direct your life and you will call it fate." There is nothing more empowering than learning that we have the wheel, so to speak. We can turn ourselves in any direction we desire. While we do not control the roads, we do control our minds and the way we react.

There are no facts, only interpretations.
—Friedrich Nietzsche

Medium Mystic

The strongest memory I have of attending Sunday school as a child is when I was trying to get out of going. The second strongest is far more enduring: it was when my class was told that a piece of God is within each of our hearts. For me, those pieces together are part of the essence of God.

When I first began a more formal study of how my abilities operated, I continued to be drawn to the word "mystic" because it fit for me. Mysticism is the practice of achieving an inner knowing of one's self and an understanding that we are all one giant stunning ball of energy. That energy is the Universe and all that exists within it. When you reach for the sense of the larger identity, loneliness slips away. A merely intellectual or logical comprehension about existence pales in comparison to the meaning and sensation that exists in the interconnection of souls.

As a medium, I hear souls from the other side and want to help them feel recognized and heard. Souls on this side are not so different; everyone longs for a feeling of recognition and connection. Helping my client reach that end is a pivotal component of a reading.

Precision and clarity for a medium are key. Because I have a keen sense of my own vibration, I am able to identify any energy that is not my own. When someone from the other side is near, I feel the vibration—every soul has an idiosyncratic vibration. And a residual energy remains in the room even after the soul withdraws. Similarly, if a stranger is in my home prior to my arrival, their energy leaves a residue that I am able to accurately identify as foreign.

A steady sense of self helps makes me strong as a person and accurate as a medium. Understanding what I do well and where I need additional development assists me in growing professionally. In recognition of my sense of self, I am able to distinguish what makes my heart and soul sing.

Each of us has something exclusive to offer the world. This is true, of course, for mediums. Each has special talents and abilities. There may be many mediums that specialize in solving crimes. However, each medium's personality and experiences are what make their work unique. There are mediums who are medically attuned, some who are brilliant at teaching, and some who have such a strong, charismatic presence that as long as they are honest, they are heard. Like everyone else, psychics and mediums do best at what interests them.

One of the greatest honors of my life is to help people connect with the parts of themselves that have been held captive, blocking them from achieving what they most wish for in this life. Whether I illuminate a long forgotten tragic life event or help my client connect once again with a loved one in spirit and consciously pass love from one side of the veil to the other, I am witness to people in bloom. The profound respect I feel for those who seek to grow in consciousness is infinite.

According to my clients, my strength and unique ability as a medium is not only in the uncanny accuracy of the information I relay but the manner in which I deliver it. The genuine empathy, love, and compassion I feel for others is conveyed through my work. That is what makes me who I am as a person and a medium.

Do you remember what you wanted to be when you grew up? Perhaps a firefighter, police officer, teacher, or artist? I can assure you that "psychic medium" never made my list, though I feel blessed beyond words to have the ability and talent to do this work.

Everyone is sensitive and everyone is psychic. Really. Both factors define themselves as we grow from childhood into adulthood. The finished product is evidence of how that sensitivity was accepted. Growing up can be a noisy experience, especially for highly insightful children. Memory of emotions such as joy, delight, fear, and terror seem to be time travelers bearing gifts. Those gifts influence all of your life's choices.

The persistent roar caused by disembodied spirits, along with my awareness of other people's emotions and thoughts, dropped me into an invariable state of overload as a kid. Unguarded and alone in my distress, I promised myself that I would come out whole and help others do the same. This book, *The Happy Medium*, is an extension of that promise.

A Read on the Reading

What is "out of the ordinary" is all relative for a medium. In my work, I have conversations with people who have died, so "bizarre" in my world may differ from what is considered bizarre in most. Overall, my client base is made up of pretty typical people, living regular lives, who for one reason or another are seeking support from what is fast becoming a mainstream resource.

From early 1999 until 2007, I rented office space in a building filled with experienced professionals in the healing arts, including Master Chunyi Lin, a nationally renowned certified international Qigong Master. Three Rivers is a wonderful complementary medicine clinic offering, among other healing modalities, acupuncture. The clinic setting was conducive for professional referrals. In 2008, I moved to a more corporate setting.

My own process in scheduling and conducting a reading has blossomed and matured over the years. The steps are the same whether my client is a partner of a Fortune 500 company or an individual seeking personal intuitive direction. Prior to the scheduled appointment, a confirmation email is sent to my client. It includes the date and time of appointment, payment options, cancellation policy, and driving directions. Also included is the statement that A reading is more of an art than a science. Ms. Livon makes no promise or guarantee of content during a session.

With the exception of name, contact information, and referral source, personal facts about my client are not exchanged prior to the appointment. During the reading, aside from "yes" or "no" answers, the client shares nothing until it is his or her time to ask questions. In order to provide the highest quality of reading, which everyone deserves, it is essential that I know as little as possible about my client's personal life before the appointment.

My first step in preparing for a reading is to take time to do grounding exercises, which includes asking God for divine protection (and sometimes drinking a latte!). If it relaxes me, it works. Then I meditate to clear myself and open up to the sacred energy I refer to as God or the Universe. I establish a formal level of protection from any energy that is negative in nature. Next, I inwardly pray that my work will be a blessing for all, of only the highest good, and for only the highest good. I ask that my client find honorable use for what is shared. I thank the Universe for allowing me to be part of this miraculous process and for all other blessings in my life. An overflowing feeling of gratitude permeates my soul for my life, for my loves, and for being given an opportunity to do this work.

Once I am grounded, I loosen my hold on the circle of protection that helps me guard my personal space. As I consciously open up my intuition to the universal bank of information, a preclusive energy, like an invisible security field, surrounds me. This is similar to a stadium security system, as opposed to the home security system I use to guard my personal space when I am not working. It takes a good deal of energy to maintain this level of protection.

Next, I greet my client and show him or her into my office. As I describe how I conduct a reading, information about my client downloads from the highest part of him or her to the highest part of me. I literally feel images pertaining to my client's story drop into my head and arrange themselves in a particular order. I explain once again that a reading is more of an art than a science. Maintaining perspective and an open mind produces the most effectual outcome.

As personal particulars continue to download, I explain that everyone is intuitive and compare intuition to singing. Both utilize the creative component. Some people are more musically inclined than others, of course. We can all sing (those without the physiological capabilities aside, of course); but some people squeak out their notes and some people belt out a song. Experience and intense training for nearly three decades has enabled me to belt out a reading.

As a conduit between worlds, I am also an interpreter. Any time you have a reading, you must carefully research the psychic or medium you choose to hire. A clean and non-biased interpretation of the information is crucial. The psychic's personality and interests naturally shine through. When using your own intuition or listening to that of another, trust your gut, follow your heart, and use your head. The combination will help both protect and inspire you.

I remind my client to keep their mind open, and to take the information with a grain of salt. All psychics, as I have said, are simply interpreters. As an example of what I mean, I suggest my client look at an object in my office such as the clock. I then ask him or her to describe three things about the clock, with the reminder that there is no right or wrong answer. After they have done so, I explain that someone else looking at the same object could describe it in a completely different way. The clock is a clock. It is all about the skill of interpretation. Trained mediums are highly adept, accurate, and skilled interpreters. Instinct, skill, and experience are a powerful combination.

Once the client is comfortable, I ask for his or her name. As pictures are dropped immediately into my head about the client, I talk, and I talk fast. These rapid-moving images are significantly relevant to what the client is experiencing in their life at the time of the reading. The pictures, often enormously vivid, illustrate how the client may stand in the way of their own success and why. This type of material is a mainstay in my readings because it has been such a powerful, constructive component of my own spiritual and emotional development. It is so true that a medium's personality and life interests play a part in the reading.

While scenes from my client's life, past and present, are played out, I can actually feel their emotions. I see, feel, hear, smell, and taste the information being sent my way. When someone from the other side appears, they, too, drop images in my head to assist in the communication process. A sort of added visual aid!

Cars and Coincidences

As well as bringing us profound messages from the other side, guides can provide helpful hints in our daily lives. One time that I'm sure that my guides were at work was when my husband and I were shopping for a new car. Keep in mind that whenever Jason is searching for a car, it is no small task—he logs in hours online, researching and inquiring. It is a sport for him. As a young boy, he loved anything with wheels; he purchased his first car (a baby blue 1950 Chevy pickup) at the age of fifteen, before he could even drive. But since an automobile is involved in this game, everyone wins. My husband is ethically in tune.

Late in December one year, we were test-driving different SUVs. Mine needed to be replaced. After about an hour of the fun (insert sarcasm here), I suggested we test-drive fast cars. Test-drive fast cars we did. But that was not the only thing we did fast. One car—a silver, five-speed something—really caught Jason's eye.

My finance-savvy husband does not believe in fairy tales, luck, impulse buying, or purchasing brand-new cars. "Too big of a hit the first five minutes off the show room floor," is what he has always said. So what made me sit down with him, do the math, and suggest we buy the thing, I cannot say. Okay, I can. My guides were nudging me to get a move on and buy that car. There were lots of reasons, financially speaking, to do so:

the new body style that year, an extremely low loan rate, and the fact that it was the car Jason had been checking out on the Internet for months. Usually, I stay out of his car deals, and just enjoy watching him have so much fun. But the circumstances were too sweet to pass up. More importantly, I totally trusted my gut.

There have been a number of times in my life when I seriously lacked funds. No matter how much or how little I had, however, I made wise choices and was able to get by. The interest rate thing has never interested me, or made sense for that matter. So when numbers came flying out of my mouth, even I was amazed. I told Jason that if he liked the car, he might want to consider purchasing it. He said he wanted to think about it. We hung out at the car dealership for another hour. While he talked cars, I talked to my guides. He did so out loud; I did so in my head.

After a while and a few phone calls home to beg the sitter to stay just a bit longer with a bribe of the take-out pizza of her choice, I sat Mr. Auto Enthusiast down for a second chat. I asked him if he liked the car. He said yes. I asked him if he could see himself in it. He said yes. I asked him if he wanted to buy it, and he said he thought so but didn't know for sure. The "new car" aspect was throwing him slightly. So, keys in hand and guides in head, I tried again. The conversation went something like this. "Do you remember that man in the brown suit who was checking out the car in question when we came?" He remembered. "Well, he is coming back around seven o'clock with his wife to purchase the car." He asked how I knew; did I hear the guy say so? My husband was the proud recipient of one of my you-gotta-be-kidding looks.

He ran his fingers along the car. I told him that if he did not want the car, it was okay. He just needed to be clear, because the choice would be gone in about forty-five minutes. I kissed his cheek, and told him I loved him and that the car was great. As I walked out the door, I assured him that I would support his choice. Thank God we'd driven to the dealership separately; that kind of exit is usually reserved for teary arguments or soap operas.

An hour later I was at home, cleaning up pizza boxes and helping my kids brush their teeth, the silver five-speed something far from my mind. The phone rang, and my innate caller ID kicked in. On the line was the proud owner of a new automobile! Jason was whispering something, but at first I couldn't hear him over my three sugar-intoxicated children. He repeated himself: "I just want you to know that you were right." "What?" I said, even though I could hear him clearly now. "I am in the middle of the paperwork necessary to purchase the car, and have been for over an hour. I just want you to know that the brown-suited man came back a little after seven, with his wife, to buy the car." I could tell he was smiling. "Just like you said." Now I was smiling.

The circumstances surrounding the purchase of this car felt sort of like a bonus for intuitive work decently done. It sure has been fun for us to drive—although Jason sometimes feels compelled to grumble about it being so new, and I grumble about his grumbling. Pretty much par for the course.

Life Happening

Intuitive insights remind us that we are on the right track and are confirmation that we are following the path our soul set before we set foot in this life. They may lead us to a house, a friend, or a walk around the park. They are natural and normal and our birthright! Intuitive insights, as my friend Aarah says, are "a sign of life happening." But sometimes life gets in the way of life and we cannot see what is in front of us. We can always ask the Universe for help, perhaps in the shape of a signal or symbol. If we are open and receptive, those signs recurrently find us.

A good rule of thumb is to stay in touch with your senses even after you have made a vital decision. After a small amount of time has passed, ask yourself if it continues to sit well? Do you feel a sense of calm about your choice? If so, your intuitive self is on the mark. If not, you may wish to revisit the situation.

If, for example, you have been considering joining a new fitness club and the name of one club in particular has been the topic of conversation recently with your coworkers, people on the bus, and fellow shoppers at your favorite health food store, this might prove to be a sign. Another way to benefit from signals from the higher self or guides is to formulate a particular question in your mind. For instance, if you have been contemplating a move to a new city such as Seattle, ask the Universe for something that would validate your choice. Keep your mind open—you might be pleasantly surprised at what presents itself. If a friend invites you to see a movie which happens to be filmed in Seattle, it may be a sign. If you receive an email out of the blue from a cousin who lives in Seattle, that may also be one.

A helpful way to verify a signal from your higher self is to check in with your intuitive senses. If your gut jumps with flowing butterflies in response to this verification, you may be onto something! When a potential sign shows itself, run it through the old "trust your gut, follow your heart, and use your head" assessment. Your instincts await notice. Notice them and do yourself proud.

One example of this kind of experience in my life occurred when I was studying for my real estate exam. I had become locked into the fear of failing. The test contained highly mathematical content, and because I am dyslexic, numbers present a particular challenge. I had failed the pretest miserably, and melted down emotionally.

In an effort to make the meltdown complete, I went to the store the day before the formal exam and purchased chocolate. Rather a lot if it, actually. While filling my cart, I bumped into a woman whom I'd gone to cosmetology school with years before. When I got home, there was a message on my answering machine from someone I used to work with when I cut hair! All this reminded me of how the cosmetology test was a breeze because I was prepared. I realized that my guides were doing their stuff—so that I could do mine! I telephoned a close friend who had recently passed the real estate exam. She taught me a few relevant mathematical computations, without which I would have failed.

Connecting with the two people from my hair-cutting years was no accident. I could have ignored the sign and failed the test. Instead, I acknowledged it and passed the test. Everything in life happens for a reason.

Understanding the Clairvoyant in You

In what way does data most effectively reach you? What is your favored mode of communication? We are all intuitive psychic beings. One way to discover how you tune in is to ask yourself, "In what way am I most sensitive?" What is your most sensitive sense? Do you have a strong ability to differentiate scents? Are your taste buds able to distinguish one spice from another? Is your ability to hear exceptionally sharp? How about your dreams, day visions, or "gut" feelings—do they frequently come true? When you walk into a room, are you able to sense what transpired prior to your entrance?

The part of you that is most sensitive is frequently your opening into the world of intuition. It is your most receptive sense. It will center on one of your five senses. Our intuitive instincts are so basic; it is just a matter of being in tune with them!

If your most keen sense is your gut instinct, this equates to the clairsentient (clear sensing) Claire. Let's say you accepted a position recently with a starter company. You had a nice rapport with your coworkers and a not so nice rapport with your direct supervisor. She was critical of your work and at times corrected you in front of your peers. As a result, you felt enormously self-conscious. Also, she showed favoritism toward men. Though her supervisor recognized your good work and supported your efforts to improve, the tension between you and your direct supervisor continued to escalate. Your stomach hurt whenever you came in contact with her.

After six months of hard work and a decent effort to resolve the conflict, the growing tension caused you to search for a new position elsewhere. During the third interview with a potential employer, you met with a new partner. While at the meeting, your stomach hurt in the same way it did at your current place of employment. A job offer is extended. Later, when you thought about the last interview, your stomach began to hurt again. This very likely is your intuitive voice making noise by way of your stomach. It is giving you a warning. Take note! To acknowledge this is to show it honor. The new partner may have insecurities similar to those of your current supervisor, and behave in the same way. The more you notice your intuitive voice, the louder and clearer it becomes.

The archenemy of intuition is lack of sensitivity. Know this: There is no such thing as being overly sensitive.
—Judith Orloff, *Intuitive Healing*

Facing Forward

Working with so many wonderful clients has given me great insight into the human soul. I have deep respect for those embracing a dark night of the soul, which is frequently a predecessor to gaining a higher state of consciousness. In this space, there is a profound absence of faith, light, and peace. A feeling of being caught between old patterns and new patterns permeates. There is a sensation of being exiled by the old self, and a need to find a permanent entrance into the new self. It is not always necessary to hit rock bottom to discover an inner truth. It is significant however, to be willing to do so. Being brave and facing forward takes guts.

If your goal is to raise your level of consciousness and increase your own psychic prowess, you are well on your way. If information is what you crave, read with an open mind, and read often. Keeping your mind open keeps your awareness up.

You may find yourself wanting to grow as a psychic and medium without having to do any internal work. If an exact map or blueprint is what you seek, I must tell you that there is none. Actually, there is no blueprint to reaching a higher level of consciousness with or without being willing to do the work. And yet, a higher level of consciousness is exactly what you will need to pump up your psychic muscles.

How you get there is a personal choice. What has worked for me, as well as for countless others is to feel the emotions that make you uniquely yourself. Search for and be available to the higher message in any given situation and make the best out of exactly where you are in your life. As Gita Bellin wrote, "the fastest way to freedom is to feel your feelings."

Our individual stories are all distinctive. The destination of each of our journeys, however, is not. At the end of the day, or at the end of a life, we always see our deeds: how we loved, how we chose against love, how we followed the path of our soul, and how we followed the path of our fear.

Be Brave with Yourself

It is only in being brave with ourselves that we can face the world unafraid. From such a space flows the essence of why we are all here. There is no absolute blueprint, of course, for understanding how to work life, but it seems to flow if we go in the direction we are led. The process of increasing your intuitive abilities works pretty much the same way.

Some of the questions my clients ask are sweet and silly. "My schnauzer just died; when it's my time, can my dog and I live together again on the other side?" "Will my wife still snore in heaven?" A common question my clients ask is how they can best become more skilled, or skilled at all, as a medium and/ or psychic. It is by far one of my favorite questions to answer because it involves embracing the beauty of soul.

My answer: It boils down to this—understand who you are, how you feel emotionally, and why you make the choices you do. Be brave with yourself. How well do your intentions meet your actions? As your emotions expand they pave the way for your spirit to soar. Your spirit naturally wants to be closer to the source, the all-knowing bank of love and wisdom that is everyone's inheritance. The only things that must die to bring it forward are the lies you tell yourself!

Every one of us must face him- or herself. It is why we are here. In the end, or somewhere along the way, things tend to fall into place. There is a particular brand of humor, irony, that acts as a beacon to some of those moments. You may have recognized one or more ironic eye openers in your own life. What once was a source of deep pain may now be a source of wisdom and joy. It is a matter of balance. Once you set a pattern of knowing how you feel, you know better who you are. A heightened state of the intuitive senses is a natural by-product of this process.

My vocation involves helping people identify just where they are standing in the way of their own success. During childhood I was prone to tears, and was teased mercilessly for crying in public. Ironically, I now help those wishing to move forward in their lives to find the source of their own tears—both the ones that choke them and the ones held hostage inside. My chief liability in junior high and high school was not fitting in—my biggest source of pride as an adult is knowing that I do not need to.

It is empowering to think in terms of divine order. We are all loved children of this infinite and beautiful Universe. There is a raison d'être for where we are and why we manage to endure. Looking for the lesson in something dark is a powerful way of not becoming absorbed by it.

When grieving spouses come to see me in hopes of making a long-distance connection with their other half on the other side, they commonly gain a sense of calm and relief. People worry and wonder if their loved one is in fact safe after they cross over. The highly personal, detailed messages and images that come through to me in a reading help them find some peace and perhaps the resolution they crave. Their spouse, child, parent, or sibling is well, and wanting them to be also.

Ask any eighty-year-old, and they will tell you that life is over in a flash. Those on the other side understand that they will be reunited with you in the blink of an eye. In the meantime, they can visit. Whether you recognize them consciously is up to you, and your higher self.

> *A wise man can see more from the bottom of a well*
> *than a fool can from a mountain top.*
> —Author Unknown

Tuning In and Figuring It Out

As a self-taught psychic medium, I've discovered that converting present circumstances into training opportunities can be very helpful to my understanding of my own psychic code. Analyzing how a series of events developed over time provides hints about future outcomes. Remembering the feelings I experienced during the events is also helpful. In thinking this way, I have unraveled more than a few mystic messages.

For example, I once worked for a small, privately owned company. The manager was not a totally honest man, to put it mildly. Let's call him Ray. Ray played by his own rules and broke them when he saw fit. He was slick and dishonorable. Within a month of accepting the position, I quit—a brave move, because I was broke. For a long time, whenever I met someone who was not on the up and up, the feeling I used to have around Ray flashed through me. After several of these "Ray" moments, it became clear to me that my guides were making use of the strong reaction I had had to the man.

Learning to read such signals is like learning a language that changes as often as do you. By tuning in to your inner feelings, you are led to your basic instincts. Basic instincts are, basically, intuitive instincts.

Have you had the experience of hearing and seeing what is going on around you seemingly from a distance deep inside of yourself? As if you were hovering above, yet firmly seated within? When those moments arise, they are priceless, so take note. Watch, feel, and listen. Those emotions are the road map to your intuition. If you can recreate them on your own (without the use of drugs), you are onto something big.

It is no small coincidence that reaching certain points of higher consciousness, or making a connection with the higher soul, transpires following extremely difficult times in our lives. It is at those times that we allow ourselves to slip into ourselves instead of into our self-consciousness. In allowing what lies stagnant inside to find air and understanding and thus fly free, you open yourself up to a beauty unimaginable. As Kahlil Gibran wrote in *The Prophet*, "Your pain is the breaking of the shell that encloses your understanding." Be brave with yourself, so that you may face the world unafraid. Allow your understanding to take flight. The bank of love and wisdom that is your inheritance awaits.

> *Have no fear of moving into the unknown.*
> *Simply step out fearlessly knowing that I am with you,*
> *therefore no harm can befall you; all is very well.*
> *Do this in complete faith and confidence.*
> —Eileen Caddy, *Footprints on the Path*

Tools and Techniques:
Intuition

As we've discussed, we all have within us an individualized psychic code, much like a language. Learning this language of intuition is an art. Art should not be judged and neither should you, especially as you learn to trust your instincts—they help you to find balance in your life. What can throw that balance off is fear.

If we are not in a place of fear, we can be in a place of love. The way to become more in tune psychically is to make peace with any fear you have about knowing yourself. We all dread being emotionally exposed, even to ourselves. People are more resistant to genuinely feeling love for themselves than they are to owning up to their vital mistakes.

After nearly thirty years of reading thousands of individuals and conducting workshops, I have come to the following conclusion: the key to deciphering your individual psychic code relies on utilizing your intuition to move forward spiritually, draw from the light, and learn more about who you are and why you make the choices you do.

Exercises for Your Intuitive Senses

During the next few days, observe how you experience input, not how you process it. Which of your senses do you use to process most things? Are you cognizant of which sense your mind registers first? For example, if you witness an argument between two strangers about a parking spot, how does your body initially respond in your first seconds on the scene? Recognizing your own procedure will serve to strengthen your intuition.

Having fun with skill-sharpening tools is an excellent way to increase your intuitive awareness. If the following exercise appeals to you, give it a try: When the telephone rings, ask yourself who the first person is to enter your conscious mind. Is this actually the person who phoned? Do this as often as possible for seven days. Notice how you improve over time!

Intuitive Alignment

No matter how sensitive you are or are not, absorbing the energy of other people is a part of life. It is important to learn to wash the excess energy away. Take this example: my children do not like to take showers. Unless of course, my husband and I allow them to eat bright red Popsicles while soaping up. After the showers, however, they all behave better and seem much lighter in mood and vibration. Red Popsicles aside, this is true for adults as well. Water cleans more than your skin. The next time you shower, imagine any vibration that is not your own washing away. Picture all negative energy, anger, frustration, and disappointment sliding down the drain. For a quick fix, wash your hands with cold water. Splash some water on your wrists as well. Think of it as an intuitive alignment!

Taking Emotional Notes

Think back to a time when you were about to be hired for a job you loved. Record that feeling in your mind. Now think of a time when you were offered a position that turned out to be a poor fit. Do the same with any situation of substance. Keep the thoughts and feelings you record simple. When next you are in a situation that resembles those you have intuitively recorded, a reminder message may drop down as a heads-up. It may take any number of forms—a dream, a nagging feeling, or a flashing picture in your mind.

Try this exercise when you are making small decisions as well. For instance, the next time you are grocery shopping and trying to decide on a brand of food, pick one and internally record how you felt when you picked it. After you have used the item, record how much you enjoyed the product. If you liked it, your gut will respond in a certain way. Let's call it a twang. Your next purchasing experience may prove to be more efficient. As you shop, be aware of the same twang when you are considering trying a new item.

The more aware you are of how you feel, the more aware you are in general. Make it a habit to take emotional notes. The song your intuition sings will astound you. It may not change your world, though it is sure to rock it.

Envelope Exercise

Think of three people you dearly love. Find a photo of each person; he or she must be alone in the picture. Next, find three identical, unmarked envelopes. Sit in a quiet place, alone. While you hold each picture for five minutes, think of your favorite memory of the person. After you hold the first photo, place it in its own envelope and seal it. Be careful not to mark the envelope. Do the same with the remaining photos.

Mix the envelopes up and place them in a line on a table. Next, wash your hands with cold water. Place your hand over the first envelope. Notice the picture that pops into your mind, or the sensation you feel. Record a brief description of your impressions on a piece of paper. Place the paper on top of the envelope. Do the same with the remaining two envelopes. When you are ready, read the description before opening each envelope. Whether you had one hit or seven, your skill will build in time, if you have an open mind.

This exercise is an excellent way to build intuitive skills. Once you become accustomed to deciphering the nuances of a soul's vibration, you have a greater chance of sensing a spirit from the other side when you are paid a visit.

I love those who yearn for the impossible.
—Johann Wolfgang von Goethe

Maintaining Balance

The word "meditation," from Latin, encompasses both physical and intellectual exercise. The daily practice of some form of meditation is an essential step in growing your intuitive abilities. It clears the mind of thought, keeps us in the here and now, and sharpens awareness of our senses. Wandering thoughts obstruct stillness of the mind and the path to insight.

The route to clearing the mind may take any number of forms. I used to roll my eyes when the suggestion was made for me to meditate. I had a difficult time sitting still and the sound *omm* made me giggle. Eventually I learned that whatever worked to help me empty out worry and thought, promote attentiveness, and observe without reaction would allow room for peace.

One key element in meditation is breath control, or the capability to direct the breath. This will help clear your thinking and center and ground you. In Sanskrit, *prana* means "breath."

Breath is considered the life force. As a result, you control your life force when you are able to control your breath.

If you enjoy taking classes, a course in meditation would be helpful. Ask the instructor for permission to test-drive a class to see if it fits. There are countless formal and informal methods that may work flawlessly for you. An excellent hands-on book on the subject is *The One-Minute Meditator* by David Nichol and Bill Birchard.

When we remain conscious of our thoughts, we can wash away the dark ones and focus on the glory of the here and now. According to Nichol and Birchard, "We discover through our own experience what researchers have revealed through experiments: What makes all of our most pleasing moments most pleasing is absorption in the present moment."

The authors detail how a change of mood can be accomplished in just sixty seconds. Each chapter offers three highly effective one-minute meditations that help readers move past the "reactive, preoccupied one-minute mind."

When I conduct a workshop and want to raise the attendees' vibration, I lead them through my own elementary method of meditation. I call it "belly breathing." There are hundreds if not thousands of variations of the belly breathing method.

Try it. Look down at your belly (no negative comments please). Let your eyes rest there or close them. As your belly rises and falls, focus on your breath. Listen to the hum as you inhale and exhale. Then, as you inhale slowly through your nose, count to five. As you exhale slowly through your nose, count to ten. This method does not make me giggle. It helps me relax and clears me of unwanted energy in between readings.

Belly breathing and a repetitive form of exercise make an excellent combination. Some examples of repetitive forms of exercise include bike riding, skiing, walking, swimming, and jogging. The traditional sitting in a lotus position and repeating a mantra works beautifully for some as well. They are all decent choices.

Other activities that act as meditative aids are reading, singing, cooking, gardening, painting, drawing, and even cleaning! If you are able to do the activity, relax, and stay present, it can work. They are all decent choices. The blueprint for finding your own meditative perfection and intuitive code is within you.

As an example, let's say you choose an exercise such as walking as your form of mind-clearing. Set aside at least thirty minutes, wear comfortable shoes, and head to a place that brings you joy. A park or quiet neighborhood—whatever is convenient.

During the first few minutes, allow your mind to empty of thought. Acts as though you are a good friend, listening to another friend unload pent-up emotion. The approach must be healthy and self-respectful, with no criticism of any kind. During the next phase, repeat something positive and life affirming about you and your life.

For instance, if you are a cancer survivor, repeat that you are completely healthy and cancer free, living and loving the life that serves your higher purpose and the Universe. If you have recently started a new job, repeat that you are working in a wonderful place, respected, compensated well, and doing excellent work. Place a positive spin on whatever you are focusing on and always phrase your thoughts in the present. Keep it simple. Breathe, and maintain appreciation and awareness of your surroundings.

In doing this kind of exercise, your vibration has an opportunity to elevate. The combination of physical exertion and focus grounds your body, which better seals the deal! You raise your conscious thought to a higher level and automatically draw in a positive force.

The next time you feel peaceful, back up and uncover what you did to get there. For me, so much energy is running through my body that it is essential for me to unload without bumping into anyone else emotionally. Being silly, really silly, has worked well for me all of my life. Since I feel in high frequency and at top speed, I need to reset my dials. I balance the serious subject matter I deal with everyday by drawing on the opposite: non-serious energy!

2

The Groundwork
of Grounding

*Be not afraid of life. Believe that life is worth living,
and your belief will help create the fact.*
—William James

A Thing of Honor

People become interested in the intuitive process and open up
psychically for a range of reasons. Perhaps a near-death experience started the newly attuned on their voyage into higher states
of consciousness. Or the cause of the altered outlook is the sad
loss of a loved one. But no matter what its origin, the inner voice
that you hear is a thing of honor. Though the journey may have
been dark, opening up to the intuitive voice is a beautiful thing
to achieve.

At one time in human history, mystics were greatly revered. A sage was considered noble, and held in the highest of esteem. The secrets to obtaining a sense of oneness or connection with divinity must be earned, and were praised and handed down from generation to generation. Today, people are once again realizing that psychic intuition is not simply an heirloom or a source of simple entertainment, but a pathway for those who sincerely strive to acquire a deeper connection between themselves and a higher power. Wisdom and insight naturally follow this journey. Our intuitive senses are so basic that accessing them is just a matter of being alive and in tune.

There are practices that can help us become strong and alert psychically. Not a chart—more a way of life. Two critical elements you should strive to develop, while developing your intuition, are addressed in this chapter and the next: grounding yourself, and defining your boundaries.

Grounding and Your Health

Being grounded is all about being connected to your soul while centered in your body. It is essential to be grounded in yourself in order to develop and maintain good boundaries with the rest of the world. Needless to say, these are both essential elements for a medium's emotional health (and everyone's health, for that matter!). The most effective way to ground yourself is through physical exercise. Getting your body moving and promoting breath control is a means to that end. Feeling anchored means being present in the here and now—it entails feeling connected to the earth, rooted in your body, and aware of your surroundings.

Being grounded is also the initial step in self-healing. When we are in pain, we commonly lose contact with our conscious selves because the agony is too much for us to bear. Working through our sorrows will help us fulfill the soul's master plan for growth, since we are more responsive, self-aware, and willing to change when we are grounded. This objectivity helps us create through love instead of fear.

I think most people would agree that it takes much more energy to avoid dealing with a situation or emotion than it does to face it head-on. What you do not deal with, deals with you. Once you understand this, you lose your fear of what will jump out at you in life because you have a deeper understanding of what is happening to you internally. You can then be anchored in the present moment, living in the here and now, while maintaining a sense of what you are feeling and thinking.

The Princess and the Pea

As an example of how blocking your pain can unground you and unsettle everything else in your life, let me share the story of my client Annie. Impatient and restless, this twenty-something woman arrived for her reading with a lovely face but a heavy vibration. It was not until near the end of the reading that I learned the source of her grief. While she was vacationing, a tragic event had occurred: her fiancé had fallen off a balcony and died, leaving her emotionally crushed and unable, years later, to move forward.

Scenarios similar to this reoccur in readings so often that I have named them *the Princess and the Pea* effect. The story varies in style, but the theme remains the same. Big or small, an unspoken problem makes a lot of noise.

When people seem emotionally hollow and stuck in limbo by some unidentified force, the seed of the pain must be located. It is often something a client would say they "got over," or possibly an incident that appears so ancient and small in nature that it holds no significance.

The initial pictures that dropped into my head about Annie indicated that she was having a difficult time getting past her own stubbornness, a trait inherited from her mother. I saw a perfectly manicured woman with similar coloring to Annie's. I knew she was Annie's mother because I felt my own mother's vibration. Her body was turned toward Annie while her head was turned up and away. Next, I saw two bumper cars crashing into each other.

Do you remember, in elementary school, receiving math or reading questions that had pictures in place of some words? Smack dab in the middle of a sentence was a picture of something significant to the story or problem. In this case, the picture of two red bumper cars smashing together popped into my head after the picture of Annie's mom with her nose in the air.

Her mother, who is still on this side, had allowed her stubborn side to prevent her from experiencing a moment's relaxation. I described Annie's mom as a woman who cared very much about the way she looked physically, but not a great deal about the way she felt emotionally. She raised her children, including a younger son, to do the same. Annie begrudgingly agreed that this sounded like her mom, and confirmed that she had a younger brother.

Annie's stubbornness was causing her heart to lock and her mind to close. She exuded a sad bitterness that belied her age. She was significantly blocked and initially hesitated to confirm any personal information. She was testing me. Clients who are afraid to open up commonly toss the "convince me" challenge into the air.

I told her I sensed that she felt especially alone in the world, and unsupported. Then I saw a vision of a young man, not very tall, with dark hair. He understood her and was always with her. The man was a huge support and loved her, and she him. She trusted him and thought he was her equal. She did not close him out from fear, as she did most other people.

Annie looked at me with empty eyes. She said she did not know who the man was. I asked her if she had a young daughter. She said yes. I explained that I saw this cute young man in her daughter's room. They were laughing and coloring together. He liked to hide behind curtains and move them around. Annie said she did not know who this person was. I continued to list identifying characteristics about him.

I thought it strange that she did not register who he was. My sense was strong that he was a big support in her life. When something comes across to me as clearly as did this dark-haired man, I know there is huge significance. But Annie kept shaking her head. She was obviously confused and a bit irritated at my insistence that she must know him. I decided to move on with the reading. Whoever this man was, he mattered to her. I was certain she would identify him after the reading.

As the reading progressed, Annie began to relax. The more hits I had, the more she cried. The more she cried, the younger she looked. Her face relaxed, worry lines falling away. This was a sweet woman in considerable pain. She had events in her life that she did not want to feel. This blocked her from feeling anything but her repressed grief.

I correctly described her place of employment and the fact that she wanted to purchase a new home. I identified the city where she was looking and what style of home appealed to her. Annie smiled for the first time and said excitedly that I'd depicted exactly the house she wanted, down to the location. Her relationships with friends, with the exception of one, were distant. As I described how she'd felt at a birthday party the week before, and why, Annie nodded in agreement.

My stomach felt less tight, a sign that my client was feeling more relaxed and secure in the process. Toward the end of the reading, I again mentioned the tendency she had to close her heart. I explained that when people are not moving forward, there is a place in their hearts they do not wish to touch because of the pain.

If painful issues are not openly dealt with and resolved, they act as lumps under the carpet that everyone is forever tripping over. The energy consumed in the unconscious attempt to bury and evade an area of discomfort is astronomical. But walking around the perimeter of a room instead of through it becomes preferred to facing a wound that has colored our response to life and love. The problems then become a much bigger force in our lives than necessary, since we spend so much time avoiding that area of the carpet so as not to trip.

When I stated that she wasn't moving forward due to pain, Annie looked at me with a cool glare and said she did not understand what I was talking about. She was stuck, guarding her wound again. I took another tack, describing the story about the princess who could not sleep because there was a pea under her mattress. No matter how many mattresses were placed on top of the pea, the princess' unconscious state detected it and would not allow her rest.

The pea must be acknowledged. Once a life-altering event is brought into the open, the pain behind it begins to dissolve. The pea is no longer in control and loses its power. The princess is now able to find peace and move on with her life.

After hearing my rendition of The Princess and the Pea, Annie was quiet for a few minutes. She said she was hoping that something about her old boyfriend would come through in this reading. There was something familiar about the vibration of the man she spoke of, and I knew it had been present earlier in the hour.

Then I heard a voice say, "I did come through!" I felt tingling on the back of my neck, which indicates that someone is saying hello from the other side. Annie then whispered that her boyfriend had died several years before.

The spirit energy I was sensing had a quirky sense of humor. A picture of John, one of my old boyfriends, flashed onto the screen in my mind. At first, I felt afraid that the John I knew had died. Taking a breath, I asked Annie for her boyfriend's name. She said John, and I realized that my guides had shown me the face of my friend as a way of telling me the spirit's name. Feeling relieved and a little silly for allowing my own fear to step into the reading, I let her know that John had been with us the entire time.

He was the not-so-tall, dark-haired man who supported her always. Generally, I can sense if someone is "living" on this side or the other, but when John had appeared earlier I did not realize that he had crossed over, because he indicated an ongoing (meaning daily) connection with Annie. Usually the person on the other side signals me that theirs is a crossed-over energy, but John hadn't until now—the tingling on the back of my neck had been totally absent before. Energy is energy, and it is not always clear as to which side it belongs.

Yet here John was, standing next to me, and in Annie's life every day. He wore a soft, yellow, well-worn sweater, blue jeans, and a gentle grin. When I described other defining characteristics, such as his quirky sense of humor (proper enough for children yet with a hidden agenda for adults), his relationship with his parents and sister, and the way he had of putting people at ease, Annie's eyes sparkled. She said she'd often heard her little girl laughing alone in her bedroom while she colored. Also, the curtains moved, as if by themselves, often enough that she'd suspected it was John. She had been too closed, early in the reading, to acknowledge the truth behind my words.

John also gave me a description of his family, which Annie confirmed as she relaxed into her chair. He wanted her to know he was okay and that his death was not her fault. He was apologetic for the pain his accident had brought into her life.

Three years ago, Annie and John were together and in love. Though the relationship had its bumps, they were talking about getting married. The tragedy had occurred while they were vacationing in Mexico. John showed me a sudden, unexpected death caused by a crashing of sorts. I felt a tremendous blow to my body as if the stuffing were being knocked out of me.

As I relayed what I sensed from John about his death, Annie told me she was not a witness to it, though she had been nearby. She said it was not a car crash, yet I continued to feel a smack to my entire body: a quick, forceful, and totally unexpected blow. John showed me he didn't immediately know he was dead. I saw him looking down on his lifeless body with disbelief.

Annie's eyes were sad as she drifted back to the scene that would shape so much of her life. Her voice all of a sudden sounded very young as she described in great detail how she'd learned of John's death. They were staying in a luxury high-rise hotel with beautiful views of the ocean. Annie awoke one morning to a loud knocking on the hotel door. She noticed that John was not in the room, and felt a strong urge to look out the window. The balcony curtains were blowing and she felt a chill throughout her body.

Fifteen stories below, police were covering up a corpse. She knew it was John's because she recognized his shoes. He had fallen off the balcony while she slept. No scream had awoken her. Two hotel employees were on the other side of the door, waiting to ask if she could identify the man found dead below her balcony.

Her guilt at bringing John to Mexico and to his death had kept Annie emotionally stagnant. John was indicating that it was not her fault, shaking his head "no" and pointing to his chest. He'd made the choice to sit on the balcony railing to enjoy the view. He did not hold her responsible, and neither should she.

The final message John had for Annie that day was his most poignant. He did not want her life to be about the loss of his.

In his short time on earth, he experienced more joy than most people do who live twice as long. Annie nodded in agreement.

John's exit from this world and into the next was certainly not the usual route of departure for a young man. His beautiful message for Annie about the wisdom of living life fully, however, is one that I have been privy to more times than I can count. A spirit so filled with love, such as John's, wishes to convey a deep sense of support for those on this side and a sense of tranquility about what comes after death.

My work as an intuitive coach is seldom monotonous. I love to witness people in bloom. To sit in front of someone doing this work is to learn how to recognize and value a deeper part of the higher self.

A Spooked Psychic

Learning to ground yourself, if you are susceptible to that sense of disconnecting from the present and from your body, takes time and practice. Sensitive children, of course, often have a very hard time, since they have not yet learned to ground and guard. I was one such child.

There are scores of children who, like me, are casually referred to as "free spirits." Some, as it turns out, are mediums! My Grandpa Max would be proud to know that I continue to live up to my nickname, Mazik, which he bestowed on me when I was less than two years old. *Mazik* essentially translates as "spirited one." Ceaselessly responding to what is, instead of what others wish it would be, has been one of my long-standing characteristics. Max had mixed his insight with his humor, giving each of his seven grandchildren a nickname that, even now, is ironically apt.

One of the benefits of growing up in a large, extended family is that I get to relive hilarious childhood memories with others. My cousins, brother, sisters, and I love to reminisce at family gatherings. As children, my siblings and I spent a lot of time with both sets of grandparents. Lou, our maternal grandfather, would take all nine of his grandchildren out every Saturday. The day always included a sugar-filled lunch and a trip to the Minneapolis Institute of Arts.

During the summer we occasionally would visit the cemetery where much of his family is buried. This may sound truly odd, but to us it was a part of life. I was not afraid, though I do remember feeling overheated and unquestionably crowded by what I now realize were spirits attempting to communicate with me. Lou would quietly sit beside his sister-in-law's or mother's grave and tend to the flowers while we tried to pronounce the Russian and Hebrew names of the deceased.

It must have been quite a sight, nine children fearlessly laughing and running up and down the isles of tombstones. We certainly meant no disrespect. We were simply celebrating life. In hindsight, I appreciate how all of us were introduced early in life to the concept of a lasting connection with those on the other side.

At the Minneapolis Institute of Arts, my grandfather would cart us up the gorgeous marble stairway to view the breathtaking treasures filling the individual rooms. It was a loud place for a young medium, rich in spirits floating around as well as art. My cousins would listen intently as our grandfather read the carefully worded description of a painting or sculpture.

Repeatedly, I would move a few feet away from my family. I could feel the spirit energy around me and was unconsciously responding. Souls can be so attached to their work, or rather the emotion that was the inspiration; they feel the need to guard their work, even from the other side. I always felt like I was being watched.

One time, when my family walked toward a particular sarcophagus (a funeral receptacle for a corpse), I felt uneasy, like we were where we should not be. I remember sensing details about the dead king who had been placed in the sarcophagus. He was a young, frightened boy forced to make adult decisions, and he died as a result.

A few minutes later, we were looking at a painting depicting a girl lying on the bank of a river, her arms tied with rope, her long flaxen hair circling her head. The plaque accompanying the painting said she had been drowned for having an affair. As I looked at the picture, it seemed to shift, coming alive in my mind. I remember knowing that the girl had been wrongly accused by a jealous, greedy husband, and I felt her terror as she sunk in the water. The story had been a true one, and the spirit of the girl was not at rest. For years, I had trouble shaking the image of her from my mind.

After our visit with the art, Grandpa Lou would pile us into his car and transport all or most of us back to the Spanish-style south Minneapolis home he and my grandmother had lived in for over fifty years. I remember helping my Grandma Dolly clean out a drawer in my uncle's old bedroom one afternoon. My hope was to snag a toy or two that I knew she had hidden in the dresser.

But all I snagged that day was the feeling of my great-grandmother Frances' spirit. As Dolly pulled out an aged plastic bag with something white in it, my arms became instantly chilled. The bag contained an ancient silver hairbrush and a few strands of hair belonging to my dead great-grandmother. I felt a weird tingle, like someone unseen was standing near. I actually remember seeing a picture of my great-grandmother in my head. I felt like she wanted me to tell Dolly that she knew her daughter loved and missed her and that she loved her as well; words of affection, I later learned, were rarely spoken in that family. But since I wasn't too certain what was happening, I ran out of the room yelling, "Are you sure you want to keep that, Grandma?" I did not know which was worse—not getting a toy or getting the creeps.

Ghosts and Religion

When I was a child and my parents watched a news story on TV about a missing person or someone found dead, my body felt flushed and I had the sensation of spiders crawling on my skin. This tingling or flushed feeling is a popular calling card of the intuitive voice. The spirits I had known when they were alive on this side of the veil, however, did not scare me much. It was the "other" energy I sensed that undid me. Like most people, my big reaction to ghosts was my big fear of the unknown.

Ghost or no ghosts, I felt deeply compelled to study the metaphysical. Anything about the supernatural or new age that did not have to do with dark magic interested me. I read books, read people, studied world religions, learned yoga, and made up my own form of meditation. All this newfound knowledge was oddly familiar and became an integral part of me.

As afraid as I was of ghosts, I was more afraid of the voice of ignorance. I knew from the wisest place inside of me that the sensitivities I had were part of the light, not the darkness. Yet whenever I heard someone mention the word "psychic" (which was more widely recognized than the word "medium"), it was almost always in disdain. The three things I needed most were knowledge, validation, and comfort.

In my initial investigations into Western religion, it seemed that the subject of life after death beyond the ideas of heaven and hell was not considered an appropriate area for study. Looking back, it astounds me that my familial and religious roots offered some of the most valuable and validating principles out there for me, yet I did not come across them until later in my travels. In my youth, I didn't know that age itself provides a certain vantage point.

People with minds and souls brighter than my own have long been sensing, speaking, and writing about disembodied spirits and reincarnation. As my own research on the subject intensified, I read about biblical characters and well-respected clergy members throughout history speaking of, and to, the dead. Some extended permission to consult the spirit of those who had crossed over. Calling on the spirit was accepted because the spirit never dies, but calling on the body of the dead was completely unacceptable. Likewise, fortune-telling was not tolerated.

Instinctively, I had known all this to be true. Overall, I had a sturdy and proven sense of right and wrong. I am not a fortune-teller; I am simply adept at reading energy. If sensing the vibration of those who had crossed over was wrong, I would have sensed it. I have always been drawn to positive energy and literally repelled by negative. Reading about the ancient rabbis' acknowledgement and validation of the work of mediums helped ground me. My spiritual hometown, Judaism, in fact recognized the language of my soul.

The Roots of Grounding

Being well-grounded is the essence of protecting yourself. You are also better able to take responsibility for your actions and thoughts when you are in your own space. Grounding is a key to happiness.

In order to stay in your own space, you must be comfortable in it. Doing emotional work, as Annie did during her reading, is crucial to this end. You need to also be comfortable and centered in your body. A tree is grounded; it has sturdy deep roots connecting it to the earth. We humans rarely seem naturally anchored. When we observe that somebody is acting clueless, spacey, or as if their head is up in the clouds, we know that person is not in a grounded place. They may have an intense headache, or feel agitated as a result.

People are grounded when engaged in an activity that is meaningful to them and requires a strong presence of being. Exercise that resonates well with our body is especially helpful. Activities that bring joy naturally center or anchor us. A feeling of deep concentration can bring a true sense of groundedness. To maintain a sense of balance, do things that help you feel connected to your body. Work out, do yoga, dance, clean your home, eat something that makes you feel good afterward, hike, bike, listen to music, write, draw, paint, get a massage, garden, hang around an animal or two, take a long quiet walk. Do whatever makes you feel energized and connected to your body and the earth.

An instantaneous way to anchor yourself is to visualize your body as a solid oak tree, roots penetrating deep into the ground. The goal is to feel firmly connected to something solid. Another great method is to say your name, either in your head or out loud. When you do, you are actually calling your soul back to your body!

Intuition on the Go

My children play a really fun game called "trash your shoes." The object of the game is to ruin your shoes before you outgrow them. The more expensive, the better. The winner gets a trip to the shoe store with out-of-body mommy.

I tend to leave my body within ten minutes of entering a mall. The number of people, the lights, the loud music, and the wild marketing techniques combine to do me in. Department stores and mediums do not mix. If you are at all psychically sensitive, it is not easy to stay grounded when you are in a crowd. While in some cases tuning in to your intuition in less-than-ideal circumstances is helpful (as in the story I am about to relay), in general it can be exhausting, and is best avoided. Messages from your guides will reach you in another way.

On this particular day, I was required to accompany Aaron, the winner of "trash your shoes," to the mall. Sitting on the floor of the shoe store, helping my seven-year-old stuff his feet into a shoe two sizes too small, I glanced up and thought I saw my friend Trisha. But Trisha lived in New Mexico. Then my child dropped an adult shoe, size twelve, at my feet. He looked at me pleadingly and said, "Mom, these fit, really! And they give me room to grow!" I suggested he try them on and walk around the store. He sauntered off, wearing what looked like snow shoes.

I found a mini-version of the coveted shoes just as I was beginning to lose my grounding. The winner of the soon-to-be-trashed shoes was now hungry. The sales person was on the phone with her boyfriend, apparently breaking up for the fourth time. A picture of a skinny boy smoking a joint dropped into my head. I could smell the pot. She was better off without him. My contest winner now was thirsty. The soon-to-be ex-girlfriend of the pot-smoking kid was crying on the phone. Someone's little girl fell and bumped her head on a nearby bench. Behind me stood a pregnant woman. I could feel her baby kick in my tummy! My head hurt.

Twenty minutes later, my son and I were sitting on a bench in the mall, enjoying some non-dairy yogurt when, once again, I thought I saw Trisha. I made a mental note to call her. Aaron snuggled closer to me. He loves watching people, and I love watching him. I turned my focus to his beautiful, wonder-filled face and wondered how much of the emotion in the mall he unconsciously sensed.

When we arrived home, my husband told me that Trisha's husband had phoned. She had been diagnosed with breast cancer two weeks ago. They were just beginning to share the news.

When I say I do not always see the bad stuff coming, I mean it. I hadn't had any intuitive buzz warning me about Trisha's cancer. The first hint I had that there was something going on with her was at the mall. From that point on, I started remembering how I feel when I see a look-alike, and I'm alert to any new intuitive patterns setting in.

Receiving Mode

The universal bank of information is available to everyone. People all over the world are seeking ways to tap into this bank and receive insight. Two popular paths used to tune in are meditation and yoga. Both help reset thought and breathing patterns, opening a portal into the intuitive self. A well-chosen meditation feels like cleaning house mentally.

Psychic mediums tend to be in a receiving mode all the time. I describe it as being like a radio that lacks an "off" switch; I have an "on" and a "pause" switch, rather than "on" and "off." Learning to put myself on pause helps bring balance into my life. It cuts down on overload and overreaction. Instead of being in a space that makes me feel over the top, I am in one that helps me feel I have it under control. Turning the volume down goes a long way toward obtaining balance and a sense of equilibrium.

When I have not had time for exercise and meditation, my tuner switch is stuck on "on." I am not grounded, and my boundaries are also a mess. It feels like I am in a library where all the books talk simultaneously. It is an agonizing experience. Overload is no fun. The lines between what other people are feeling and thinking, and what I am feeling and thinking disappear. It makes me feel sick to my stomach, irritable, angry, and claustrophobic.

Mediums are not the only ones who experience extreme overload. The same can be said, though perhaps not as often or to the same degree, for the majority of people. The next time you are at a mall, look around. When you see a "vacant" sign flashing in someone's eyes, it's a good bet that their conscious self has temporarily left the premises. If this goes on for any length of time, overload begins to feel like an emotional bender, complete with headache!

When there is so much noise within, I cannot hear my own inner voice and am unable to clearly and cleanly connect and receive. I am lost without my guides and their support. It took years for me to understand what was happening. As I have learned to recognize it, the still inner voice has become much more audible over time.

Thankfully, I have learned the steps necessary to put myself into "pause" mode. Exercise, meditation, decent nutrition, and time spent alone all help toward this end. It is when I am in a peaceful, well-grounded space that I am able to open up and perceive more clearly the messages I am meant to receive. Fine-tuning my grounding skills has helped me fine-tune my intuitive skills.

The key to receiving information, intuitively speaking, is connecting or reconnecting with your body, spirit, and mind. The line connecting to the universal bank of information must be clear to be effective. The line is you. If long walks and kickboxing help you feel more fused, soul to body, you have chosen well.

Elevator Ride

Curiosity and awareness about metaphysics continues to be on the rise today, as is evident by the number of bestselling books and popular television shows about psychics and mediums. The psychic in all of us is now more able to "come out" and ask questions. Thankfully, inner seeking is much more outwardly respected.

Living with a foot in both worlds, as mediums do, is never dull. Those who have close friends or family members who are mediumistic or psychic may be offered an unusual inside view into that world. As much as it is a privilege to do this work, a potential by-product is a sense of social isolation. A powerful remedy for feeling alone, however, is feeling understood.

The support I receive from my husband is priceless. Time has been good to us. As in any decent relationship, we have worked hard on expanding our communication skills. I no longer become so bent out of shape because he cannot read my mind. Now he doesn't get so bent out of shape because I can read his! I help him breathe life into situations that have gone flat by offering insight and a fresh perspective. We help each other weather life. He has been the calm in my storm more times than I can count.

As Jason's awareness of the intuitive process has grown, so has his own intuition. As his intuition has grown, so has his understanding of himself and me. One Saturday night, we were headed toward the parking ramp after a night out. I was eight months pregnant with our first-born son. Standing in a moving elevator felt like a roller coaster ride. My "pregnancy glow" was turning paler and paler as the elevator rose.

We had only three more floors to go when the elevator stopped yet again to let people in. The people were slightly inebriated. Not drunk, though they smelled of alcohol. When the elevator doors opened again, all three exited without incident. I turned to Jason and asked him if he thought they were tipsy. He said yes. I asked how he knew. They did not act drunk, and had no bottle with them. He said he could "just tell." "How could you tell?" I pressed. Preferring not to repeat himself he gave my belly a sideways glance and said, "They smelled a little like wine."

How would you feel if you were the only one who could smell the wine? It was as obvious to you as the color of the carpet. How would you feel if you were one of the few who had a sense of any aroma at all? Since there was no real physical evidence, you would be told you were wrong because no such sense as smell even existed. Yet every day you could smell the aroma of bread baking, lilacs in bloom, or a fire burning. It gave you joy and helped warn you of danger. Those around you had no sense of smell, so they deprecatingly insisted that there must be no such sense at all.

That is what it feels like to be me, much of the time. I can sense spirits around me even when no one else can. To some, they do not exist. To me, they are a very real part of life—as much as my sense of smell, sight, or sound.

While as a medium I am able to interface with those who have crossed over, as a psychic I am able to see down to the core of someone's soul by simply looking at the person. Their fears, emotional patterns, level of joy, ability to love, and personality traits are all presented in one tenth of a second. My abilities also help me zoom in on their lovability factor—the sweet, genuine underside of people. That part is amazing! Still, it's a lot to take in. As much as I love people, I am not interested in knowing their "stuff" unless I am working.

My training as a medium has been largely in learning how not to read people, as apposed to how to read them. I have worked at length to understand how to tune out the waves of information. Remaining grounded and in tune with my guides are major components of this. As a result, I am now more available to my family and friends. Disembodied spirits no longer see a flashing sign above my head that says "hi, I sense you, bug me!" When I am finished with a reading, spirits from the other side usually leave.

The Not-So-Nutty Professor

Prior to her appointment, Blanche was definitely a skeptic. A licensed surgeon, she had a confident air and a sparkle in her eyes. Nothing in her medical training remotely covered life after death— her job, and her understanding, ended when a patient died. She was perhaps an example of the pitfalls of over-grounding... living so much in the here-and-now that she wasn't connected to her intuition.

But Blanche quickly opened her mind. Or her brother Clyde opened it, anyway. After explaining to her how I work as a medium, I opened up intuitively and soon met someone wishing to connect with Blanche. It was her brother, a science professor who was deceased. In fact, he was quite possibly murdered.

I described Clyde's physical characteristics, along with his sense of humor. He said he had died of a wasting disease or complications associated with it. Blanche confirmed that the man I described was her brother, and that he had died of cancer. Then Clyde said he had made some decisions that resulted in speeding up the time of his death. Blanche just stared at me. She clearly wanted more information about what I was perceiving before she confirmed anything.

Clyde showed me a beaker, much like the ones used by scientists. This one had an Rx printed on the glass, along with an exaggerated version of a Mr. Yuk sticker. He then dropped me an image of a dark-haired woman who was much younger than he was, holding the tube. Frankly, I didn't like her vibe; she was sort of like Elvira without the cool nails. Her hand was covering the Mr. Yuk sticker. I felt like he was telling me that this woman, who may have been his nurse, had "mismanaged" his medication. I asked my guides for clarification, just to make certain I was interpreting the picture correctly. The same scene dropped onto the screen in my head, Mr. Yuk sticker and all. Blanche animatedly confirmed the image.

She had suspected foul play in her brother's death, and also felt immense guilt that she had not visited Clyde more often during his illness. They lived in different states, and she'd had a tight surgical schedule to contend with. But Clyde showed me an image of himself brushing her comment off—I could feel that he had great affection for his sister. There was nothing in his vibration that resembled resentment.

I saw a scene where Blanche seemed to be calling some sort of authority figure. Her brother pointed a finger at his chest. I didn't understand the gesture initially; I sensed that he had felt he put far too much trust in the caregiver. Then I realized he was taking responsibility for his actions. I subsequently learned that he had instinctively known he had little time left.

Blanche confirmed that she had wanted to hire a private investigator to look into Clyde's death. She said that the dark-haired woman was her brother's new girlfriend, Andrea, not a nurse. Blanche suspected that Andrea had deliberately over-medicated Clyde. She had also attempted to change the beneficiary in Clyde's will (but she did not know that Clyde had never signed it).

After seeing the results of her brother's autopsy, however, Blanche gave up the pursuit of justice. Nothing could be proved; Clyde's cancer had spread significantly. Though Blanche harbored ill feelings toward Andrea, the confirmation from Clyde during the reading was what she needed in order to find some resolution. It was clear that Clyde favored his sister over their other siblings. When I explained the feelings he was sending over, Blanche confirmed this, but said she never knew he felt that way until after his death—several of his friends had told her as much when she went to Clyde's home in Arizona to get it ready for sale.

At the reading, the two siblings shared a long-distance last laugh together. Clyde showed me a picture of a legal document;

in the signature portion, where his name belonged, was the word "no." Somehow, the will Andrea had prepared was never recognized.

I have had the pleasure of reading Blanche for the past five years, around the holidays. She reports feeling her brother around from time to time. Her sense of intuition has improved with her opening mind. The more she acknowledges Clyde's presence, the more in tune she becomes.

Physicians by trade are not taught to feel. Their training is around diagnoses. It is no surprise that there are times when all of us, physician or not, over-ground and are stuck in our heads, ignoring our emotions and instincts. When we open up to the intuitive process, those times eventually become a thing of the past.

Balancing Act

People require balance in life, and balance and intuition are like peanut butter and jelly. Or wine and cheese—take your pick. They are far smoother and more enjoyable together than apart. As a medium seeking to find balance, the heat is turned up a few notches. The challenges of work and school, familial obligations, finding time for exercise and friends, maintaining physical and spiritual and psychological health, and understanding world politics are all waiting to be equalized. Then there is the compelling need to be loved, feel love, and nourish beautifully relevant love. This really throws everything into high gear. Life holds surprises. Just when the scent of equilibrium is near, change occurs. Equilibrium is but a dream.

Or perhaps not! If you remember to stay in the present, as you feel every sensation, color, song, and word around you, you are ahead of the game. Being in and open to the moment brings its own gifts! Growing yourself spiritually helps add a sense of balance and dignity to life, even in the most awkward of times.

For those new to, or in the intermediate stages of, understanding their awakening intuitive senses ("medium mediums," as I like to refer to them), the extra added nuance of indiscriminately hearing someone's thoughts, knowing who is on the phone before caller ID kicks in, and hearing the dearly departed voice of Great-Grandfather Roger from beyond might prove a bit much.

Unless, of course, the medium works to respect what is happening inside. Honor emotion—your own and others'. Observe the process without becoming absorbed by it. To honor something does not mean to offer it full control. If you are convinced that you are the only one who can smell your deceased brother's all-too-sweet cologne in the air every morning, or clove cigarettes like the ones your friend used to smoke before cancer took him, do a little research. Remain open minded. That very mindset can be validating.

How often and when do these aromas occur? Is there an anniversary or a birthday approaching? Perhaps you are sensing someone from the other side. Possibly, your new next-door neighbor smokes clove cigarettes. The golden rule is not to fall too far over on the side of either ignoring your feelings or being ruled by them. Find the happy medium, and stay there.

Create Your World

You are vacationing in Vermont. The ski chalet is hosting a generous happy hour, complete with a highly talented orchestral quintet. You drag yourself into the chalet after nine hours of vigorous snow plowing. As if you have not had enough of the cold, you need a pack of ice to reduce the swelling because your arm aches from muscles unaccustomed to such strain. Not only that, you crave a good eight hours of sleep. Yet the scene greeting you in the chalet is so inviting, you feel drawn to it—to the wine, the beautiful view of freshly fallen snow on the nearby trees, and the savory scent of hors d'oeuvres. Deciding to sleep later, you and your companion sit down to listen to music and sip wine.

Your legs feel like lead. Everything on you aches, including your eyelids. Still, you love the atmosphere. To what is your mind drawn? Where do you focus your eyes and your thoughts? How does holding the image make you feel? The choice is yours, and will set the stage for the rest of the vacation and, in no small way, for the rest of your life.

What does this have to do with grounding? Well, the same magical force that supplies the bank of intuitive information we all tap into is the one that helps each of us create our individual reality. Where your mind is focused, so goes your life; catch a falling thought and see where a new and improved one leads you. However, we must maintain a silence inside us to be able to take notes and observe what we are thinking. That silence comes from being grounded.

There are those who have readings in hopes of hearing something supernatural that will make their unhappiness disappear. What most people do not understand is that their own words and thoughts are magical. I have found that some people consider this a happy fact, and some find it a sad one. Those who are stuck in a pattern and wish to be released are delighted to be told they have the power to break free, while those seized in a pattern of fear and victimization have difficulty hearing that they must assume an additional burden if they wish to start improving their lives. Nearly all people are somewhere in between. Change requires guts.

Changing our minds about how we view ourselves can and does transform our lives. This is fact, not fiction. When a client is teetering on the edge of believing this truth, about to accept the idea that they themselves can change their life, my guides offer an array of suggestions meant to illustrate the point. In certain instances, they draw up a picture of me as a fifteen-year-old girl. The emotion I throw off about myself at that age must speak volumes!

During a reading, as I have mentioned, a spirit or my guides show me scenes of my own life to help illustrate what is occurring in the lives of my clients. There is an element of personal exposure involved in this process, and information is delivered so rapidly I do not always have time to change the names to protect the innocent—meaning me! As much as I like to keep my private life private, my own experiences are a testimony to the strength of our individual personal powers.

So, taking a deep breath, I share the ugly truth. As a teenager, I lacked confidence and any semblance of self-esteem. I was harassed mercilessly for having frizzy out-of-control hair, being weird, and not fitting in. Standing out in a crowd, as I did without any effort, felt terrible. Several insensitive kids would regularly remind me of how hideously ugly I was; it was a game to them. Somehow, though, even as they wounded me, I understood that they were suffering some sort of inner trauma.

Although I felt miserable, I was also striving to be grounded. So I followed my intuition and changed schools the following year. Allowing myself to trust my gut proved to be one of the most pivotal decisions of my young life. As I prepared to start fresh at a much larger high school, I made another life-altering assessment that led to a changed thought pattern: it was none of anyone's business how ugly or lovely I was. No one had the right to wound me. From that moment forward, each time I looked in the mirror, I smiled. Confucius wrote, "Everything has its beauty but not everyone sees it."

With the exception of my little brother, who was just doing his job, no one ever teased me about the way I looked again. The funny thing was, it did not surprise me that I was respected. My entire being radiated an altered vibration, one with good self-esteem. My grade-point average shot up from C at best to mostly

A. Each day I reminded myself that I was a loved child of the Universe and deserved to be happy. This episode marked the first time I realized how being grounded could help me observe and control my thoughts, and therefore my life circumstances. I was able to change my thoughts, and therefore change my world.

I was only a teenager at the time; adults have far more power in their lives to enact change. Either you set new patterns or commit to living in the old ones. If you focus on your arm, the world will spin around it and its pain. But if you focus on the music, the beauty of the view, and how relaxed you feel, your world will be filled with more of the same. Whatever your choice, that choice sets a new pattern or strengthens an old one. Your thoughts offer a platform from which to view your world. Transformation is based on shaking up old patterns in your life. And, of course, it requires guts!

It's simple. The more aware you are of your feelings, the more aware you are in general. In a state of heightened consciousness, your intuitive hunches become illuminated. When you acknowledge them, they recur. Personal insight can help you move forward in life if you allow it, for intuition is alive and well in all of us. It helps us live our lives more fully and serves as a mode of communication between loved ones on both sides of the veil. It assists us in determining which options best serve our souls.

Growing your intuition does not require a club membership. We all are intuitive beings. It is just a matter of being alive and in tune with our intuitive selves! The more aware you are of your feelings, the more aware you are in general.

> *All that we are is the result of what we have thought. If a man speaks or acts with an evil thought, pain follows him. If a man speaks or acts with a pure thought, happiness follows him, like a shadow that never leaves him.*
> —Buddha

Tools and Techniques:
Grounding

In an effort to become more permanently grounded, there are specific techniques that can be put to use. They involve connecting with one's spiritual source of energy or one's own vital life force. People feel more grounded when engaged in something important that requires a strong presence of being.

Maintaining Balance

To maintain a sense of balance, do activities that make you feel energized and connected to the earth and your body. As I have said, creative activities such as painting, drawing, and gardening are great choices. Connecting with animals and nature is highly effective, as is any form of physical exercise.

Practice any one or all of these helpful, protective techniques: imagine a giant invisible bubble around your body that allows nothing negative to enter. Envision a white light pouring in, through, and around you. Picture a dark green cord attached to either the base of your spine, if you are sitting, or the soles of your feet, if you are standing. The cord is flowing down to the center of the earth, anchoring you there. Do some belly breathing (gentle breaths) and envision yourself firmly rooted to the earth through the cord.

Wear clothing that brings you joy. When you feel spacey, look down at your shoes, pants, and shirt. Thinking of your clothing snaps you back into your body. Say your name out loud. Say your name to yourself. Find the picture in your mind that brings you the most comfort and safety. Is it of you being surrounded by friends? Driving in your car? Singing in your favored place of worship? Find the place that helps you feel safe and protected. Bring it with you wherever you go and put it to work when you need protection.

As a result of this work, you are no longer held captive to the pain of your past or the fear of your future. You are present in your life and gain an inner knowing, and therefore are not swayed by other people's reactions. Your response to them become less reactive, less governed by emotions you never before understood that you had.

The Once-Over

As I have illustrated, large crowds do me in. When I am about to conduct a well-attended workshop, I need to stay in my body in order to work effectively. A tried-and-true technique to keep me anchored is what I refer to as "the once-over." In my mind, I check out what I am wearing, beginning at the top. As I breathe evenly, I take note of my shirt, belt, pants, socks, and shoes. By the time I have finished giving myself the once-over, I am in my body and ready for what is next.

House Clearing

House clearing is about restoring balance. It helps change your emotional settings, also known as patterns, because it helps lift your personal vibrations. The clearing and cleaning of personal space enables us to reclaim it. We are then less vulnerable. Think of it as spring cleaning for the soul.

Emotions leave a residual vibration. Have you ever walked into a room following a heated discussion between two people and felt tension in the air? Depending on the intensity of emotion felt by the participants, the room could feel very heavy and dark. Old, stagnant, and negative vibrations need to be washed away from a home. Emotions, both heavy and light, leave debris. Energy attracts energy. Clearing out any energy that is not your own is a healthy way of maintaining a decent living environment.

Disembodied spirits radiate energy. While usually we experience the positive energy of our loved ones, it is possible that you may encounter a spirit radiating a negative vibration. This spirit is an unwanted guest. House clearing is a powerful and effective way of clearing them out.

House clearing is also referred to as smudging. Smudging, or the ceremonial burning of gathered herbs, is part of many Native American traditions. Also known as Original Americans, Aboriginal Americans, and American Indians, Native Americans are recognized for deeply respecting the earth and understanding how its properties can heal. For centuries, Native Americans have used sage successfully to purify and show respect for all parts of creation. Smudging calls on the spirits of sacred plants to drive away negative energies and restore balance.

The burning of herbs such as sage, sweet grass, and cedar has also been used for emotional, psychic, and spiritual purification by great numbers of other healing, religious, and spiritual groups. Most rituals involve some element of cleansing. Incense, fire, or herbal smoke mixtures are burned around the world, including in places such as India, Southeast Asia, China, Israel, Africa, Australia, and Europe. Smudging is also treasured for its aromatic properties. It should be done with love, reverence, care, and an attitude of respect for the process and for the plants themselves.

The most effective way I know to clear a space, or "sage" it, as we refer to it in my home, is to clean it first. If you do not have time for a good old soap-and-water house cleaning, simply wash a few dirty dishes and empty your garbage. Your intent matters. Getting rid of clutter is also a highly effective way to change and raise the energy vibration. The act of cleaning and clearing clutter sends a wonderful message to the Universe of an openness, and willingness to change.

The smudging ritual can be defined as a powerful spiritual or mystical house cleaning. It leaves a space fresh and clear of unwanted energy. Smudge to enhance or create positive energy.

Clearing the debris is a way of reclaiming your space and making room for further joy and prosperity.

To do this powerful spiritual clearing, you will need a few items: something to burn, and something to burn it in. Please be mindful of using appropriate, fire resistant tools, and be aware of the possibility of upper respiratory issues arising due to the smoke.

The most commonly used herbs are white sage, cedar, cilantro, mugwort, lavender, and sweetgrass. I often use white sage alone. Or I combine white sage, sweetgrass, and cedar. The most popular combination of herbs is white sage and cedar: white sage clears the negative energy, while cedar fills the space or hole that the sage left behind. Sweetgrass is thought to welcome in good influences. The fragrance of sweetgrass combined with sage and cedar is often found to be soothing. You will find these herbs online, in co-ops, and in health food stores.

Another option is purchasing a smudge stick. Smudge sticks are bundles of dried herbs tied together with colored thread or a strip of hide. Look for one that combines sage (preferably white), cedar, and sweetgrass. You will also need matches and a ceramic or stone bowl, a seashell, or a natural, fire-safe bowl. An ashtray also works well. Though large feathers fan the smoke nicely, they are not a must.

Next, open a window. If possible, leave it open during this process. If it is too hot or cold out, just open the window for a few minutes at the end of this process. If you are completely unable to open a window, run a fan and crack the door open. The unwanted and negative energy moves out the window with the smoke. The goal is to move the air around and out, as well as to introduce new air.

The next step is to stand in the middle of the room. Light the dried sage and cedar and turn around in circles three times, moving clockwise. Allow the smoke to wash over your body.

Never allow the lit herbs to stay aflame—smoldering smoke is the goal. Let fear-filled thoughts move up and be taken away with the smoke. See all the negative energy in and around you being cleansed away. Picture yourself as healthy, balanced, and centered—emotionally, physically, and spiritually.

You are now ready to move on to the next step in smudging. Concentrate on the four corners of each room. Traditionally, you would start your cleansing in the east, fanning the smoke with a feather or just your hand. Continue around the room in a clockwise direction. The smoke from the smoldering herbs attaches itself to negative, old, tired energy. Remember there should be no actual flame, just a smoldering. As it clears away, it takes with it the negative energy, releasing it to another space where it will be turned into positive energy.

The amount of smoke the sage produces can be an indicator of the intensity of unwanted vibrations in your home. Once you smudge your home a few times, you will be able to gauge a baseline amount of smoke. The process works no matter how much smoke your sage or smudge stick produces, as long as it is lit.

As you walk through your home, remember that it is your space. Keep a picture in your mind of happy times spent there and those to come. Maintain a positive emotional attitude. Allow old, unnecessary emotions and thoughts to dissipate. Picture them flying out the window with the smoke. Remember, this process is an ancient and powerful one. Whenever possible, I light sage in between client appointments. It shows the exit sign to any visiting spirits who remain on this side after their loved ones have left my office.

Some people find it helpful to say a prayer or prayers during smudging. Religious tradition, or lack of it, is not a prerequisite. What makes the process holy, and thus more effective, is that the prayer or thought is one of love, and comfort. For example, there is a Cherokee blessing that is both beautiful and filled with a protective, loving meaning: "May the warm winds of Heaven blow softly on your home, and the Great Spirit bless all who enter."

The short version of this process is to open a window, then safely light the herbs you choose (including sage) and walk through the room or rooms you use most. The herbs can be used to simply uplift your mood.

Once the benefits of the smudging are felt, things take on new meaning. A powerful time to meditate follows. Use the positive energy you have created to envision a beautiful life for yourself. Help draw to you that which your heart and soul wish for you by keeping your emotional, physical, and spiritual space clean. Fill your mind with this energy, and with the photographs of your life taken by your soul.

The foolish man seeks happiness in the distance,
the wise grows it under his feet.
—James Oppenheim

3

Your Space or Mine?

Happiness is when what you think, what you say,
and what you do are in harmony.
—Mahatma Gandhi

Lost in Space

It is nine o'clock on New Year's Eve, and you're attending the party of a dear friend. Dressed in festive sparkles and black, you've been looking forward to celebrating the New Year and tasting the food your friend has so carefully been preparing for days. Always decent at schmoozing, you're chatting away with a tall, cute man who has recently broken up with his girlfriend. He has just told you a funny story about a mutual friend, then asks if you would like another glass of wine.

As if out of nowhere, you feel so sad and out of sorts that you want to go home. You excuse yourself and find a quiet space away from everyone. The sad feeling disappears. What happened? Well, your energy had moved into the tall, cute man. What you felt were *his* feelings, not your own. You were in *his* space. Though he was not speaking of it at the time, his grief over the loss of his girlfriend was leaking out. Once you found your own space, however, the feelings that were not your own departed.

If the tall, cute man had chosen to share his emotional load by spilling his broken heart in your lap with story after story about his love, he would have been exhibiting poor personal boundaries. You would have been quite aware of why you felt exhausted; his emotional vomiting would have made you feel ill. But poor psychic boundaries are problematic as well.

Have you ever felt drained after just sitting next to someone? "Off" somehow, and confused as to why? Whenever you are unaware of where your space begins and another person's ends, your boundaries are misaligned. Remember, expanding your intuition involves more than just following gut feelings. Grounding yourself is essential to your health and happiness— and so is the ability to form decent boundaries.

Handmaiden of Dysfunction

If you are serious about tapping into and growing your intuitive capabilities, the most fundamental thing to learn is where your space begins and where it ends. An outstandingly effective way to grow psychically is to gain an understanding of what you are feeling and why. As a result, you will no longer be a slave to fear. I know this does not sound sexy, spooky, or special. It is, however, one of the most powerful, life-altering measures you can take. If you do not learn to protect yourself from absorbing vibrations that are not your own, you leave yourself vulnerable—mentally, physically, and spiritually.

When your boundaries are skewed, everything feels off, noisy, and congested. You may feel strangely spacey. When you are afraid to experience your emotions, you abandon a part of yourself, which leaves you vulnerable. Anxiety is your backdrop, and insecurity and poor judgment may be your shadow. But negative energy is difficult to eliminate if its source is unknown. Once you are aware of how your personal vibration feels, you become a master at sensing when another energy is encroaching.

Decent boundaries are the building blocks of intuitive work of any kind, and personal and psychic boundaries are truly one and the same. When you establish and maintain them, the benefits are infinite. Because you are consistently aware of how you feel, the chance of feeling like you were in a hit-and-run by emotions like sadness and fear decreases significantly. You may find that you are better able to stand up for yourself, and as a result, people take you more seriously. Perhaps you will be more motivated, healthier, and less tired and drained. Goals may be achieved at a faster pace due to your new ability to focus. Conceivably, you will feel more peaceful and eager to live in the here and now.

Knowing how to stay in your own space and recognize your personal vibration helps you gain an understanding of other energies as well, including the presence of those who have crossed over. Because you can now more rapidly detect any vibration that is foreign to your personal energy field, you are obviously in better control of your environment.

People often do not know how to recognize when another person is in their psychic space, or vice versa. For instance, when you take on someone's feelings, as in the example of the New Year's Eve party, you are in that person's space. If someone extends unsolicited advice and/or insists you take it, that person is in your space. When you do not stand up for yourself, you are not exercising decent boundaries. If simply standing near another person drains you on some level, a boundary has been crossed.

Blame, a traditional method of boundary crossing, is destructive on numerous levels. It is a friend only to fear and entails one party blaming (dumping) a mistake or bad mood on another party. Poor boundaries are the handmaiden of dysfunction. Maintaining decent boundaries is an art form. Be an artist!

Bricks and Mortar

If boundaries are the building blocks or foundation of intuitive work, exactly what is the mortar that holds the blocks or bricks together? Grounding. Grounding and boundaries are intimately interconnected; grounding is what enables you to build your boundaries.

Decent boundaries are barriers that ward off fear and darkness. We cannot construct them without the benefit of feeling grounded. To be grounded we must have a strong presence of being. It is difficult, if not impossible, to have boundaries without grounding.

Becoming Bridget

Bridget, a tall, Sophia Loren look-alike, sat down, steaming cup of coffee in hand. I had a strong urge to refer to her as Brianna, and had from the moment she contacted me for an appointment. As I ran through a description of how the reading process was to ensue, my nose began to itch and colorful pictures whirled through my head. Someone wanted an audience with Bridget.

As words describing how her actions collided with her intentions rolled off my tongue, my nose actually began to hurt. That someone who wanted an audience with my client was neither patient nor overly kind. His vibration felt demanding and was draining. I knew from her guides that it was important to describe the unwillingness she had in her life to speak up for herself with family, and how it had affected every aspect of her life. Her heart and her actions were doing battle. It seemed, however, that the pattern had begun to vary.

Bridget was a person with a shining spirit and a willingness to love far beyond the norm. She excelled at opening her heart—and lowering her boundaries—and overcompensated for other people's shortcomings by doing their work for them. But a one-way sort of love has nowhere to go except down. My client felt down.

When I read a client, I temporarily loosen my own boundaries and feel the client's emotional reactions as if they were mine. (In the 1980s, the term used was "becoming one" with another soul.) During the reading, I could feel the heaviness in Bridget's heart and how it settled in her stomach. It was as though she was walking around carrying guilt-related boulders in her belly. She barely looked at me. My heart ached for this woman who had given far too much of herself away.

I saw an image of her son, a shining mirror of his mother. As I relayed some potentially useful health information about her son's lungs, the ardent spirit who had been waiting for an audience moved to stand behind Bridget. He now had a father-like demeanor. He had died from a wasting disease in the chest area; while alive, he had wanted his daughter to focus on his needs rather than her own needs or her son's. The spirit's energy was turbulent and somewhat repentant, and he acknowledged how unfair his expectation of Bridget had been.

He showed me a picture of himself with a desperate expression on his face and demanding words spilling out of his mouth. His eyes were sad as they looked away from his daughter's. Bridget's father had allowed his fear and assumptions to overtake his judgment. But he clearly loved his daughter. As I have mentioned, when a spirit journeys back to this side of the veil it is to offer messages of love and accountability.

Bridget confirmed the information I shared. Her father had died from emphysema-related complications. There was an expectation that she abandon her life to help him live through the last stages of his own. He'd insisted that she move across the country to be with him. However, she'd worked hard at building her self-esteem and personal boundaries and was no longer a slave to her fear. Though she wrestled with guilt, she did not uproot her life and move.

As her father's energy became softer and his affection more obvious, the spirit of Bridget's mom moved in. She was with a beloved man. The screen in my mind showed a close-up of the brother. At the same time, I felt a love and protection so deep and sharp I knew he must have been her mother's younger brother when they were both on this side of the veil. The love felt similar to how I feel about my own little brother. I am fiercely protective of him and always have been.

I saw the mother standing, with her brother silently at her side. Her energy was loving and pragmatic. She had much to say about wishing she had done something to acknowledge the inequality of expectations in the family when she was alive. She was proud of her daughter and proud of her grandson as well.

Bridget's mother's soul radiated with love. She did not drop pictures into my mind; she gently placed sensations in my heart. It is like emotional speed-reading but without the potential to miss anything significant. In order for this sort of communication to transpire, the spirit with whom I am connecting must abound with a high voltage of love. The spirit's lovability factor must coincide with or surpass my own.

I sensed that Bridget could use further validation about familial issues. She was stuck in self-blame. She was in the grips of truly coming to terms with the knowledge that being expected to take care of everyone's proverbial stuff is too much to ask.

As a way of substantiating the truth of her mother's presence and sentiments, I silently asked the mother to send another picture or sign. She showed me a lovely, stylish hat propped at a tilt on her head. She sent a feeling of love that she had for her husband straight into my heart. I accurately described aspects of her parents' close relationship.

Bridget smiled through tears, saying that her mother had lost a younger brother in a car accident decades ago, along with a younger sister. The sister's name was Brianna. Bridget was supposed to be named Brianna, after her aunt. Her mother had adored wearing hats and, even though her husband was an onerous man, she had treasured the relationship she'd had with him.

Bridget had reached a pinnacle in her life when her father became terminally ill. She had worked to understand herself and build her self-esteem and boundaries; as a result, she was no longer willing to say "yes" when she meant "no." During the reading, she heard messages that validated who she was and who she had become. Bridget clearly appreciated what her parents had to say.

Still, the words were long overdue. Her parents' acknowledgement of past events validated how far Bridget had come. Had either of them been able to truly see her, beyond their own stories and needs while on this side of the veil, it would have benefited all souls involved. Bridget knows this and now moves forward with ease.

The personal life deeply lived
always expands into truths beyond itself.
—Anaïs Nin

Uninvited Guests

For years I felt spooked out by something I could not explain. I suspected that I was alone in my perceptions, because my family and friends were not having a similar response to certain people, places, and things. As a child, the most well-traveled emotion I experienced was fear. The odd things going on around me were far from validated. There was much less information available at the time about the "sixth sense." People around me thought it was nonsense. This upped the fear factor, which left me more vulnerable. It would have made a huge difference if someone had said, "You are not alone. There are other people who experience these things as well. Let's find out together what it all means. I believe you."

All mediums on some level register the vibration of those who have crossed over. Their own souls radiate a certain glow, whether they are expert or untrained. Disembodied spirits recognize a medium's glow. They are drawn to it because they long to be heard and acknowledged! Some spirits will go to great lengths to catch the third eye of a medium. Perhaps it is the same for them as it is for small children—negative attention is better than none at all.

Souls on either side of the veil are drawn to vibrations that are similar to their own. Think about it—have you ever referred to someone as "being in good spirits"? Or perhaps heard friends or family members say something like, "Dad's in good spirits today"? What do you think it all means? Soul energy is alive and well on both sides of the veil and very much a part of our lives. When you are in a good mood, good energy is magnetized your way. The same is true for a bad mood. Dark energy is attracted to dark energy.

Spirits retain a residual of all of their former personalities. Some are loving and kind; some, not so much. The spirits in the not-so-kind category have been known to swoop in on the vulnerability of under-trained and untrained mediums who have not yet learned to define their boundaries. A little knowledge without self-protection can prove to cause a lot of trouble. Young people in the throws of puberty especially need strong emotional filters, because hormone changes open them up psychically.

Low-level spirits are drawn to those they can manipulate in much the same way muggers target little old ladies. Just like there are unsound people in the world, there are unsound spirits out of the world. Remember, knowledge is power, so there's no need to be afraid. Understanding when to shut down the third eye takes time. Until then, there are highly effective techniques to employ that help to protect everyone!

Learning how to shield ourselves psychically is closely related to the way we protect ourselves in every other way in life. If, as a child, you were taught to stand up for yourself and others and to not accept doing something that made you feel uncomfortable without asking questions, you had the start of good boundaries. If you learned early on that you were loved, accepted, and deserved good things, you knew that the Universe had your back. Much like a toddler who crawls away from Mom to explore the world, then quickly crawls back to make certain she is still there, people of all ages need to feel there is a safe place to go. Remember: when you know when you are safe, you know when you are not. That inner knowledge builds great boundaries. If you have not received these messages, start giving them to yourself now. It is never too late to learn this valuable skill.

As far as disembodied spirits go (whether kind or unkind), they are in some way on *our* turf. Once I understood that the life I am experiencing is "my turn" over here, and that the spirits have had theirs and are now in my space, the spirit activity around me calmed down. Lights, TVs, radios, and other electrical objects no longer had lives of their own. Sharing space is one thing—giving it up completely is another.

Simply put, the Universe gave me the gift of this life. Living life is complicated, more so than any one of us can understand absolutely. But I recognize that the way I view my personal space helps me build it, and therefore helps me shape my life. By "personal space" I mean my body, the home I choose to live in, and even the car I drive; these are mine, off-limits to unwanted spirit activity. Everything that exists is owned and provided by the Universe. And the Universe says it is my turn.

It is not my intent to oversimplify, but to demonstrate the power you have over your life. The only soul that belongs in *your* body is yours. You are naturally entitled to keep your space (your body, apartment, house, or car) clean and clear of negative spirit activity. If you find yourself living in a home, for instance, that feels eerie to you, as if someone from the other side left a memory or their soul behind and is now stuck, there are professional mediums who specialize in helping.

A turning point in my life was when I was eighteen, living in an inexpensive (really seedy) part of town. My phone would ring, day and night. When I answered, no one was there. I could almost hear laughter emanating from somewhere in the air. At one point, I found myself stuck on the ceiling, unable to move, watching my body walk around the apartment.

At that moment, I recognized two things. One was that this had been happening in one form or another all my life. The second was that whoever was in my body better GET OUT! In an instant, I was back in! Some drunk dead person had been having way too much fun with me and I was angry, really angry about it. I reclaimed myself that day and have not struggled in the same way since. Sometimes anger is good. In this case, it eradicated my fear.

Being "used for my body" took on an even deeper meaning that day. The level of awareness I had about what disembodied spirits could actually do when I drifted away from myself, or my body in this case, was forever changed. I was terrified. I was no longer a flight risk. For years I had traveled to other places and dimensions while out of my body. Usually this occurred when I was listening to music. I felt I was protected. As time went on and my abilities developed, the level of shelter I threw around myself needed expansion.

That translated, for me, into remaining more conscious and in my body. The terror I felt that day shot me into the arms of a comfortable chair, owned by a remarkably skilled therapist. She helped me face the pain I was attempting to break away from. I was then better able to stay in my body and experience whatever it was I needed to feel. Then and only then could I drift off to another dimension with an upgraded protection plan. The fear I felt that day in my apartment, when I could not find my way back into my body, unswervingly propelled me forward.

From time to time, uninvited guests are spirits who either died tragically or are drastically tied to something on this side of the veil. For instance, the spirit may have experienced severe abuse as a child, and spent life on this side trying to escape the pain (and unfortunately causing more). Perhaps their mode of escape was substance abuse. Another example is a soul who, out of pain, ceaselessly hurt other people with no regard for the outcome.

The soul made a decision not to resolve matters when offered opportunities by the Universe to do so during life on this side. Then, instead of following their guide to the other side, they stayed stuck in fear on earth, with no body and no way to resolve what ails them. It is complicated. My understanding is that their energy is not wholly stuck, as help is by their side awaiting a signal of acknowledgement. There is always loving assistance accessible for the spirit, no matter what their actions were before death. If they don't accept the help, they remain where they are—which may be where you are. Or where you live, anyhow.

Whether the energy I feel around me is from a disembodied spirit or residual emotions, uninvited vibrations are a bother. Have you ever walked in on two people who are having an argument? Perhaps they suspended the discussion before you arrived, yet the tension in the room remains thick. You feel the energy or vibration. The degree of the fierceness of the argument is the same as the intensity of the emotional debris left in the room. You will be affected by it less if you understand that it is not your own.

Another turning point in my development as a medium might have, at the time, put my father to shame. Showing proper decorum was invariably expected of my siblings and me at all times. We were never allowed to swear, for instance, and had to eternally show great respect for our elders. These are important qualities to develop in children. However, they deftly stood in the way of my ability to push an uninvited spirit away. I took being polite too literally. It was a boundary issue.

When I was thirteen, the majority of the spirits hanging around my space were older than me, so I felt I had to be respectful. In addition, I felt sorry for them. After all, they were *dead*. They wanted to be recognized, so would not back off when I gave them the brush-off. I would repeatedly and politely ask them to leave. Some spirits did, some did not. Years later, I discovered that I didn't have to be polite about knocking some intrusive spirit out of my space.

What worked for me was actually the use of foul language. When an uninvited guest would not leave, I learned to get tough. For me, that meant swearing. Even as I write this, my face turns red. I'm no goody two-shoes—I can hold my own in a rough crowd of the living. But my intention to eject a spirit from my space had to be stronger than it was—much stronger. Swearing helped me reclaim my space. At this point in my life, I only pull out the four-letter words when I need to remind myself that the spirit is being rude, not me. (I also use four-letter words when someone cuts me off on the road. I guess I am not that polite.)

Pushy Spirits

I love my work. Helping people achieve a sense of closure or just make a connection with a loved one on the other side fills my heart with pure joy. We are all here to learn to love more fully, and to be loved. Whatever steps in the way of that development, once identified, will then begin to dissipate with some work. If connecting with a loved one helps, I am all for it!

When I'm working, I am open and receptive to messages. The protective energy that always flows around me is turned up several notches when I do readings. Most spirits are respectful. They want to communicate, not irritate. Once the reading is over, they disappear.

But not always. There are times when someone's crossed-over someone stays after hours to bend my ear. When I ask the spirit to leave, they usually do so. During one reading in particular, over a decade ago, my client's crossed-over, pushy cousin Arlyss tried to climb into my body. Perhaps I was not communicating her messages fast enough, or perhaps she failed to read the rule book on the ride over. Either way, I managed to blast her out, even though I was mad and a bit afraid. No one had been able to do such a thing to me for some time. I wondered what was up with my own leaky boundaries.

Since my experience with the drunk dead person, there had not been a spirit who had been able to steal his or her way into my body and set anchor. When Arlyss first tried to enter, I just thought I had a headache. But since it came on fast, I figured it out swiftly. The protective energy I had set around myself pulsated; the alarms were going off. I literally blew the soul of Arlyss out by zooming in on her energy and separating it from my own. I pictured it as being blasted out of me with a force used only for intruders.

I was honest with Brad, my client. I explained what was happening, and told him that if it happened again, the reading would need to end. He said his cousin was loving and a little aggressive when she was alive. My bouncers, as I refer to my protective energies, were alert and ready. The reading continued without incident. There were so many direct hits during the appointment, I had to marvel at Arlyss' communication skills. She had wanted to reach out and touch Brad's heart more directly than this long-distance service is wired for.

Those on the other side are as real as we are. Their presence is worthy of notice. No one enjoys being ignored, especially when their company is so missed. Simply acknowledging an awareness of their energy is often just what they need. Still, an uninvited guest can be annoying. If you sense one, tell it to take a blessing and leave. Another way to clear the room of unwanted spirits is to say, "I salute the God within you; now leave."

When disembodied spirits recognize the energy of a medium, they zoom in. They react like they found an interpreter in a sea of people speaking a foreign language. Still, uninvited guests in your space are no fun.

If you are a young medium, or are raising one, congratulate yourself for having the confidence to explore the possibilities. Read books, take classes, and ask questions—this will help build your level of knowledge, and as you know, knowledge is power!

Bouncers

My office is located in a large professional complex, complete with security guards and cameras. If there were a problem, it would be easily solved. A similar type of protection is necessary when working with those on the other side. My guides shield me from dark energies on both sides of the veil. I am grateful for the help they consistently offer, though I was not always aware of how the help arrived. My guides act as bouncers when dealing with disembodied spirits.

In a club setting, bouncers are employed to help keep everyone safe and to remove those who are destructive. My guides help eject disembodied spirits with a negative vibe and intent. Dark spirits are not allowed anywhere near me as a rule. If a reference to a spirit who is or was malevolent must be made for clarification during a reading, humor is often employed by my guides to keep my energy clear of fear.

During my meditative process, prior to conducting a reading, I picture my bouncers as alert and ready. The reason I chose the bouncer image is because it provides a feeling of security. While in my late teens and twenties, I became friends with a few sweet men who were bouncers by trade. They were the ones who helped build the image I use today as a way of protecting myself psychically.

My friends and I loved hearing the live music Minneapolis has become famous for. (Okay, not famous—perhaps "noted for" is more apt.) We were never huge drinkers or into causing trouble. Either we arrived with dates or all stuck close together. When an overzealous man wouldn't take an answer of "no thanks" to an invitation for a slow dance, a kind bouncer was there in a snap. They were always willing to walk my friends and me to our car if we felt uneasy for any reason. Independent and street-smart as we were, there were a few times when we intuitively recognized the need for help.

An excellent way to secure further protection psychically is to ask yourself what pops into your head when you think of feeling safe and protected. Notice what image is conjured in your mind and exactly how you *feel* about it. Is it a locked door, or a team of body builders? Whatever peaceful image it is, if it produces a feeling of safety, keep it on retainer! Your guides are excellent at multitasking. They can act as a channel for insights, and a map when you become lost. When you are tuned in to them, your intuition is turned up.

As I have said, you do not need a club membership or to be a cardholder to tap into your intuition. The universal bank of information is open twenty-four hours a day, seven days a week and is available to all. Withdrawing from this principle source serves only to increase it. Bear in mind that you do not necessarily require a prior formal meeting with your spirit guide to do so.

If you wish to become more aware of your guides, simply quiet your mind. Tune in to your own still, inner voice. When it is the voice of your guides, it will sound like your own yet feel totally different. A guide's voice is wholly confident and wise. Memorize its vibration; *that* is the key. Intuitive knowledge, for instance, may appear in your mind in pictures or as sounds in your ear. Your guides will hold the wand that consistently points you in the right direction. The sole purpose of your guides is to act in concert with your higher self and alight the path you carved out for your soul before you were born into this life.

Auntie Ide's Three-Way Call

One of the best things about learning how to define and master your boundaries is that you can choose to drop them at will, knowing that they will be there again for you as soon as you need them. This convenient trick enabled me to enjoy a wonderful family conversation in the most unexpected of places.

My Great-Aunt Ide is one of those people in the world who become more beautiful and wise with age. She is Faye's sister, the youngest of five and the only remaining sibling on this side of the veil. Her grand-nieces and grand-nephews have been known to fight over where she will celebrate the holidays. My cousin Ellyn and her family have frequently won the battle over the years. Something about imported chocolate. We are all onto that now, so the scales are more even!

Auntie Ide is stunning and appears at least twenty years younger than her age. She prefers that her nieces and nephews, adding up to thirty in number (including grand and great-grand) refrain from discussing her age. Let's just say she was born before Prohibition. Ide lives alone in a condo, drives a car, and can argue politics with the best of them. My siblings and I love to watch her and my father "talk" politics.

Ide and Faye shared an abundance of friends. When the last one died at the age of ninety-eight, my aunt, of course, wanted to attend the funeral. She insisted that she drive herself, though driving conditions were not decent. In Minnesota, "not decent" translates as ice, snow, rain, sleet, and dangerously cold temperatures. Having had a number of decades of practice in the art of stubbornness, she would not be swayed from her decision.

My Grandma Faye had popped in on me from the other side more often than usual during the five days before her friend had died. Unless a family member is celebrating a wedding or birth, I tend to think someone is dying when she drops in. (Like my Grandma Faye, I sometimes worry unnecessarily—I've always thought it's the combination of being of both Jewish and Italian descent.)

After her friend's death, Faye very clearly let me know that she wanted me to take Ide to the funeral. She did so by continually showing me a picture of her sister getting into my car! For good measure, she sent me on a guilt trip by dropping snapshots of the little yellow, knitted doll clothes her now-deceased friend had made for me when I was seven.

Now, how many people do you know who are able to receive a request for a favor from a grandparent who has been dead for twenty-some years? It was an honor. I called my aunt and told her I wanted to accompany her, and that she could argue with me on the drive to the cemetery.

My great-aunt is a sharp and open-minded woman, more so than most thirty-year-olds. She and Faye used to tag-team in their effort to watch over me, especially during the time of my parents' divorce. Ide stepped in when other key people stepped out. The love and trust between us helped open her mind to some spiritual possibilities she would not have otherwise considered.

As a little girl, when referring to death, I remember her saying in a hushed tone, "No one knows whose tomorrow it is." She has since confided that what I say about life after death has been of comfort to her. Though I do not share when one of our deceased relatives or friends is in the room, I do approach the subject of life after death when the timing is right.

During the drive to the cemetery, Faye had a few things she wanted me to ask her little sister. As if making casual conversation, I asked my aunt how old her mom was when she died. Ide said eighty-two. I heard Faye say eighty-four, so I said eighty-four. Ide paused and said, yes, that's the age she was! As we drove along, Faye dropped a few more questions and answers into my mind. A deep feeling of sadness hit my belly. I remembered an obscure story of my great-uncle and his rather untimely passing. Once again, I "guessed" how old he was when he died.

My aunt looked at me with a big smile and said, "Yes, that was his age when he passed! How did you know that?" As sad as the subject matter was, she was amused that I knew such ancient family history. I must admit I have always loved making my aunt smile. I felt a bit like a kid jumping rope as fast as I could to please a favored relative.

In the next instant (and while driving, I might add), I was standing in what appeared to be a small, extremely modest home or apartment. The scene was in black and white, which indicated the early to mid-1900s. I felt very cold and hungry. I saw a little girl that I recognized as Ide.

I described a range of identifying characteristics of the home in which Ide and her siblings grew up. My grandmother added various quirky personality traits belonging to my great-grandfather. My family is not much into gossiping about deceased relatives so I would have no way of knowing some of the silly facts she shared. I could feel that Faye was having fun with the three-way exchange.

This line of questioning went on until we reached the cemetery. Each time I added the small details Faye shared from the past, Ide's face showed surprise and delight. She asked how I knew such ancient history. I told her that Grandma Faye was whispering things in my ear. I am pretty sure she thought I was kidding.

As I said, these details were not well-known family facts. We were all having such fun, I did not want our time together to end. But once we arrived at the cemetery, end they did. As a medium, I need to firmly shut down at a cemetery. The disembodied spirits hanging around a graveyard can make me feel uneasy. They want an audience; I want to grieve over a lost loved one. The two do not mix.

The exchange between my great-aunt, grandmother, and me was a pure joy. It depicts the upside of being a medium. All the years I have spent pushing other people's energy out of my space and minding my own boundaries has paid off, and I am able to safely open up to the divine energy the Universe has to offer. Once in a while, it results in a family reunion and a game of "Do you remember when…"

The Family Brunch

Do you have any idea how difficult it is when a close relative asks for an answer to an oddly personal question at a family brunch? "Should I get the tumor removed?" or "I'm in love with so-and-so; how does he feel about me? Can you read him?" Those who pooh-pooh the intuitive process are the funniest of all. "Oh Jodi, do you really believe in all that? Well, I don't! Say, just the other day, the television went on by itself. Odd thing is, it was the anniversary of my mom's death and it went on at the exact hour she died. What do you think of that?"

Those who are open minded and willing to see life through differing vantage points are invariably delighted with my input. Those who cannot face their pain hate it, and me along with it. There have been times when I inevitably felt a bit set up. Brunch is no time to ask a psychic cousin about a tumor.

Helping clients by tapping into my abilities as a medium has assisted me in becoming a more conscious, compassionate person. When the ones grieving are friends or family, the boundaries I have learned to use to protect everyone can become watered down by tears. As a general rule, I do not help if I am not asked. Even when I am asked, it is not always appropriate.

My demeanor changes when I am working. As a mom, wife, relative, or friend, I am regularly full of hugs and humor. As a medium I strive to remain in the happy medium category—balanced, supportive, and neutral. People seem to hold the highly personal information I deliver with an elevated degree of regard when they see me as a trained conduit without emotional motive. There are different boundaries associated with a loved one, however. It can be confusing.

Ultimately I have found it wise not to read my friends or family. It has taken me years to reach this end. Though there are a few old friends with whom I have worked successfully, it seems too complicated overall. It is a boundary issue. The information I share during a reading is not mine—it does not come from me, it comes through me. Because my readings identify where people play games with their soul's plan and stand in the way of their own successes, it is far easier for someone to be angry with me rather than take responsibility for their own behavior and move forward. The phrase "don't kill the messenger" is relevant here! If a client has a similar reaction, it does not affect me in the same way because I don't see him or her at family gatherings or parties.

There are two exceptions to the rule of not reading friends and family. When a spirit from the other side pops in with a message for a loved one who is also my loved one, I typically deliver it when it is appropriate. Those on the other side don't much care about my personal boundaries. What they have to say is far more important, in their view.

The other exception (to date) is when friends wish to attend one of my workshops. If they feel strongly about working with me professionally and have fabulous boundaries all around, I consider it. Like attracts like in this universe. I am drawn to my friends, and they to me in part because of shared interests. A number of my close friends are exceptionally perceptive.

The workshops I conduct have developed a solid reputation with new and existing clients. A few of my friends love to attend them and have done remarkably well in growing their own abilities. Though as a rule I like to keep personal and professional relationships separate, the workshop setting offers a great compromise.

One of my dear friends, Anne, lost two adult siblings within six months of each other. Her interest level in life after death, which was previously high, went up several notches following her brothers' deaths. She attended various workshops and increased her library of books about metaphysics.

I'd met her brothers only a few times, because they lived in another city. It was not unusual for one or both to drop in on our conversations after they crossed over. I felt fine with sharing what they had to say because Anne had always respected me and what I do. In fact, she was concerned that her brothers' visits were too heavy a burden for me. I assured her they were not. Anne became adept at recognizing signs from her brothers, which helped her grieving process considerably. As it turned out, it aided one of her friends as well.

Your Fan or Mine?

Greta, a beloved neighbor of my friend Anne, had brain cancer. Though I had never met Greta, I knew her illness impacted many. The morning after Greta died, I was driving my daughter Sophia to school when Anne called to share the sad news. After offering my condolences, I felt someone tapping on my curls (literally) and was aware of a few other signals that symbolize a spirit is calling. Pictures of a woman smoking, drinking, swearing, playing cards, and laughing danced onto the screen in my head.

But Greta had only just crossed over, so I knew it would be rare for her to make an appearance. Someone from the other side was sending a message for her. This is kind of like a personal, hand-delivered telegram from someone in heaven. The messenger had father or grandfather energy and a sparkling sense of humor. I described the scene to Anne, who immediately began to laugh. It seems that her friend Greta had loved to swear, smoke, play cards, and drink cheap wine. She had been extraordinarily close to her father, who had passed years before. The message was clear. Greta was more than all right. No longer was she suffering from the cruelties of terminal cancer, but having fun with her own crossed-over friends and relatives!

Days later, Anne asked me to help with something that was of deep concern to her. She said she did not want me to work, though she needed confirmation that she had done the right thing. I asked her what was going on with Greta and her daughter. Anne laughed at not being able to hide details from me. She then began to relay a memorable story.

Jena, the grieving daughter of Greta, had replaced an old ceiling fan in her bedroom with her recently deceased mother's elaborate fan. The ceiling fan's first night in the house was memorable. It turned itself off and on, over and over again. The next morning, an electrician checked the wiring in the fan and in the house. Everything was as it should have been. That night, the fan came on at full speed at 3:00 a.m. The following night, it began to spin on its own at 3:10 a.m.

When Jena shared this story with Anne, Anne told her it was her mom and suggested she ask Greta to stop. Anne called me after her conversation with Jena. I told Anne that she was right on and had done beautifully! She was truly tuned in to what was going on. Anne asked me if I minded sharing any other information.

Keeping my boundaries in check, I opened up and asked my guides for clarification. Jena's mom was clearly aware of how worried her daughter felt. The two had truly been best friends, but Jena didn't necessarily believe in what she called "the whole life-after-death thing" and worried constantly about her mom. Her mom, dramatic in death as she was in life, wanted her daughter to know that she was doing fine.

I suggested that if the fan continued to turn on mysteriously, Jena should tell her mom she knew it was her. She should say that she was relieved to learn that her mom was okay and to please stop moving the fan because it frightened her.

This mother and daughter had had a beautiful relationship that obviously did not end when one of them died. Greta understood that her daughter's stubborn nature could lock her mind shut and hold her captive to fear; Jena was afraid of the impact her mother's death had had in her life. Her footing was off, so taking a step in a totally new direction was terrifying. Life after death, ghosts, and mediums had not been part of her general vocabulary, or in her personal dictionary. But when Jena talked to her mom, it put her fear to rest. All the fan now provides is a warm memory and a breath of fresh air.

Alive and Well on the Other Side

From the moment Dana came into my office, I could tell that she had a skeptical mind. She was a blond-haired, blue-eyed woman with a striking beauty and conservative nature. She had recently moved to Utah, but consulted with me due to a referral from one of her close friends in Minnesota. She had a history of success in the business world and an active social life. Dana was skeptical, but open to the metaphysical possibilities of a reading.

From the beginning of the appointment, I had an unsettled feeling about Dana's level of comfort and safety in her new home. Rather than sharing this information too quickly, I asked my guides for more concrete information. I gathered that her new condo was a source of pride and joy, yet she did not feel fully comfortable there. She said she felt like a dog kept jumping on her bed at night. The problem was, she had no pets, dog or otherwise. When I asked for more defining information, I saw an image of a unique-looking man with a detached, lonely grin on his face. I asked Dana if she knew an older gentleman who wore blue jeans, an oxford shirt with a vest over it, and deck shoes. Dana replied, "Holy shit, that's Jack!" I told her that a man matching that description was a frequent visitor in her home, and that he had died of cancer during the previous year. He had seemed to hang around often over the past few days.

I described the uneasy feelings I sensed she felt. The uneasiness was due to his visits. Dana's face turned pink, then went pale as she nodded. Jack, she said, was a recently deceased family friend who had been on her mind. I saw a man sitting on the edge of her bed and pacing back and forth in her bedroom. She said she had been feeling someone do this and was alarmed about it. She was afraid to tell anyone for fear that they would think her crazy. She had begun to wonder if she was wacky.

At that point, Jack shared some of his emotional background, including the feelings of loneliness he experienced before he had died. He was a man of few words, so he'd struggled alone to prepare for death and say goodbye to those he loved. In some way, he never faced that his life was ending. He showed me a picture of himself with dark circles under his eyes. His mouth appeared to be painfully full. When I see this, I know there were vital words left unsaid.

Dana asked me why Jack was around. I said it felt like an anniversary of sorts, for him, was near. He needed to be recognized and felt that she would hear him. She confirmed that Jack had died in early September the year before, and sure enough— her reading was in late August. She wanted to know what she could do to encourage him to go away.

Jack needed his presence to be acknowledged. He had been in denial about his health before he crossed over. As a result, he never said the words he felt in his heart to those he loved. He badly wanted someone to know he still existed on the other side. The despondent image he sent of himself spoke volumes. Still, he was in her space, and scaring her! I told her to tell him that she knows he is around, wishes him well, and wants him to leave because his visits frighten her!

Dana's reading was far from unusual. People pick up on peculiar occurrences around them all the time, and are afraid to expose themselves by talking about it. They fear that they might appear strange or odd. There is a white elephant in the midst and it is a deceased loved one who wants a nod hello! Not so improbably, once people speak candidly, these lurking occurrences dissipate or completely disappear. Imagine the results if we all were so direct with our experiences with the people around us—both on the other side and this side, as well!

Tools and Techniques: Boundaries

Your Psychic Temperature

Have you ever felt really angry after being in a crowd of people? Or perhaps you felt nauseous or teary-eyed? These may be signs that your own personal boundaries are merging into the crowd. This is also referred to as being a psychic sponge.

When you are near someone who is depressed, take your psychic temperature. Do you find yourself feeling low on energy? Are you suddenly sad? If this is a pattern, your ability to control how you empathize needs to be refined. We are all here to learn. When you over-empathize, you overstep your boundaries and enable the other person to skip class. There is a lesson in those feelings, and it may not be yours! We are all on this planet to learn.

Are you a person who offers to solve problems for people on a regular basis? If a friend continues to make the same mistake, do you find yourself attempting to "fix" it? When you do this, you take away the lesson your friend needs in order grow. He or she will continue to make the same error until they themselves learn to change their behavior. You are actually in their space when you do this.

Do you have friends—or better yet, acquaintances—that only call when something awful has happened in their lives? Do certain friends carefully recount the incident in a monotone voice? How do you react? Unconsciously or consciously, they are infecting you with their unfelt emotion in hopes that you will feel it for them by reacting to their ordeal. Passive boundary busting is not pretty. It is an odd little way that some people employ to deny themselves the gift of feeling. Don't be party to it. Align your boundaries and you will have far more energy.

Vanishing Energy Vampires

Have you experienced an "energy vampire attack"? Following a conversation with certain people, do you feel totally drained? Does spending time with that same person continue to drain you, no matter the duration? Energy vampires come in all shapes and sizes and may be loving and kind in nature. When you spot one, feel free to politely keep a distance until you are better able to protect yourself from being drained. In your mind, picture yourself surrounded by a clear, impenetrable shield. Your energy stays in, theirs stays out. It works.

Energy vampires wish to help themselves to your bank of energy and will do so in whatever way they are patterned. For example, if an energy vampire is experiencing a problem in life, you may be pulled into trying to help solve it. No matter what your suggestion, however, it is rejected. The point of the conversation for the vampire is not to solve the problem. It is to spill out fear and gather in the energy of the unwary.

The person who drains others is significantly unaware of their own energy source. They seek to fill an empty space, not drain you and step into yours. Walk away from them with compassion.

We are all here to shine. Taking the steps necessary to fulfill our goals as souls is what makes us glow. Moving away from judgment, being accountable for our own behavior, and allowing the people in our life the space they need to move forward is a way of loving them, and ourselves.

When you establish and maintain decent filters in your life, the benefits are infinite. You may find that people take you more seriously. Goals may be achieved at a faster pace than before due to your new ability to focus. Other people will not feel as inclined to dump their feelings on you. You will feel more peaceful, less reactive, and better able to take care of yourself.

Hands On, Spirits Off

Oh, if only there was a spray that repelled harmful energy! Unfortunately, this type of self-protection cannot be purchased in a bottle, but consider the phrase "Hands on, Spirits off" to be your motto!

The first rule of thumb, when dealing with pesky, uninvited spirits, is to have fun. Honestly, humor and common sense make a great team—not only against the spirits, but against thoughts that have been aimed at you by the living! Remember, what other people think of you is none of your business. There is tremendous power in visualization, especially when combined with words of deep wisdom. Do you recall the funny and wise rhyme, "I am rubber, you are glue, bounces off me and sticks to you"? Okay, it may not sound wise, though I assure you it is! When you assert something in your mind, and visualize it happening, on some level it does. The nasty thought is propelled back to its originator, and the uninvited, not-so-dearly departed spirits back off. As long as you intend no harm and wish only to diminish bad energy and strengthen your personal boundaries, you are in good shape. Go ahead—create your own rhyme, visualize your own scene, and have fun.

Another powerhouse technique (if you enjoy flowers) is to visualize yourself or someone you wish to protect, such as a child, surrounded by an impenetrable bubble of harmless, brilliant, gorgeous flowers. Bright colors repel darkness. Years ago when I was in property management, we sought a cost-effective approach to generate a poor first impression of a property on gang members wishing to rent apartments. Law enforcement officials suggested planting numerous, bright-colored flowers outside each entry to the building. It helped!

My closing suggestion is doubtless the fastest and most effective. Invoke the protection of the divine. Utter a loving prayer and feel its protective embrace.

Multiple-Choice Questions

1. Your son has made an offer on a house not far from you. What could be better! He asks you to check the house out with him that afternoon when the inspectors are there. You skip over to the house, walk in, and feel heaviness in the air. The house is bright and lovely, but you cannot shake this obscure feeling. The heaviness is strongest in the living room. What is causing it?

   A. You are feeling heavy and sad because the house does not have a mother-in-law apartment.

   B. A heavy vibe or spirit may be in the room. The feeling you have is not a comfortable one.

   C. You recently put on a pound or ten and the mirror in the corner of the living room is screaming at you.

Answer is B.

2. You are registering online for a class on impulse control. You finally find a date that does not conflict with your Temper Your Temper class. Toward the end of your online purchase, you are kicked off of the Internet and are unable to get back on. It might have something to do with the coffee you spilled on your computer hard drive. You contact the site directly by phone, as they have online tracking

capabilities. A young upbeat-sounding rep answers your call. She is unable to track your transaction. You suddenly feel totally put off. She remains professional and apologetic. You become agitated. She still is unable to find your transaction twenty minutes into the call. Now you are angry. You tell her she is way too happy and not very smart and you want to speak with her supervisor. What is happening here?

A. You are picking up on the salesperson's attitude because of your astute psychic skills.

B. You are sensing that you should not have even considered the impulse control class. It was a momentary decision. The whole thing just makes your temper flare. You want your money back from the Temper Your Temper class.

C. You are dumping your frustration on her due to poor boundaries.

Answer is C.

3. Your wife mailed the invitations to your Super Bowl party last week. Ernie, your best friend, called to ask where the party was to be held. It seems your wife forgot to include that information on the invite. Your reaction?

A. You love this because you always forget to take the garbage out when it is really, really full ... and your wife never believes that you actually did forget.

B. It does not bother you that she forgot to include the address. What does bother you is that she refused to include on the invite "bring your own beer and food."

C. Your wife is lovely, and she has a difficult time staying grounded. You need to buy her something special, something that sparkles.

Answer is C.

4. You are at an Engelbert Humperdinck concert. The room is abuzz with good vibes. He does a song you absolutely love! You sing along at top volume. The person next to you asks you to sing a bit softer, as your voice can be heard over Engelbert's. You feel really sad. In fact, the rest of the night you feel sad. This is because…

   A. You just know that your voice added to the concert. Now the experience will be less than wonderful for all around you.

   B. You took personally someone's reaction to you, and their mood. Not an uncommon reaction.

   C. You suddenly realize that it is no longer cool to say Engelbert Humperdinck, let alone be at an Engelbert Humperdinck concert.

Answer is B.

5. Babysitting has never been your gig. However, being a decent friend has. Therefore, you agree to watch little Parker while his mother goes to Kmart for her new spring wardrobe. Parker is a busy lad, and today is no different. He runs around the house screaming, "Catch me if you can!" After an hour of this, you have a sharp sense in your gut that Parker may fall down the stairs. You cannot seem to shake the feeling. As a result, you are able to get him off the stairs right away, distracting him with a double hot fudge sundae. You experienced…

   A. Precognition. You discover later that little Parker had fallen down the stairs before when he got this wild!

   B. Wishful thinking. You really hate to babysit, no offense to Parker.

   C. Real men do not baby sit. You would rather be home with a pint of Ben and Jerry's watching *Steel Magnolias*.

Answer is A.

6. While interviewing for a part-time position as an ice cream taster, you have a chance to meet three people who would be your coworkers. Things were going well until you met them. Two of the three have a menacing vibe. You really need the job to supplement your income while in school, and it is close to home. Management offers it to you and you decline. Why?

   A. You simply chickened out of a good job once again, sweet toothy.

   B. You remembered that you are lactose intolerant just in time.

   C. Your gut feeling told you to decline, loud and clear. You would have been miserable working in such close proximity to such dark energy.

Answer is C.

7. It's a cold, rainy day. As you pull into the Target parking lot to pick up a few last-minute items for the holiday party you helped arrange for the office, a parking spot marked "compact only" opens up close to the door. It's a tight fit for your not-so-compact, super-sized SUV. As you put your car into park, another much larger spot opens up. Oh well. While you rush to the door, a pang goes off in your belly. Your eye is drawn again to the roomy spot at the end of the parking lot. Fifteen minutes later you tuck your items in the back of your shiny blue SUV and walk around to the driver side door. A larger-than-life door ding sparkles under the lights. You could have prevented the door ding…

   A. If you had paid more attention to the pang in your belly and the way your eyes continued to roam over to the larger parking spot.

B. If only Fred from the office had volunteered to pick up soda and day-old doughnuts at the store near his home.

C. If people would be more careful. It's a free country and you can park wherever you want.

Answer is A.

8. During the last two months you have been debating about whether or not to attend your twenty-year high school reunion. You were an overweight teen obsessed with popularity. Not an unusual combination, you learned later in therapy. You cannot wait to see Katrina, the ever-skinny, lucky, and popular girl who tormented you for being chubby. She had everything in high school except compassion. You heard she's gained weight and lost her luck. This time it will be your turn to shine your tight abs and sparkling teeth at her!

You and a small group of friends from high school doll up, have dinner, and saunter into the reunion. The room is abuzz with high energy, laughter, and '80s music. At first, you feel you are back in high school. Once you notice the lack of big hair and shoulder pads, you make your way into the room, relaxed and anxious all at once. Caught up in the wonderful liveliness, you forget about Katrina until you see her standing with her old clique of friends, where she evidently has been all night. She looks pretty and sad. No one is flocking around her. Instead of waltzing over and dazzling her into envy, your heart opens. You see before you the same person you knew in high school—pretty, insecure, and almost perfect. You also see the ravages two divorces can leave behind so you smile, wave hello, and move on with your life and the evening. All this is a sure sign that . . .

A. With compassion as a teacher, you learned to forgive and love who you are. As a result, you can better understand and forgive others.

B. The boomerang effect is real. Katrina never could spell the word "divorce," let alone spot a loser. As a result, losers and divorce found her.

C. Big hair and shoulder pads are back in style.

Answer is A.

Finding intuitive balance and maintaining clear boundaries are natural when other areas of life are running evenly. Emotional, spiritual, and physical steadiness work together as a team in helping you find and maintain a happy medium. It is within that happy medium that mastering the intuitive code, sustaining compassion, and living life with joy meet.

4

Small Mediums

I believe in the laughter of children's eyes
before the world teaches them not to cry.
—The Happy Medium

Moms, Dads, and Mediums

Children exhibit pure genius of soul. Their free flow of happiness, sadness, and wholesome joy at simply being alive is a blessing to witness, not to mention experience. Children are naturally intuitive. Having not yet learned how to turn off this ability, they are able to distinguish truth from lies. They do not question their senses because to do so would make no sense.

Do you remember *The Flintstones,* Hanna-Barbera's cartoon featuring Fred, Wilma, Pebbles, and their neighbors Betty, Barney, and Bamm-Bamm? The show first aired on ABC in the early 1960s. Bamm-Bamm was a toddler with superhuman strength. With ease, he could lift people, autos, and even houses! Hilarious scenes were written around this little guy and his out-of-the-ordinary talent. Bamm-Bamm did not know how to deal with his muscle might, let alone reel it in. If he had been blessed with a model, someone he could compare himself with, he may not, for example, have accidentally placed a house on Fred's toe. Thank goodness Betty and Barney loved the little guy and had the foresight to help him find a place for his unique strength. All children should be so lucky.

If my clients have children, or recall being one with any clarity, they may also remember how it felt to see and hear things that no one else did. I am not talking about the bogey-man under the bed. What I'm referring to is the sparkling light behind someone's head, or a radio that continues to turn on and off, or a knowing feeling about a future event that cannot be explained. This can be a lonely experience for a child if the response from others is one of fear. If you are afraid, your child will be, too. If you tell your child that what they are experiencing does not exist, they will lose trust in themselves and in you.

Children and Signs of Signs

Children are naturally in tune with their higher souls and the energy around them. Parents would do well to be receptive to possible signs from the other side if for no other reason than to offer a safe place for their little ones to bring questions. Questions ignored can create feelings of tremendous anxiety, since children take their emotional cues from the adults around them. Moms and dads learn early in their career as parents that if they are afraid, their children will pick up on it. All authority figures, in fact, have great influence in shaping a child's lifelong impressions about matters of substance.

In general, children are more aware of electromagnetic energy than adults are. They are better able to sense what is around them, from tension in a home to a spirit's energy. Children more easily hear voices, even conversations between spirits! It is also common for young people to see auras. Spirits often want to protect or watch over young children; to the spirit, it is an added bonus when the children see them.

If the signs you or your child are noticing bring both of you joy, recognize them knowingly! Whatever we focus our attention on grows. If the signs frighten you, however, acknowledge them and then firmly insist that they discontinue. Most spirits will cooperate. There are universal rules to abide by in life and in death. Remember, this is your space!

If you or your child seem to have a real reason to feel afraid, most likely a visiting entity with no connection to you or your loved one is dropping in. Employ humor as a protective measure. For example, some entities are like playground bullies. They feed off fear. When you are not afraid, they lose interest and leave you alone. Say, "Hello, I see you—now go away! This is my space and you are not allowed in it!" Color the spirit with imaginary colored pencils; next, erase it with an imaginary eraser. Or visualize a mammoth balloon filled with magical water landing directly on the entity's head, which in turn makes it disappear. In a splash and flash, the spirit is gone! Your sense of humor protects you. It is difficult to remain in a place of fear when you are filled with laughter.

Finding comfort after the loss of a loved one is essential. Encourage your child to wear your dad's favorite sweater or bake your grandmother's caramel chocolate cake—these are positive ways to remember those who have died. And be sure your children know that a visit from a loved one on the other side is the spirit's way of saying, "Thank you for remembering me. I love you too."

Middle Ground

Children naturally respond to what is happening versus what *should* be happening. Adults have learned, and become conditioned, to keep certain truths peripheral. In other words, older children and adults have learned to tune out the truth if it will bring discord. Around five or six years of age, if not before, children realize that they are better received if they cease to notice or act on the occasional white elephant in the room—also known as the truth. The amount of energy it takes to ignore the obvious is enormous. The healthiest of parents work to find a middle ground, helping their child to maintain a sense of honesty and respond appropriately.

A child speaking truthfully—telling Aunt Isabelle that he will not kiss her because she has prickly gray whiskers on her chin and her breath is stinky—may not be illustrating the best of manners. Nevertheless, the child is being honest. We want them to be truthful yet we do not regularly model truthfulness. It's puzzling for a child, to say the least.

But there is a way to put a positive spin on almost anything without needing to lie. Acknowledge the truth of Aunt Isabelle's whiskers and stinky breath to your child, while also explaining some special way (other than a kiss) of showing Aunt Isabelle affection and respect. Likewise, if your child requests that you read a *Winnie the Pooh* book to her because Grandpa is visiting from heaven and wants to hear it, do it! There is a solid chance that your child is tuned in to Grandpa's visit from the other side. Honor your child's ability to recognize truth. The truth is freeing and bestows harmony. Be warned, though—harmony can be contagious!

Matilda, the Little Medium with Manners

Matilda's mother Gail describes her daughter as a pistol. At twelve years old, Matilda is less than five feet tall and has a high-pitched, tiny voice. However, her vast communication skills are outstanding—or in this case, out of this world.

Gail has worked in the mental health field for fourteen years, as a psychologist. After receiving a number of client referrals from me over the years, she put her preconceived ideas about psychics and mediums aside and scheduled an appointment to meet me. I later learned she did so for two reasons. The first was to become better acquainted with my work because the clients I referred had arrived in her office with uncommon information from me that genuinely helped facilitate their healing. The second was because she feared for her daughter's psychological health. She did not yet understand that she had her own little medium living right under her roof!

In Gail's line of work, "hearing voices" has a different implication than it does in mine. When her daughter began having conversations with an Uncle Kenneth, long dead, and was found trying to feed the invisible (and also dead) family cat, Gail became alarmed. She worried that her daughter's mental health had taken a nosedive. Matilda had always been an outspoken and unusually wise little girl, with a no-nonsense attitude. She recently told her mother to buy herself new glasses because she had just stepped on the cat and sat on her uncle.

In truth, I had to put my own prejudice aside before meeting Gail. Psychiatrists and some psychologists consider hearing voices to be nothing other than a sign of mental illness. I have always thought that that line of thinking was small-minded. Though her work with my clients had been excellent, I was not at all convinced that Gail was an internally aware person. The minute I met her, however, I liked her! She told me she had a concern about a family member and that any resolution to the dilemma might be more related to my work than hers.

The minute she said the words "family member," a picture of a tall girl with a wide mouth shot into my head. I could hear a little voice. The girl's clothing appeared to be mature for her years. A funny scene of a little girl and a big stuffed chair played unremittingly in my mind.

Gail confirmed that she had a daughter. The clothing that Matilda was wearing in my vision simply meant she was mature for her years, and the over-exaggerated mouth meant she was able to speak up for herself. She could open her mouth when necessary, and perhaps, even when not! The hilarious scene was of Matilda standing next to a chair in a lavishly decorated living room. What made it amusing was that it was presented in fast-forward mode, over and over again, by a tall, likable fellow in spirit. He wore a lot of yellow.

When I described the picture to Gail, she roared with laughter. Matilda's Uncle Kenneth, who had died over a decade ago, was the presenter of the scene. He obviously thought it significant. When I relayed who in spirit was providing the pictures, Gail laughed even harder.

Matilda and Gail had recently been invited to an opening tea. An opening tea, as explained by Gail, is a formal party given in honor of a recent wedding engagement. It is similar to an engagement party except that no men are invited. When it was time to be seated for lunch, Matilda had refused. Gail was immeasurably embarrassed, as her daughter's actions appeared to be extremely rude. After a few minutes of agony, Matilda sat down.

A look of relief washed over Gail's face as I affirmed her daughter's story. Apparently, Uncle Kenneth did not much care for etiquette. He had invited himself to the opening tea and seated himself in Matilda's chair. She refused to sit on her uncle, because she's a little medium with manners.

I had a few suggestions for Gail. The first was that she retire the antiquated idea that anyone who so much as acknowledges the possibility of life after death or hears voices is batty. The second was that she endeavor to understand that it is far more common to feel the presence of disembodied spirits than she might realize. The third suggestion was that she acknowledge her daughter's ability to see and/or feel spirits who have crossed over. The only thing remotely crazy about the truth is the way we feel when we ignore it!

Proud Mommy Moments

When my children ask heavy questions that they may not yet be developed enough to understand the answer to, I do my best to stick to an abbreviated version of the truth. This includes anything from questions about sex to fears about the bogeyman. Children seem to develop best when they do so at their own pace. As they grow older, I marvel at how their innate instincts unfold and bloom so naturally.

One spring, I was interviewing a young woman for a part-time nanny position. She was qualified and friendly, yet something did not feel right about hiring her. Though she had answered "no" to the smoking question on her application, I intuitively suspected that she did smoke, and perhaps dabbled in recreational drugs as well.

As I was describing my children (two of whom were due home from school momentarily) to Puff Nanny, I mentioned how perceptive they all were. "For example," I said, "if you smoke cigarettes even occasionally, my son Cole would ask you or me about it." Her eyes rounded. Bingo. I could feel her fear. She had been found out. In situations such as these, I take note of what my intuition has to say, and wait to see how everything plays out. My gut and my head were the lead players in this scene.

Upon further questioning, I learned that Puff Nanny had not worked anywhere for more than six months at a time in the last two years, and had been issued two speeding tickets in thirty-six months. A few minutes later, I heard the bus and the sound of loud, happy, hungry children in my yard. After introducing my boys to the interviewee, they asked her enthusiastically if she liked bugs, baseball, and climbing trees. Although she was great with kids, this smoking nanny was not asked back for a second interview. When it comes to my family, my intuitive voice wins virtually every time.

After she left, I was preparing afternoon snacks and asked my boys if they liked her. They both said yes, she likes baseball and climbing trees! Cole looked at me and said in a matter-of-fact tone, "Mom, I think she smokes."

In my mind I was proudly thinking, "That's my boy!" Out loud, I casually asked if he had smelled smoke or had seen cigarettes. He had not. I looked at him and asked what made him think she smoked. He said he *just knew it*. I told him I had suspected the same, and that it was likely his instincts at work.

My daughter Sophia has drawn pictures of events that have yet to ensue. She is a wonderful artist. My son Aaron has a sharp sense of "scary" future events. This is not uncommon in someone whose intuitive skills are beginning to develop, including adults. Aaron has provided heads-ups about flat tires, speeding tickets, unexpected inoculations at the doctor, and thunderstorms. (Children have not yet been conditioned to shut down their intuitive eye. In terms of adults, I believe our fast-paced society plays a role in priming us for fear. It nourishes fear by default, because it does not support slowing down, breathing, or just simply being. We are pummeled with scary messages and are in fight-or-flight mode more often than not, "on call" for trouble.)

Instructing children to be aware of and alert to their instincts is an act of love. When you do so, they learn a method of self-protection. Horses' instincts alert them to the presence of a snake. Don't you want your kids to know as they go though life whether a snake is nearby?

My children are not unlike those in your own life. Beautiful and creative, they embrace each day with a sense of wonder. In encouraging them to trust their instincts, I help them learn to have confidence in themselves as well. Truth encourages faith, and faith has a power all its own.

Small Town, Big Instincts, Little Boy

Homebuilders and haunted houses don't mix. My client Bill is a designer and builder of homes in a small town in Minnesota. Over the past five years, we've met annually to discuss practices that maximize creativity and create and attract opportunity for his company. This appointment, however, was not connected to his business. It was related to someone he was related to!

Bill was concerned because his son, Jake, was terribly afraid to go into the house his grandmother had recently purchased. Jake was a gregarious, confident, and sensitive boy. He reported feeling prickly when he walked into the house and complained of the smell of smoke. His clairsentient and claraillient abilities were showing up for duty.

When I scanned the house (meaning, when I read its vibration), I felt that someone had died in it, years ago. The cause of death was related to fire. The smell of something terrible burning filled my senses. My old friend Clair of Scents (clairallience) was helping me to understand more. I then saw what appeared to be a pink fainting couch. A lit cigarette kept popping into my head.

Bill's son was feeling the spirit of the man who had died there, not a dislike for his grandma. He might be confused by his own reactions. I suggested my client do some research about the house and its past.

Eight months later, when my client called to schedule another appointment, he confirmed what he had learned in the reading. One of the neighbors told him that about twenty-five years ago, an elderly man was a victim of a fire in the home. He died due to smoke inhalation. He was a bit of a drinker and had fallen asleep while smoking a cigarette. The fire was contained to the bedroom and no one else was hurt.

My client's son was a highly sensitive little boy. He was fortunate to have a father who trusted him. But this was far from the first time this little guy had sensed a soul from the other side. Children are naturally able to feel the presence of spirits. Because he had a long pattern of feeling this sort of energy, he was showing the early signs of a growing medium.

I suggested that Bill tell Jake that happiness and sadness leave a sort of residue in a home. Like the smell of a newly painted room, it can take some time for the residue to go away. A long time ago, there had been joy and some feelings of very deep sadness in the home. Just acknowledging the sensations Jake had when entering the house might help him feel less afraid. Saying a prayer for all who enter and have entered is also highly useful.

Depending on the age of the child, more can be shared with them. Common sense and intuition are partners, and giving children too much information is not helpful. I am a fan of less is more. In this case, there was no need to share information about the fire and death—just acknowledging the feelings behind the circumstance was an empowering thing to do. Once the little boy's feelings were validated, and a simple reason for them was identified, he no longer refused to visit his grandmother. Also, the unwanted vibration of the spirit dissipated simply because it was acknowledged.

Recognizing the nuances in intuitive messages is invaluable. Intuition is natural, but learning balance is essential. Remember, it's all about finding the happy medium. When you trust your gut, follow your heart, and use your head, you have balance on your side.

Validating your child does not mean you must agree with, or fully understand, what your child is saying. When you listen and ask questions without judgment, you are validating their *feelings* about the experience. This is extremely powerful. It authorizes your child to trust in him- or herself, and in you. It also knocks out fear.

Raise your child to be open to the possibilities. Everyone is born with some level of intuitive ability. Your child's emotional sensitivity may be closely tied to his or her intuitive potential. Embrace sensitivity and experience the delightful upshot!

How an ability is recognized, understood, and accepted is key. Not every person with strong intuitive and mediumistic capabilities will choose to develop them. The point is to honor the child and validate the ability. No one wants to feel isolated. Let your child, either the one within you or the one you are raising, know that he or she is not alone. Allow your love to be felt. Expressing love and acceptance protects your child. Please do not be afraid of what you do not understand. This is the stuff life is made of.

If you or your child do not choose to cultivate the intuitive ability, that is okay. But much like a natural athlete who chooses not to exercise or play a sport, muscle energy (or intuitive energy) becomes backed up. You or your child may feel a sense of disconnect or haziness, unidentified at times. This may be a longing for a soul-to-soul connection, for a spiritual workout of sorts. Find some creative outlet and let yourselves go.

Watch for signs of emotional wounds in your children, also. They will happen because life is filled with the yin and the yang. Remember, you may unintentionally hurt your children because of your own unsettled past. You are human and here to learn and develop too. Take responsibility for your actions, intentional or otherwise. By simply doing so, most parents can create more love than pain.

The Universe is on our side, helping guide us toward living to our souls' potential. We are not alone. The Talmud says, "Every blade of grass has its angel that bends over it and whispers, grow, grow."

Help your children heal from their injuries. Be loving and approving. Teach them to mend themselves. Take notes. Years later, if a scar from an old or new wound begins to burn, help tend it by sharing what you remember about the scene of the emotional crime. If, once again, the same injury or another reopens and you are no longer on this side of the veil, the care you once gave will forever be on whatever side your children reside. Love does not take sides. It exists on all levels.

> *Recently a young mother asked for advice. What, she*
> *wanted to know, was she to do with a 7-year-old who*
> *was obstreperous, outspoken, and inconveniently will-*
> *ful? "Keep her," I replied ... The suffragettes refused to*
> *be polite in demanding what they wanted or grateful*
> *for getting what they deserved. Works for me.*
> —Anna Quindlan

Big Reactions, Little Girl

Most adults would be able to recount any number of anomalous spirit-related goings-on throughout their own childhoods, if someone had validated them when they occurred. Those odd happenings were in fact not particularly odd. They were ignored out of a sense of fear. The good things we ignore go away; the bad things get in our way.

As I mentioned earlier, as a young person I was constantly teased for being weird, unattractive, and too sensitive, and for having frizzy, out-of-control-hair. My reactions were frequently extreme because I was responding to how people truly felt, not what they said. Bullies did not scare me, because I could see where they hurt and responded with kindness to it. I knew people down to their souls. My responses often reflected this knowledge and were crucial at times of trouble.

I grew up in a large family and had more aunts, uncles, and cousins than I could count. Some of them were not actually related to me anymore, due to divorce; they just stuck around for the entertainment. I remember at one family gathering, when I was around eight years of age, I sat next to one of my many bald-headed uncles and asked him if he missed Darlene. He turned red, bald head and all, and walked away. It turns out that Darlene, his mistress, had recently died, leaving behind my grieving uncle and his not-so-grieving wife. At the time, I had no idea that my comment inadvertently exposed a family secret.

Lilly and Benny

My grandfather Lou had a heart of gold. He financially supported his big sister Lil and her husband, Benny, throughout their old age. Every so often, he would bring his nine grandchildren to visit them. Lil and Benny were sweet and gave us silver-dollar coins; they also smelled like mothballs.

Lilly and Benny died within weeks of each other and left everything, including $50,000, to my grandfather. This was a huge surprise, as he had the impression that they were severely lacking financially. All of the nieces and nephews, grand and otherwise, were invited to take what ever chatchkas (knick-knacks) they desired from Lil and Benny's tiny apartment.

As an eleven-year-old walking through their apartment, my senses were on fire. I heard my great-aunt laugh, felt her hug me, and smelled the scent of the mothballs. Later, she sat on one side of me, my uncle on the other, and directed me as to what to take from the apartment. She asked me to offer certain items to my sisters and brother. At the time, I thought this was all a game. I did not fully understand that Lil and Ben were actually there in spirit, enjoying the spirit of giving!

I had learned long ago not to share these happenings with anyone. It was considered poor manners to speak of the dead and even worse still to speak of ghosts. Anything unknown was considered better left unsaid—so I said nothing.

Imaginary Friends

Young children love to play. They do not care if a new friend has one arm or two. Open to the core, they are in it for the fun. It is worth it to note that a great number of my clients' children seem to see things and/or play with imaginary friends. Also interesting to note is the high amount of spirit activity around kids. You may not have met your Great-Aunt Bertha before she died, but no matter, Aunt Bertha is watching over your son. Chalk it up to past-life relations or just plain good luck, but your child has someone watching over him. What is even more interesting to note is that, on some level, he knows it.

One of my clients is the owner of a mid-sized business and has a standing appointment with me every quarter. The appointments center predominantly on her growing company, marketing plans, employees, and choices she must make to continue to enjoy such success. One afternoon, she began asking me questions about the spirit world. Her grandmother, who died four decades before, had always been a part of our meetings. She had been a mathematical whiz, and wanted to help her granddaughter strengthen her precision in business.

For a number of reasons, I do not directly share information about visiting relatives when working with corporate clients. They are meeting with me to benefit from my intuition, and to discuss business, not personal matters. It's a boundary issue. If clients indicate that they wish to know who is visiting from the other side, I always divulge.

On this particular day, my client, Angela, wanted to share her own story with me. She told me that her twins, one boy and one girl, slept in separate rooms. Andrea, the little girl, was an early riser. Her mom would often hear her singing and talking to "Aubrey" while playing alone in the morning. When asked who Aubrey was, Andrea would say, "Your daddy's grammy." My client, ever practical, had never heard of Aubrey and thought Andrea had an imaginary friend. That is, until one Thanksgiving when old photos were taken out for viewing.

It was late and the twins were both on a chocolate high. Angela wanted to buy time until her children crashed. She handed them each a photo album. Twenty minutes later, giggles could be heard from the corner where her children lay on the floor, smudging the pages of the photo albums with chocolate. When asked what they were laughing at, Andrea said, "Aubrey looks chubby as a baby, Mommy. She's not chubby now."

Feeling flushed, my client looked at the photo. The writing underneath the photo said, "Aubrey at three years of age." Angela had not seen the photo before. She also did not know that her great-grandmother, whom she had never met, went by "Aubrey" as a child. Her given name was Audrey, but Audrey's little brother used to call her Aubrey, and it stuck.

Though you may think you are the voice of wisdom, it is children who are the most amazing teachers. It's important to validate how your children feel in any given situation. When you authenticate their experiences, their self-confidence and trust in you and in themselves blossoms.

Tools and Techniques:
Children

One Through Ten

This is a magical and entertaining game that can be played with children of all ages. It builds intuitive skills and passes the time all at once. I play it with my children while waiting to be seated at a restaurant, traveling in a car, and as general entertainment.

Start by asking participants to do some belly breathing. Suggest they place their hand right below their belly button and breathe deeply. With each inhale and exhale, their hand should move slowly up and down. After a few minutes of this exercise, which helps clear and quiet the mind, ask everyone to picture a giant eraser clearing their minds of worry and thought. Next, have them silently count to ten. Remind participants to listen to the way each number sounds and watch to see if a picture of it pops up in their minds.

Then, the first player thinks of a number from one to ten. The player must picture the number in their mind and say it silently over and over for one minute. There is skill involved in doing this!

At the same time, the other players open their minds and wait to see what number pops into their heads, audibly or visually.

Next, each player takes turns guessing which number it might be. Everyone takes turns. As in math, only the actual answer counts! Whoever "guesses" the correct answer wins.

In this game, "guessing" is obviously related to the intuitive process. Whoever has chosen a number must clearly think about the number inside his or her mind. Whoever guesses the number on the first try just may have seen it on the screen in his or her head, or heard it with his or her inner ear. Chances are pretty good that just playing the game not only passes time but builds intuition. The game is fun and develops confidence and perception.

Color My World

This colorful game works much like the "one through ten" game explained above. Players take turns guessing the color the lead player is thinking about. The game acts as an aid in building the "creating your own reality" skill. If a color can be thought into the mind of another person, think of what else the Universe has to offer! Contestants can learn to think their reality into love, peace, and joy.

A Serving of Positive Energy

Positive thoughts help create a fabulous life. Teach your children to think about others and themselves with love, and good things are sure to follow. A serving of positive energy is amazingly effective with young children. Older kids benefit also (there is just a lot of eye rolling to suffer through before the positive energy takes hold).

My husband and I, like most people, work long hours. As a result, we do not eat together as a family each and every night. Every Friday night, however, we do. Friday after sundown, Shabbat begins. It is the Jewish day of rest, and rest we do. Well, we play "old" '80s music and the kids (and perhaps an adult or two) dance. Shabbat includes candles, wine, challah (bread), prayer, and a serving or two of positive energy.

After we light the candles and recite the prayers, we take turns talking about something meaningful that happened during our day. Next we say something positive about every person in our family, which includes saying something kind about oneself. I love to tune in to the personal energy of each family member as something wonderful is said about them. Their energy explodes in light and delight.

Detective Mom

This technique is one I use every day while cleaning up after my children. I also use it in my job, to pinpoint who may be stealing company funds from a client. If the technique is merely attempted, it fortifies understanding of the intuitive code.

Children are not known for their skill at picking up after themselves. My own children have imaginary (and I'm not referring to spirit) friends who mess up their room and draw pictures on the wall. They think I'm pretty cool when I can identify whose candy wrappers are on the floor or whose toy truck is stuck in the laundry chute. When they ask me how I do it, I show them.

Objects radiate with my children's vibration. For instance, my sons' own identical school backpacks—when one is left where it should not be, such as on the bathroom floor, I am able to pinpoint whom it belongs to simply by tuning in to its vibration. When I lay my hand on it, a certain feeling radiates from my heart. It is the same feeling I have for the owner of the object. The backpack tells a story; it names names! I love the way all five Clairs are activated when I play detective. In this case, my clairsentient voice is heard.

Just as a reminder, the five Clairs are clairvoyance (clear seeing), clairaudience (clear hearing), clairsentience (clear sensing or feeling), claireallience (clear smelling), and clairgustance (clear tasting). Once you begin to perceive, you will know which of your senses is activated. For instance, if you experience a specific scent that is somehow related to the owner of the object, clairallience is at work.

Examples of objects that marvelously retain personal vibrations are shirts awaiting the wash. Find two or three shirts with different owners. Mix them together in a pile. Close your eyes and pick up one shirt. Be aware of exactly how you feel when you do so. Then open your eyes and see who the shirt belongs to. How did your "guess" do? Simply doing this exercise strengthens the intuitive inner eye.

To play this game with your child, you may want to be the first one to "guess" which object belongs to whom so your child can see how it works. Remember, too much information too soon is too much for kids. Approach this exercise simply as a fun game. Start by closing your eyes and asking the child to place a small object in your hand. The object and its ownership should not be particularly unique or recognizable; a hat or a coat works well. Remember that it must be something worn or used often by someone in your home. It may even belong to your family pet! What feelings arise? Is it the feeling of love you have for someone in particular living in your home? Whose face appears? Do you smell or hear something related to a family member? Does an image flash in your mind and dash out just as quickly? If not, don't fret. It takes time to build this skill.

5

Love and Intuition

Let us always meet each other with a smile,
for the smile is the beginning of love.
—Mother Teresa

Soul to Soul

Of all the gifts you will receive in this life, love is the only one with everlasting power. When you accept love and return it, it becomes a part of your sparkle and your soul. Love is your companion in this world and into the next.

Love and intuition are born from the same source, and intuition is nothing less than a tool for tuning in to our internal selves. By our very nature, we seek companionship. Our inner wisdom can be a guide in finding what we need in this life. Of course, what we seek may not appear in the exact way that our imaginations conjured it. It may be even better.

Feeling loved and understood are two essential elements in achieving a successful relationship. As Merle Shain wrote in *Hearts That We Broke Long Ago*, "Loneliness is not a longing for company; it is a longing for kind." The exhilaration that transpires when we meet someone with whom we "click" overrides all other intuitive perceptions, of course. Or at least our ability to take notice of them!

When we are deeply moved, our souls are speaking. Feeling drawn to someone or something is a call from another part of ourselves. Learning to take measure and find balance during times of high exhilaration is a sign of maturity. A good rule of thumb is to remember first impressions. Often, when judgment does not stand in the way, those impressions are right on.

Love, or Not?

It is not necessarily finding love that is difficult, but accepting it when it is offered. Believing ourselves worthy of being loved opens us up to accepting other people whole. If we see ourselves as deserving of love, we are able to recognize that others are as well.

Have you ever met someone who felt mysteriously familiar? You and this magical someone just seemed to fit. There was an understanding, a rhythm flowing between you from the start. But when the initial infatuation began to evolve into something substantial, that magical someone somehow turned ugly. Her nose was too big or her parents too nosey! His career choice was poor or he was simply too boring.

It is only after the infatuation retires that the real work, and the real love, begins. In situations like the ones described above, you were most likely channeling your subconscious fear of love into small dislikes, and seeing these issues as red flags about the relationship. You may have been responding to your own fear of being ugly, or your fear of being exposed or vulnerable.

Has the following scenario ever happened to you or anyone you know? You have recently met a truly darling man and have been seeing him for almost three months. The two of you have much in common, including a similar sense of humor. He makes you laugh more than anyone else ever has. When you are together, you finish each other's sentences. When you are apart, your mind is on him and the way you feel around him. He is kind, cute, smart, employed, single, and interested in you. You are also interested in him. That is until you wake up in a "mood" one morning when you are scheduled to run around the lake with Mr. Darling. Instead of being up-front about your dark mood, you show up late, offer no explanation, and don't say more than three words during the entire run.

Afterward, he asks you to have lunch with him. You decline, feigning a headache instead of acknowledging the attack of hormones mixed with fear that has truly taken hold of you. He seems confused. Ever respectful, he kisses you and promises to call the next day.

When he calls, you cannot wait to hang up. His laugh grates on your nerves. You are vaguely aware that your response to this kind man is not in alignment with how you truly feel about him. You have been pressing the fast-forward button in your mind, which is located directly next to the fear button. You are a neat freak, he is not; he is not an animal lover, and you are. How could this possibly work? The relationship is doomed!

If you are brave enough to press the rewind button and stop right before the place where your feelings changed, you will find your emotional hot button. You are now an observer and no longer captive to your fear. Your intuitive senses have been ignited.

Sitting quietly and listening to yourself breathe, ask the Universe to reveal what you need to see. Enclose yourself in a protective bubble, then open yourself up to your intuitive insights. Right before your mood changed, Mr. Darling invited you to accompany him on a ski trip. Things were becoming more serious, more intimate. You knew that if you went on a trip with him, he would see the real you, moods and all. Then, that very night, you met a few of his friends. They were loud. He ignored you most of the night and drank too much. You were tired and wanted to go home. You have a project deadline looming, and now your plans to run around the lake with Mr. Not-So-Darling are not so appealing.

That was it! The evening you met his friends; the evening he invited you on a trip, and to get closer to him. Instead of talking about how you felt, you backed away.

You now have a few choices. Brave up and talk to him about your concerns. Or chicken out and continue to be stuck in a pattern that has long reached its expiration date. Your choice, your life.

Love is about letting go of control. As Carl Jung wrote, "Where love rules, there is no will to power; and where power predominates, there love is lacking. The one is the shadow of the other." You have no power with love; love has you, you don't have it. You must believe that when you let go in love, the Universe offers a net. The net is your connection with soul, your own intuition, and the protection of all the people who have loved you before this moment. Love is an outward expression of an inward connection to soul.

Love is about surrender. If you wish to maintain control, you will remain alone. If you trust in the process of life, then love just might extend its hand. Allow yourself a chance at love by letting go of judgment of yourself and others. People who really know how to laugh do not worry about what they look like when they do. Control is for emotional misers.

Surrendering to love does not necessitate throwing out reason. It requires locating it and moving in! How many times have you reflected on a relationship that ended and thought, "Why did I not see this? It was so obvious!" Perhaps your ex-love was constantly approached in public by angry ex-loves. Or possibly you sabotaged it yourself because you were afraid of how you felt, so you failed to notice how your fear was trashing a potentially good thing. Had you taken note, you might have been able to alter the outcome. Your fear opened the door and tossed out reason.

The voice of reason is the one that says, "I have met some-one who is a real person. I am excited and afraid. Though I have always wanted to be with someone who has never been married, this woman has been, and I like her a great deal. I am sticking around; I choose love instead of fear." Reason also says, "Though I just met this beautiful man, I feel I have known him all my life. He tells me now, instead of when we first met three weeks ago, that he is married. I need to end it now. His wife deserves better, and so do I!" The voice of reason is reasonable.

Human beings thrive on love. Love wears many faces. Perhaps it wears the face of your child, your parent, your friend, your neighbor, or even your cat! Romantic love is not the only meaningful love the Universe offers. It is actually loving and being loved that is essential.

> *Your task is not to seek for love, but merely to seek*
> *and find all the barriers within yourself that*
> *you have built against it.*
> —Rumi

The Discovery of Love

Love is not a thing to be handled or sold. It is ethereal. Wars have been fought and lost over love. Countless ballads, poems, books, and movies have been written about love by authors willing to abandon their egos and surrender their pride. Still, attempts at describing how it feels to be in love, though heart-wrenchingly beautiful, fall far short of the actual experience.

As with love, when you experience a moment of intuitive insight, your body becomes alive, almost electric. You experience a knowing beyond words. The only way to comprehend it is to experience it. Love and intuition are truly siblings.

Witnessing two people who are bound to fall in love connect for the first time is an enlightening experience. It is second only to being one of the souls about to fall in love! Though I have been a bystander to the beauty of such a moment only twice, the memory is so engaging that it has a permanent place in my heart.

Have you ever observed people when they are totally absorbed in watching a fascinating movie? Their eyes are unreservedly focused on a point of interest. They are in the room yet visibly somewhere else at the same time. It is similar when the eyes of future lovers lock. The sound of their memory unbolting is almost audible! An unconscious half smile rests on their lips and a sense of deep peace outwardly pulsates from them both. Perhaps this is the soul's way of celebrating a reunion.

There is only one happiness in life,
to love and be loved.
—George Sand

Silly Psychic

It is not easy to maintain a sense of openness when you feel shot down by love. Rejection is heartrending in any language. Pain, however, clears a path that makes room for something new to grow. When you are mourning the loss of a love, or the loss of the dream of a love, remember that something important flowers out of every experience. Look at it as thinking in fast forward.

Following the break-up of one of my deepest relationships, I was overdosing on attitude. Mine. So two of my brainy and gorgeous friends took me out for a night on the town. Translation: two PhD candidates (let's call them Brainy One and Brainy Two) and one medium dressed up and went downtown for dinner and drinks.

We ended up in a semi-swanky bar/restaurant where everyone was beautiful. Or perhaps it was the glass or two of wine—two being my limit, I was sillier than usual. Sadder, also. One of my most significant relationships had just ended. I understood it had been the right choice to head for the door, but I also knew I would miss him for a long while.

At the bar, we ran into one of my close friends from college. He's a brave and beautiful man who humored me as I pretended to flirt with him. It was outrageously funny, because everyone knew he was gay. My boundaries were not so perfect that night! Beware of anyone who has suffered a significant loss and is desperately pretending there wasn't one.

While my boundaries were not in good shape, my psychic "hits" were. Our waitperson was my first target. She had a nice vibe, was a bit needy (like I was one to talk, drink in hand, broken heart in chest, and reading her without permission as I was), and, as I told my friends, she worked as a makeup artist and salesperson for a local department store—I kept seeing her standing behind a counter with tubes of color scattered in front of her. Meanwhile, two men where headed toward our table. I turned to Brainy One and Brainy Two and said, "The short man is a Republican, and may even be running for office. The tall man is unemployed, in his early thirties, and lives at home with his sweet and wealthy parents."

After a painfully boring fifteen minutes, all was revealed. The two men shared their life stories, complete with politics and living conditions. The waitperson handed her card to the Republican. My friends choked, trying not to laugh as they read her department store card. My "hits" were confirmed, my wine glass emptied. Brainy Two was asked to dance, leaving me with tall, blond, gorgeous Brainy One. Then a darling five-foot-something man asked Brainy One to dance (note that the top of my curly head barely reached her collarbone).

I was left alone with my attitude, poor boundaries, and an empty glass of wine. One or two handsome men smiled at me and asked me to dance. But I decided instead to tune in to something tapping on my shoulder. Two crossed-over souls had entered my space. There were huge numbers of them in the ancient building. Lower-consciousness-level spirits (those who hurt others or themselves while alive and have not transitioned into the light) often like to be around people who are filled with alcohol. They actually move into the inebriated person's space and make themselves known. They do this by encouraging poor behavior, such as offering silent approval and applause in the ear of the one who is filled with alcohol.

I was not drunk, though I was rather vulnerable, so I ordered a sparkling water with a lime and listened. Laughter echoed through my consciousness on one level. Sadness hit me on another. I could feel the aching all around. Those on both sides of the veil were yearning for a sense of recognition.

One such crossed-over spirit had been a mover and shaker in the heyday of his career. He'd made some greedy choices, and taken to drugs and alcohol and sleeping with strangers. The sense he gave me was that although he'd died wealthy, he knew he had no love except for his love for alcohol, and so he felt bitter. All this landed on the screen in my head and in my heart in one solid thud. I must have been open to this spirit because of my own sadness at the time.

Following death, most spirits do go where they are led, which is toward the brightest light. Those who do not go toward the light after they die often make the choice to stick around their common "haunts," drawn to what is familiar out of fear. I felt compassion for this spirit and acknowledged his story. He moved on, unable to feed off of my pain.

My brainy and gorgeous friends had had enough and wanted to go home. Brainy Two gave her dance partner a pretend phone number, put her coat on, and made way for the door. Too bad, because my sense was that he was highly intelligent and thoughtful, and had a loving spirit.

Carry-on or Check-in Baggage?

When I was single, my friends and I would joke about the messed-up people "out there" in the "dating world." Never mind that we were, at times, part of that mess! The funny things people do when reaching for love, or hiding from it, are noteworthy. I have always maintained that everyone has baggage. The solution is to find someone whose baggage is carry-on rather than check-in.

In other words, if a woman you are dating is divorced and has done some pretty deep emotional work pertaining to what went wrong in her relationship, and takes appropriate responsibility for her part in it, this can be considered carry-on baggage. If, on the other hand, your date is still seething with anger seven years after the break-up of her marriage and spits every time she says her ex-husband's name, she has baggage that needs to be checked.

We all have some kind of baggage. In learning to deal with it, our souls walk the path toward enlightenment—the very path we set before our birth. I have met clients whose loved ones have been brutally tortured and killed. Moving past the rage about the loved one's death is far from easy. Yet I see brave people work through appalling ugliness and come out shining and beautiful. The magnitude of a problem does not matter nearly as much as the weight it puts on our hearts and the way we carry it. No matter the size of the bag, if we cannot bear the weight, we need to have it checked.

If you feel stuck on some long-ago issue, get help. In no way am I even hinting that your pain does not matter. It matters a lot. If you allow a tragic event or events to define you, however, you are ignoring the better part of yourself for your pain. To mourn a loss does not mean you must be stuck in it forever. Don't allow something sad in your life to define who you are.

> *To put the world in right order, we must first put the*
> *nation in order; to put the nation in order, we must first*
> *put the family in order; to put the family in order, we*
> *must first cultivate our personal life; we must first set*
> *our hearts right.*
> —Confucius

Falling in Love with Love

When you were a child, did your parents go out together on Saturday nights? Mine did, religiously. My mother served my siblings and me Swanson TV dinners, which included a brownie, a medley of veggies, mashed potatoes, and Salisbury steak or fried chicken.

My client, Jeremy, was the type of guy who would have eaten the brownie first, leaving him hyped up on sugar with a crash in sight. "Indulgence" would be a perfect middle name for this charming man. Jeremy loved love, and fell head over heels at least three or four times a year.

During his reading, I was sent a feeling of a sugar high and a picture of him sitting alone on an ornate sofa next to a TV dinner (minus the brownie) and a bottle of red wine. A flash of my old friend, Mario, jumped into my head. Jeremy and Mario had something in common.

Jeremy could be described as a relationship junky. A relationship junky is a person who is addicted to the initial stages of love. Craving only the emotional buzz, or high, and none of the truly deep, emotionally intimate phases, a relationship junky ducks out when the real work (and fun) begins. Jeremy confirmed that he was rather addicted to the early stages of falling in love. He liked the free fall as long as he did not hit anything.

During Jeremy's reading, a spirit from the other side was present, feeding me details of my client's life. The images that were dropped into my head were vague and peculiar and needed some interpretation. But my years of practice helped me effectively relay this quirky information. The images of food and wine were telling a story that was part of my own intuitive code. The image of my friend Mario was sent in confirmation. (This friend, by the way, was the CEO of relationship junkies.)

It was Jeremy's great-uncle, he later confirmed, who was providing the images that were acting as a matinee in my head. The uncle was something of a ladies' man and had died in World War II. He came through with the word "dandy," wearing a beautiful old suit and a red rose. He rapidly flashed different colored roses, wine, and the faces of different women. He certainly did think of himself as a ladies' man! Though Jeremy had never met his uncle, his mother had a photo of him, dressed as I described, sitting next to a vase filled with red roses. His uncle had come through to support Jeremy in breaking his antiquated pattern.

After a decade of falling in love fast, Jeremy was now looking for a way to slow it down and keep it going. He was an art dealer from the East Coast and a sleek dresser with a refined taste in wine. He had recently met "the love of his life," Carey, at an art show. They were considering moving in together.

Jeremy was concerned that he was once again moving too fast. He said he had a nagging feeling and was not sure what to do. Nagging or persistent sensations are often intuitive insights, feedback from the higher soul. Nagging feelings differ from obsessive thoughts. Nagging feelings, well, nag. Obsessive thoughts take control of the mind. Big difference!

During the reading, Jeremy asked about Carey. There was a vitality and sweetness to Carey's vibration. I sensed also that there was a history of emotionally impulsive moves. Jeremy confirmed the information I shared. I told him that moving in together might be an impulsive choice.

The good news was that he was showing signs of transformation already, because he had stopped to consider his actions! He did not know enough about Carey or his own feelings about the relationship to say for certain if moving in together was sensible. In situations such as these, I suggest that my clients put their intuitions to use, along with their hearts and minds. He needed to break the question of moving in together down into manageable components.

I suggested he picture himself sharing space, combining belongings, and dividing cleaning duties with Carey. I inquired how he felt when he saw himself doing this. How did the everyday realities with Carey stack up? What was his body's reaction when he imagined what I had recommended? By observing his own response to questions such as these, his intuitive self could act as counsel.

I invited him to describe how he feels when he's with Carey. His reply was, "Peaceful." "How would you feel," I asked, "if you continued to date Carey and did not move in together? Did your heart leap in desperation or stay calm?" Sensations of desperation reek of fear.

"How," I inquired, "did that feeling compare with the reaction you had when you thought of moving in together? Which one was more serene and peaceful?" If the thought of moving in together did not bring peace, the thought of waiting should. It is important to consider what each reaction denotes. Use your head to reason with yourself.

Also, what does your head tell you about the person you care about? I asked him whether Carey seemed stable emotionally and independent financially. Were their exchanges equal? What would Carey bring to the picture? What would Jeremy contribute? Infatuation may not withstand such questions. Head-over-heels love can cause you to trip. Allow your gut, your heart, and your head to work as a team to keep you balanced.

After the reading, Jeremy and Carey postponed moving in together for over a year. When a sense of steadiness became commonplace in their relationship, they moved forward. They've remained deeply in love for six years. Shaking up old patterns proved to be both enlightening and heartening.

Romantic Signs

If flashes of past failed affairs of the heart dart through your mind when you enter a relationship, the meaning may vary. Do the flashbacks pop up unexpectedly? Or do you call them to mind to help compare the new love with the old? If the memory has stillness about it, arrives in a spark, and comes more than once without provocation, your higher self may be sending it to you.

What the spark identifies only you can decipher, because it is part of your own intuitive code. Remember, your guides use your own life story as a tool. Flashes of failed loves, the ones that did not stay for keeps, could be a red or yellow light. On the other hand, they may just be the color of your fear. Meanwhile, flashes of people you know who are in relationships centered on love may be a green light. To help differentiate the signs, slow down and modify the pattern of behavior you have settled into. Familiarity is not always good. Be willing to change the pace. Be honest with yourself about how you feel versus what you want.

Keep in mind that your intuitive voice speaks a language unique to your own spirit. Once you make adjustments that feel right, keep an eye out for new signs. As long as you don't dictate what they are required to be, they will show up.

Remaining grounded when making life-altering decisions is a sure way of being able to tap into all of your instincts. Combining all of your senses makes sense. Placing trust in your gut, following your heart, and using your head is especially effective in sorting out romantic equations. It does not take the romance or fun out of it. It gives the experience a chance at really taking off.

Of course, when listening to that inner voice, be certain it is the voice of intuitive knowledge versus fear. First, ask a question that you know the answer to. Is the voice truthful? Are you feeling respected? If not, you are dealing with fear. Tell it to go away. Intuitive responses feel familiar. Unless there is truly immediate danger, the sensation should be one of calm certainty sent with respectful words and a loving quality. The voice of intuition is steady. The voice of fear is not.

Little Black Box

As I welcomed my client Mark, a reticent and handsome twenty-eight-year-old business owner, to my office for his appointment, I had to consciously close my intuitive eye. A spirit was waiting for us in my office, and a visual presentation of Mark's life was commencing prematurely. This was not a typical appointment! I had to ask my guides to hit *pause* so I could explain to Mark how the reading process would proceed.

As the reading officially began, I felt like I was watching a movie from the 1940s. Beautiful faces, all perfectly made up, flashed in front of me at a fast and furious pace. One was the face of a young woman with striking green eyes. When I described this woman to Mark, he turned five shades of red! I said she was shy in public and silly at home with friends. Her career had something to do with teaching young children and she seemed to be in love.

The next face was that of the spirit who had greeted us when we first walked into my office: an exquisite woman, also with green eyes, in her late fifties. She was reaching for a black box and handing it to Mark. Her eyes held sadness and love.

My nose began to itch. The spirit was unswerving in her effort to connect with Mark. As I reached for a tissue, I described her further. I told Mark that her energy was that of a mother, his mother. I asked if she had passed away over a decade ago. He confirmed that yes, it was his mother, who had died ten years before.

As I relayed defining characteristics about her, Mark's expression softened. Her laugh, I said, was contagious, and her smile gentle. She then showed me a picture of a man holding the hand of another woman while gazing into her eyes. It seemed Mark's mom was married to a man who was not always true to her, but this did not diminish her love for him.

Next I saw a picture of three little children, an older girl and two boys. They were dressed alike. These were her kids. I knew that Mark's mom had died of something lung related because I was having trouble breathing. As soon as I said the word "lung," my breathing went back to normal. I described the black box to Mark as being small, old, and soft like velvet. His mom had such a sweet, loving vibration. She felt warm and kind.

Mark said the outfits I described were actually the uniforms worn at the parochial school he and his siblings attended until high school. His mother did have a wonderful laugh and had died of lung cancer. He did not know the meaning behind the box.

His mom continued to flash me a vision of the box and a woman's face. I told him it felt like the young, shy woman was someone he had recently fallen in love with. He confirmed this.

This is an area where interpretation and tact must hold hands. It seemed like the relationship between Mark and his girlfriend was ready to move to the next level—meaning marriage—yet Mark was giving out a very hold-off vibe despite the love he obviously felt. I did not know if his mom was meddling from beyond or if there was more to it.

As soon as I thought the question, Mark's mom showed me the face of a dark-haired man with brilliantly beautiful blue eyes. He was gorgeous and apparently knew it. Mark was equally darling, but without the swaggering vibe. Using the term his mom put in my mind, I asked Mark if his dad had run around while married to his mom. His whole persona changed as he confirmed this. I could feel his apprehension. Mark was afraid that either he or his girlfriend would turn into a swaggering someone.

We talked about the signs his mom might have missed or ignored when his dad was having the affairs. His girlfriend was nothing like his father and neither was he. Though Mark's dad was loving in nature and intelligent, he also viewed commitment differently than did his son. His mom showed me a little girl with an "M" name and an "e" sound at the end, such as Molly (names are difficult to hear from those on the other side;

it is like listening to someone talk while they are underwater). Mark said his middle sister had just had a baby and named her Marnie. His mom's energy was becoming faint. She had done an amazing job communicating. The support she sent her son definitely had not died.

Two months later, Mark's sister, mother of Marnie, came in for a reading. She said that Mark and his girlfriend Ellie were engaged. He wanted her to tell me that the ring he gave Ellie was his grandmother's. His mother had left it to him as part of his inheritance. When he opened the safety deposit box to retrieve it, he noticed that is was housed in a little black box.

Speaking Up, Speaking Out

Jo, a vibrant strawberry blond, blue-eyed, college-aged woman, arrived early one morning for her appointment sporting a well-worn backpack on her shoulder and one or two deceased relatives by her side. As I reached out to shake her hand, I took note of the energy around her. A family gathering was already underway.

Unconsciously, clients bring their emotional histories, and often one or two loved ones, from the other side. Those loved ones can stir up emotional trouble that has been hiding or in hibernation. Jo struck me as enormously good natured but a bit sleepy, emotionally speaking. Interestingly, I sensed that while athletically she was highly energized, her level of self-esteem had been recently and seriously depleted. My guides threw me an image of what appeared to be little red hearts above her head, some of them broken. I found this message to be sappier than usual, and waited for the story to unfold.

During the reading, information was dropped onto the screen in my head about Jo's forthcoming career choices, her twin sister, her love life, and where she would make her future home. This is a pretty typical start to a reading. Then the hearts appeared again, but this time they flew out of her backpack by the dozens. I knew then that Jo gave too much of herself away in intimate relationships. Her emotional resources were exhausted; she had been involved with men who were terrified of being seen as vulnerable, so they acted like emotional bullies when they were afraid. I could see that Jo was conscious of not being confident enough to speak her mind with men, and that it bothered her tremendously.

Then abruptly, the screen became fuzzy with smoke. I smelled beer and cigarettes and heard the voice of a middle-aged man as if he were standing next to me.

I could tell by the way he was communicating that his personality while on this side was a bit boastful, yet charming. His vibration was one of an uncle or much older brother who had been quite the maverick. There was also a second spirit from the other side who was sending a hello to Jo. He was older than the first and his vibration was far more reserved.

I asked Jo if she had an uncle or grandfather on her father's side who had died. She said both her uncle and grandfather had passed on. Though I felt the energy of both relatives, one was communicating with more gusto than the other. Images continued to form in my head. I asked if her uncle had died in early middle age. She said yes. I began to describe detailed characteristics, such as how he dressed and precisely what his face looked like. Jo's eyes grew big, since she had never before had a reading of any kind.

Her uncle, whose name I later learned was Marty, showed me a picture of Jo with her hand over her mouth, standing in what appeared to be her own kitchen next to a man who was looking away and smoking a cigarette. Marty wished to validate his presence in Jo's life by relaying this information. His vibration was genuinely protective; he seemed concerned for Jo and highlighted the scene where her hand was over her mouth. Marty's message was reminiscent of the earlier information about

Jo and her self-esteem. Evidently, Marty did not think Jo spoke up for herself in life, and especially not in love. Marty seemed to have been somewhat of a rebel, able to say what was on his mind. He wanted to impart some of his exuberance to his niece. He was outspoken about how he felt; she was the opposite.

Next, Marty's energy went from protective uncle to charismatic biker. I saw a shiny black motorcycle with big silver spokes. He flashed a picture of himself standing next to the bike with a huge grin. Then I felt a withering pain in my chest. This is how I intuitively recognize cancer. Because the pain was in my chest area, I suspected lung or breast cancer. I relayed the message to Jo, who smiled with tears in her eyes.

She confirmed that Uncle Marty had been a bit of a ladies' man. He loved riding his motorcycle and dating women (lots of them). He relished drinking beer and was a heavy smoker, and had died of lung cancer in either his late thirties or early forties. Also, his short temper had caused some strife with his father. At that point, Jo's grandfather stepped in. He also had died of cancer: leukemia. He dropped a lovely picture into my head of his arms wrapped around Jo's father and his family. I told her that her grandfather wanted her to know that he was watching over them.

Jo was unsure of the details of the relationship between Marty and her grandfather, but confirmed that two nights ago, while in her kitchen, she had a small fight with a boyfriend. Jo was moved by everything that had been revealed, and was anxious to test the information against her father's memory.

Jo's next appointment was about six months later. She said that her grandfather had indeed died of leukemia. Her Uncle Marty and his father loved one another, yet had ceaselessly clashed. She had called her father the moment she left her last reading and asked him a number of intense questions. He was, according to Jo, shocked about the accuracy of the information I relayed.

The timing of her first appointment had also moved her father. During the week prior to her reading, he had been especially pensive. He spent time praying that his deceased brother and father were okay. Though they had been gone for some time, they had recently been on his mind. He had asked them, during prayer, to watch over his family. Her grandfather and uncle undoubtedly had a hand in encouraging Jo to schedule our appointment.

The ability to feel the presence of someone who has crossed over is unquestionably not exclusive to psychic mediums. Jo's dad, on some level, had registered the presence of his brother and father. Both had been on his mind, seemingly out of nowhere. Keep in mind that sensing a spirit's presence and tapping into the universal bank of information does not require a club membership. Be open to the brilliant possibilities the Universe has to offer, and see them falling into your lap!

As for Jo, the information about her love life and lack of confidence had made a considerable impact on her choices. She knew that her Uncle Marty had witnessed the scene between her and her then-boyfriend Hans. Hans could be gentle and kind, but was unwilling to compromise. Jo finally spoke up for herself and changed an antiquated pattern. She and Hans parted as friends, and her confidence was on the rise. She had started dating someone new, who applauded her newfound ability to speak her mind. Jo's energy was buoyant. Sometimes a nudge from someone on the other side can do the trick!

Dating a Medium 101

To say that I was conservative about dating would be a vast understatement. I was tremendously cautious in my love life. All three of my siblings were married to their first loves at twenty-three years of age. According to some well-meaning people in my life, being single was considered something to be fixed (or fixed up, in my case). In truth, I had an enjoyable and active social life. But it was occasionally fun to be fixed up. I found it interesting to see what sort of person my aunt or cousin, grandmother, or friend thought would be a good match for me. I was sensibly open-minded and met some wonderful men as a result of the blind dates, a few of whom remain dear friends. I was having fun, making my own decisions, going to school, working, and traveling. Blessed to have been in a few relationships with some truly stellar men, I was willing to accept nothing less than fabulous.

When someone wanted to fix me up, I would ask for the man's name, and then I would know pretty much all I needed to know about him. The matchmaking relative or friend seldom, if ever, knew how I obtained my inside information. My cousin Elena knew, though, and it infuriated her! Elena is fantastically intuitive herself. She has a long history of introducing people who almost instantly fall in love. That is, with the exception of me.

After she said a potential date's name, I would ask pretty on-target questions. "Isn't he still involved with the blond woman with two kids and on his third divorce as well?" Or, "I think his company is transferring him to New York. Did he tell you that? Besides, he smokes. I do not. So no, I will not go out with him." My instincts were virtually always on target. Still, I must have been a lot of work for her in the matchmaking department. She must have believed me worth it, though, because she kept trying. The men she introduced me to time and again proved to be the polar opposite of who and what I needed at the time.

Personally, I think she was just trying to guarantee her place in heaven. There is an old wive's tale about the blessings that follow someone who introduces a man and woman who eventually marry. When someone does so three times, a place is saved for him or her in heaven. Turns out Elena must have a reserved seat with a view awaiting her!

Before any date, I would simply ask my guides for basic, non-intrusive information. Is the man kind of heart, open minded, wise, and emotionally healthy? Oh, and funny? A red-light feeling would overwhelm me if he were dangerous. By dangerous, I do not necessarily mean emotionally so. If I was drawn to him, there was something for me to learn and I was usually a willing student. Creepy is another story.

You can use your intuition as an internal alarm system. Keeping you safe is part of its job. Look for patterns. Think of a time when you met someone who turned out to be a deep love and/or a great friend. Do you remember how you felt at the initial introduction? Or how you feel about them at this time? Store that memory in your intuitive filing cabinet. Now think of a time when you met Mr. or Ms. Creep. Someone who turned out to be less than kind, and whose actions purposefully caused you pain. Store that memory also. The next time you meet someone new and one of those memories, or feelings attached to the recollection, pops into your mind out of the blue, chances are excellent that your intuitive alarm system is sending a signal your way!

If you follow an instinctively good feeling but the relationship does not go as you had hoped, it does not mean your instincts failed you. It's just that your higher soul knows best what you need for curative transformation. There is no fast-forward button to press in matters of the soul.

The combination of love and physical attraction seem to send most of our better judgment sailing. Wisdom and intuition are partners; let them both do their job. Remember, when embarking on a new love adventure, to ask your gut, heart, and head to converse.

There were times when the intuitive heads-up was a huge help. Like when I sensed the man was emotionally involved with another woman or had a chemical dependency issue. More times than not, however, I was on the same page as most people in the dating world; I just learned to read the signals and turn the pages faster than some of my friends. When the sign pointed to the door, I knew someone was leaving.

My intuitive abilities and self-esteem were growing fast. I knew this because I understood when my heart was open and when it was not. I heard my soul speaking and responded. I was blessed at times to have experienced remarkable love. There were also times in my life where I declined dating offers as well as the Fiddler on the Roof type of fix-ups. It was much more worthwhile for me at those stages to stay at home on a Saturday night, clean my house, hang out with my cats, and read. It never lasted long and I always felt rejuvenated afterward.

I found the dating process to be both kind of fun and kind of lonely. Everyone's hearts are on the line. Hopes and expectations fill the air. As an empath, other people's feelings come through to me in stereo, so I had to be certain to know what my own feelings were. As a result, I could respect and honor everyone else's. I was grounded and I was a hot-head. Nice combo. But going with the flow in dating, which I learned to do, helped preserve my sense of delight. Invariably one to approach relationships gingerly, I waited to see what would develop.

This attitude helped me maintain balance. If you have ever dated, you know that balance is not an effortless space to sustain when filled with love and hormones. Early on, I commonly felt irritated when intuitively I knew my date's words were in opposition to what he was feeling and how he was acting. I was able to sense his truth, even when he could not. It took a long while for me to comprehend that being brave and knowing oneself, and therefore one's inner voice, is a process that takes time. It also takes soul.

At a certain point in my life, I began to grasp that not everyone was open to tuning in and understanding the messages of their soul. For them, a higher sense of consciousness held no appeal. They chose to leave the gift unopened, which is far wiser than opening and exploiting it.

It has always been people with a higher sense of knowledge, who pretend they do not have it, that really dishearten me. They hoard insightful tidbits to feed their egos and take advantage of others. To know better and not do better is like deliberately playing games with the soul. The soul is nothing to toy with.

In response to such conscious manipulations by someone with whom I was romantically linked, I would characteristically offer a few choice words out of anger that were not so carefully monitored. Since my abilities illustrated the truth in others, I reacted to what in fact was true, not what he wanted the truth to be. Now and then, I acted the psychic snob. In the dating world, this is analogous to burping out loud in a five-star restaurant. Charming.

Mediums do not have small reactions to big feelings. At least this one does not. It took some time for me to learn that fear uses lies as a cover. I believed in being observantly truthful, and always respectful. My sticking around depended on a lot of factors, not the least of which was how conscious the other person was of his fear.

It is not uncommon for time to take its time in unlocking us and our frozen hearts. In situations such as these, once the heart is thawed we are able to truly see who is standing before us. When we meet (or finally see) the love (or a love) of our life, there is a sense of identification ... a familiarity we feel at first sight. We recognize that person because somehow, we know them by heart. Some say this is a déjà vu experience, or a hint of a past-life connection. This could be true. I know for certain it is the soul delighting in the moment of freedom the personality has allowed to unfold.

Accidents, twists of fate, serendipities, and even simple quaint moments are all set up by the soul. These are instances to take note of, to memorize. Our souls speak to us in times of ecstasy, chaos, pain, sleep, physical exertion, prayer, and meditation. Our spirit reaches out to us in instances spent on an elevator or alone in a garage. Take those occasions and make them a conscious part of you. They are yours and will make you steady and wise.

Intuition acted as a chaperone on my dates, hanging in the background like a security team, ready to throw out a message from my personal intuitive filing cabinet if necessary. All five Clairs came along, geared up and ready to work. I felt a little more secure in the face of possible rejection. I was not in fact out of harm's way, of course. Putting myself out there was part of what I needed to do in order to find out who I was.

I learned to take clear note of coincidences, especially when they happened three or more times. Synchronicities are patterns that repeat in time. Our souls attract them into our lives to help us grow our states of consciousness. Synchronicities place a spotlight on something or someone. The more often we recognize the spotlight and what it means, the higher our psychic frequency becomes. I found that if a relationship held special value, a wealth of synchronistic events would arise. This happened especially when a vision, dream, or déjà vu preceded the synchronistic event. I knew then that it was my soul talking and I had better listen.

Dream Man

My dreams have always been significant for me. I love floating in another reality—one in which I can fly, embrace my deceased relatives, and appreciate more consciously that all of life is a dream. Dreams are a tool of the soul.

Dreams are in code, and provide you with a chance for reflection. Since I often forget my dreams within a few minutes of waking, I keep a notepad by my bed. There is great insight to be found in recognizing patterns. If I am searching for a job, I may dream of the feeling I will have at my new job rather than the job itself. If I have several dreams in one night, or am in a place of not wanting to know about the dreams, I simply lose the memory of them once they are recorded in my journal.

My dreams have provided remarkable information about new men in my life. This kind of presage was not offered in relation to every man I dated; clairvoyant dreams were only presented when I cared profoundly for the man and was in love, or falling in love. And the dreams were always right on. Over the years, I experienced at least one dream that seemed to lead me down the aisle (although later I found that "aisle" meant something other than marriage). As time went by, I became more fluent in understanding what the signs were and what they foreshadowed. Of course, I always let relationships play out as they would, never wanting to make a move based solely on a dream, just in case I had misinterpreted the essence.

However, during the "courtship" period with my husband Jason, no such dream appeared. I was on my own with this one, it seemed. I'd met Jason at a children's fundraiser, one that my cousin Elena was sponsoring. Then, shortly after we were married and had moved into our new home, I was reading through a two-year-old journal. The content was far too interesting to keep to myself, so I read a paragraph out loud. Jason looked up; actually, he woke up from a semi-sound sleep. (I like to stay up late and read; he likes to go to sleep and snore.) He rubbed his eyes and said, "When did you write that?" He actually asked to look at my journal, thinking I was joking and had made the whole thing up. Rookie.

It was not until I read through my journal that night that I remembered anything about the dream I'd had about "the man I was going to marry"—a dream that occurred six months prior to my meeting Jason. Here is a synopsis of what I wrote:

I am standing on the lawn of an inviting, two-level home located somewhere sunny and warm. I walk up a set of stairs and let myself in the front door. The artwork is abundant and far more contemporary than is my usual taste. None-theless, I find it particularly striking and am drawn to it. Several pieces of artwork have a silver plaque on the frame with the number sixteen. The home belongs to a self-assured man I have been dating for several months, six to be exact. We didn't grow up in the same city. He is handsome with very dark brown or black hair, a Greek nose and striking blue eyes. He is stylishly dressed and there is some witty reference to his shoes or feet.

There is a sort of symmetry between us that I have rarely shared with any other love interest. We recently became engaged and I am surprised at myself for being ready to move forward so quickly. He takes me downstairs where there is still more art. He is grounded and proud of where he is in his life. The work he does is strongly connected with the law and numbers.

His parents are in the back yard by the swimming pool, waiting to meet me. They are really young, a little shy, warm, darling, and not overly tall. I see immediately how much they adore their son. There is an enormous part of me that is in a bit of shock at the pace at which everything is moving. Still, I feel totally in tune with myself, serene, and ready to move forward. The dream ends with the man and I jumping into the pool. End of dream, start of life!

Six months later, I met Jason. Six months from the day of our first date, Jason and I were engaged. As in my dream, I knew it was right for us to move forward, yet felt surprised at the speed of it all. We met on November 16th, had our first official date on March 16th, and were married on March 16th one year later! I believe that the artwork in my dream represented the differing ways in which we express our creativity. He admires and respects my abilities as a medium and writer, although he is neither—he is a successful business owner with a beautiful and unusual balance of logic and creative insight. Although his hair is a lighter shade of brown than that of the man in my dream's, he looks and dresses so much like the dream man that it makes me laugh. Jason has feet that remind me of Fred Flintstone's—flat. I love gifts from the Universe!

The dream, before I met Jason, ministered to me on a purely unconscious level. It helped calm my fears about moving quickly before these fears could hit. And a number of serendipitous moments we shared while dating also provided heads-ups of what might come. Each time a coincidence occurred, it felt like a hug from the Universe.

Though I had been deeply in love before, the pieces had never fallen into place with the ease they did with Jason. There were no games played in our relationship, so our hearts could remain open. Jason was confident enough in himself to be honest about what was in his heart, which only made me love him more.

He surpassed me in intensity and actually sought an equal partnership. This was a combination I had never experienced. As a result, I was able to remain grounded, true to myself, and open to what was unfolding. When I felt fearful, I checked in with my gut, my heart, and my head. Not surprisingly, they were in astonishing harmony—so I married the man!

In hindsight, I always had some help muddling through the ups and downs of dating. My guides, acting as supreme parents, offered sign after sign. Once in a while, the sign read Blind Intersection. For me, it came down to knowing my own worth.

In love, as in all things, it is only in being brave to ourselves that we can face the world unafraid.

> *Please give me the opportunity to expand my heart*
> *into the life of another in the holiest way, the most*
> *beautiful way, the most intimate way, if that serves*
> *Your purpose. For I would learn the secrets of love and*
> *use what I learn to grace the life of another.*
> —Marianne Williamson

Tools and Techniques: Love

Appreciation Journal

Have you heard it said that when you are ready for love, love finds you? Well, this is true, *and* there is more to the story. None of us know for sure why our lives move in the direction they do. The best we can do is to navigate well and set our sights and thoughts in the most favorable direction possible. Shaking up old patterns is a powerful start.

An appreciation journal is one that is filled with heart-felt words of admiration and self-approval. In showing gratitude for what you have, you invite more of what you want. Find a new spiral notebook with a pleasing cover. Commit to filling it with light, positive words about yourself! Begin with a list or two. Here are some suggestions:

- Create a list of every loving quality you have found in yourself and others.

- Create a list of each striking quality you have found in someone you have been romantically attracted to.

- Create a list of the qualities you most admire in your friends.

- Create a list of the love stories you have fallen in love with. What do they have in common?

- Write yourself a letter filled with the words you most need to hear. Include in the letter qualities you admire about yourself as a friend.

- From the vantage point of your biggest fan, write a letter outlining what would make you a warm and wonderful partner. Mail the letter to yourself!

Good Morning, Good Night

The first thought you have when you wake in the morning and the last before falling asleep hold a certain magic. Ensure that the words you say and the thoughts you think are filled with love and light. In the morning and the evening, take a moment to recite poetry or prayers, or read one of the countless books published that will help open your heart and mind. Books such as *A Woman's Worth, Enchanted Love,* and *Illuminata* by Marianne Williamson speak to the heart and superbly lift the spirit. Louise L. Hay's *You Can Heal Your Life* is one of the single most powerful books I have read regarding self-esteem and change. Whether they are inspirational, religiously motivating, or just plain funny, if they help you feel calm, positive, and present, they work.

If you desire a career in fashion, you need to dress the part—exquisite clothes and all! Likewise, if you seek love, give love. Love and appreciate those in your life right now, your friends, family, and coworkers, and of course your dog. When you love, you glow. People are attracted to light.

With Open Arms

Love is an extraordinary and supreme offering. When we grant our love to others, it is also a gift we extend to ourselves. Whether or not it is accepted or rejected, it still remains a gift. In order to draw love to us, we must be in a space of loving and accepting ourselves. The vibration of self-acceptance and self-assurance magnetizes people to us. Help yourself sparkle by being your own best friend and appreciating the gifts you were given by the Universe. Since like attracts like, be someone you like!

This may well involve a conversion of your thought process. To draw new love in, you must be willing to shift your current patterns. It is more important that you take responsibility for the patterns you have set than understand them completely. The need to decode them could just be a smoke screen delivered from your ego.

Create a welcoming space in your life for love. Open your arms and your heart will open further. For all intents and purposes, just reading the words on these pages facilitates change because it opens your mind to the possibilities.

Each evening before you fall asleep, thank the Universe for your life. Name three or more things you hold most dear. Acknowledge that you are willing to alter your thinking, and your habits as well. Declare that you are already doing so. Accept that you have and are shifting in consciousness and action. This helps make room in your life for what you hold most dear.

6

The Universal Code
of Ethics

Action indeed is the sole medium
of expression for ethics.
—Jane Addams

A Code to Live By

No thought or deed unfolds in secrecy. Absolutely nothing slips by the Universe unnoticed. Everyone on this planet is held to a high standard and is governed by a universal code of ethics, which demands that all action be taken for the highest good of all. This is true for accountants, physicians, truck drivers, teachers, janitors, flight attendants, psychic mediums, family therapists, and you.

We all know that undergoing intense training or earning a degree does not necessarily guarantee that someone will perform well, and ethically, in their chosen profession. Mediumship is no exception; merely having been born with mediumistic capabilities does not necessarily qualify a person to be a decent medium. When choosing a psychic or medium, be sure to employ the same caution you would use in choosing a doctor or financial advisor.

Good mediums maintain high universal standards, ethics, and morals. They also are able to sustain emotional balance, which gives birth to compassion. When compassion, skill, and sound training are combined with high ethical standards, there is definitely reason to take notice of the medium. Someone with these traits just might have something valuable to offer. These mediums are out there, and well worth the search!

Psychic mediums are interpreters of information. How well they receive and understand the information is an indicator of their ability. The way in which they deliver messages is a matter of skill and personality. Tact and kindness count. Mediums must respect how powerful the reading process is, and pay it honor. The potential it has to deeply affect the mind and tap the soul is immeasurable.

A psychic's insights are always filtered through their personality. If their filter is tinted brown with the ravages of depression, the information they deliver is also tinted brown. If the filter is tinted green with a high degree of compassion, the information that comes through is green. The color of these filters is related to how well the psychic or medium interacts with the world at large.

Something to consider when hiring a medium is how you, as a consumer, intuitively respond to the person. Aside from your initial excitement and nervousness about the appointment, are you comfortable? Readings are powerful flares tossed into the unconscious. Anyone addressing your subconscious so directly should be professional and a dynamo. Remember, fear has many faces, so consider your own during this process and do your best to remain open minded, but not naive.

Over the years, I have been asked by various people to use my abilities for less-than-reputable activities. I consistently decline such offers. I do not use my intuition to cheat in any way. Nor do I read people indiscriminately, for fun or fortune. Not in my work and certainly not in my personal life. I learned at an early age that my talent and abilities were to be used for good.

I believe that my intention meets my action. In other words, I put my money where my mouth is, and fully accept that the intuition I was born with is both a gift and a responsibility. My professional capacity is tied to how well I honor the magnificence and meaning of the intuitive process. I know that to misuse my abilities would be synonymous with tossing them out the door.

Karma is the law of cause and effect, and we are all under its rule. Our deeds, past and present, determine our future experiences. Karma is always in operation, no matter what level of awareness is involved. The higher our consciousness, the faster the law of cause and effect operates. I refer to this particular consequence as "the boomerang effect." It's a whopper to experience, especially for those who know better and choose not to do better. When a person with an advanced level of consciousness deliberately (or otherwise) brings harm to another, the Universe responds in a way that will provide just the right lesson necessary to make a point and offer an opportunity for growth. The lesson is designed to hit home and stay there. If the offender refuses accountability for a poor choice, the boomerang effect may act as a shadow and follow the erring person around until responsibility is accepted.

The boomerang effect affects us all. Every thought and action returns to its root. As it reverts, it may alter form, become stronger, or remain identical to the original deed. The law of cause and effect is unbreakable.

The Disappearing Psychic

During my teen years, I met psychics with skill levels of all shapes and sizes. Of special interest were the more "seasoned" psychics. From observing them, I learned how to hold on to my abilities. There were the psychics who shared information cautiously, with reverence for the act and the soul to whom they spoke. To them, clients flocked! The law of cause and effect can help manifest extreme joy and prosperity. But there were also psychics who used their abilities to gamble and win favor. Time after time, those who used their intuitive abilities for selfish reasons, such as winning money, slowly lost their psychic edge.

One such psychic—whom I shall call Henry—had a near-death experience while in his early forties. His intuitive abilities took off from there. Suddenly, he was able to sense vulnerabilities in people and pick the right slot machine in Vegas. He could zoom in on what people most needed to hear in order to win them over. He was a ruggedly handsome man who had yet to find the right woman. He had tried, however. When I met him, he was on his third divorce.

Henry had clairvoyant dreams and could read a palm with remarkable clarity. As his hit ratio grew, so did his popularity as a psychic in the small town where he lived. He helped people identify career choices that fit. He genuinely liked people and wanted them to succeed. Somehow, though, he became drunk on his own success.

Henry hit on pretty much everyone, including psychic teenagers who could stand up for themselves. I found him to be less than darling, and more than I cared to get to know. Whenever he found a young someone to close in on, he offered to read her for free. His readings somehow always included himself in their future. As his slime factor grew, his psychic skills shrunk. All five Clairs went undercover. Spontaneous insights were eventually all he had left. Oh, and a fourth ex-wife.

Over the years, like so many of you, I have experienced enough sadness to flatten me emotionally. I could have chosen to remain angry because I was hurt and frightened. But my strong belief in a higher power, and my ability to love, helped me learn to forgive. The intuition I was born with, and have since nurtured and developed, has helped me to understand something about why people do what they do. Compassion can be a lifesaver.

Don't get me wrong—I can feel red-hot anger and throw a really intense and unfriendly vibe at someone who is deliberately hurting me or mine. It is just that holding a grudge has proven too heavy for me. I have learned that acceptance is a form of forgiveness. Those who have caused harm are left holding the bag. And I am not talking a carry-on bag, either!

Each of us is here to express fully
our highest spiritual self.
—The Happy Medium

The High Cost of Living

The cost of living as oneself, of being different, unique, and sensitive, is high. But the cost of not being exactly who you are is even higher. Would you rather be respected for who you are, or who you pretend to be? If someone dislikes you, it has more to do with his or her own lack of a sense of self than it has to do with you. People condemn in others what they wish they had or didn't have in themselves.

The last time I checked a dictionary, the words "different" and "unique" were not defined as "wrong." My world is full of color. This offends those who live in black and white. Of course, I can feel dejected when I am criticized. Nonetheless, my goal is to live by the motion of my soul. It is empowering to shut out the voice of fear. It is not that I do not care what others think of me; I simply believe it is none of my business.

As with most mediums, I have huge amounts of energy rolling through me. I like the ride, since it keeps me real. My life is rich with emotion. To dull my senses would mean I could not feel all of my love. That would crush me.

The capacity I have for understanding the human soul has profoundly developed as a result of my work. My willingness and ability to love has deeply intensified. Most people, at the root, are filled with loving, sparkling light. Loving energy is like no other energy.

People really do sparkle. Their highest selves beam out from their eyes. I see more than what people present of themselves—I see what they would love to present, or could present, if they lived up to their own soul's wishes. As a result, I expect much of others. It is not that I insist everyone always have a higher knowing, it is that when they do, they act on it! Without a doubt, this aspect of my personality can cause difficulties.

To have insight and act blindly is, to me, an indulgence no one can afford. I know that when I have done so, I've let the best part of myself down. Development of the soul is a process. The potential shining of each soul captivates me. We all make choices, and are responsible for them regardless of our level of consciousness.

While society does not always support us in acting based on inner knowing, the Universe does. Speaking out and up for those who are victimized is a brave move of soul. It takes personal alignment and a sense of self to do so. Turning down a date with the sweet man your best friend once dated, and is still in love with, takes soul. Making the choice to sell a product to a client that is in their best interest, versus your own, is a stand of soul. Being who you are and standing up for what is right is a key element of living ethically, of adhering to the universal code of ethics.

Everyone is offered these opportunities every day. The more we take them, the more frequently they are offered. The more we accept them, the higher our intuitive capacity grows. We become observant of our own actions, and therefore an observer of the world around us. Making the right choice is often the lonely choice, of course. We must be willing and able to stand alone to truly stand up.

The wisest and most enlightened decisions are frequently the least popular. Psychic intuition is a beautiful, double-edged sword. People who judicially make use of their natural insight would be completely lost without it, and are grateful to the Universe for entrusting them with it. Develop your intuition, and you may find you have an opportunity to help other people take a chance on themselves, and learn to shine.

Brave is the Person Who Takes a Chance

Have you ever known the peace of helping someone carry an emotional load during a heavy moment in their life? Joined them in their tears, though the sound of their breaking heart was deafening? Then you have known a form of bliss sent to only the brave of heart. Your honorable action is recognized.

There is a kind of love described as "global." While it comes from the most personal part of us, it is impersonal, or at least neutral, in nature. It can be seen when a stranger changes a tire for another in the pouring rain or on a snow-filled night. Burdens are much less heavy when shared.

Scores of people are less than willing to share their troubles for fear of feeling exposed. Yet it is when the pain is shared that it has a chance to dissipate. Brave is the person who takes a chance.

I am privileged to witness such bravery on a regular basis. Doing my work is an honor. I am trusted with, and feel the weight of, my client's sorrow. Intuitively, I see its inception. My abilities also allow me to feel my client's reaction to the information sent his or her way during a reading. Usually the actual details of a reading vanish by the end of the day, if not sooner. There is one exception. If the content resonates with me emotionally, I may remember some particulars. In other words, if something in the life or personality of my client significantly parallels my own, I may temporarily remember a small portion of the experience.

A Unique Soul

Usually, it is second nature for me to be able to maintain my personal boundaries while doing a reading. However, my work with a wonderful, vibrant client named Vara challenged my detachment on a number of levels. Her silly humor and endearing spirit broke down my practiced guard, and I had to work much harder than usual to ensure that my ethical code was held to the usual high standards.

Vara had a personality that could fill a room. She was bright, dramatic and outspoken. Before she was through the door of my office she blurted out, "Will my breast cancer return?" I explained the reading process and made it clear that she would have ample time to ask questions. Until that point, "yes" or "no" was all I wanted to hear; anything more interferes with the information coming through. Vara, however, was not a yes-or-no person. She was all about details and questions and humor. Her inquiries had a punch that could stop me in my tracks!

Vara had to fight for the floor during her reading, however, because someone from the other side definitely wanted a word with her. He showed me a flash of my own brother. This meant that the energy coming through was either Vara's brother, or someone brother-like to her. He stood behind her, indicating that he was around her often, and had a charming presence even in spirit. He was handsome, charismatic, private, and a bit of a pushover. He skillfully dropped pictures in my head and heart of his life and his relationship with Vara.

I asked Vara if her brother had died. She said yes. I continued quickly—he was coming through so clearly I did not want to waste time. Vara jumped up and asked how he'd died. A reading, I explained, is often presented to me in picture or movie form, and I had yet not reached that frame. She sat back down and looked at me expectantly, eyes sparkling.

When I told Vara that the man's energy, presented in spirit, was so lively and delightful, she nodded in understanding and began once again to shoot questions my way. I told her (somewhat apologetically because I do not like to be rude) that her brother said she would get her money's worth if she shut up and let me do my job. She erupted into laughter, and later indicated that this was truly her brother Ashley's humor. Even though death had separated them, their love and shared humor kept them connected.

The love he sent radiated around her in full color. He wanted her to know he was peaceful. He had an understanding of a larger plan and was not trapped by feelings of rage or distress about not being able to live to an older age. Ashley loved his family from the other side and was with them in a way that prevented him from missing them the way they missed him.

When you see a movie and the music indicates that something terrifying is about to happen, your body reacts in a certain way. You may find that seconds before you even hear the first note, your body gives warning of danger. Your instincts are sending out a red alert! The intuitive process is filled with moments such as these. When a spirit or your guides want to capture your attention, your senses are typically the tool. This reading was no exception.

My senses were alerted. Suddenly, my arms felt chilled. Ashley was placing a feeling of utter panic inside of me. His death had been a violent one. I tentatively asked Vara if Ashley had died suddenly. She nodded. As he gave me a feeling of terror and shock, part of me began to shut down. His passing had not been from illness or accident. Again, the feeling of fright ran through me. Choking out the words, Vara told me that Ashley "had been murdered."

My guides monitor the information sent my way. When a crossed-over someone wants to tell me how they died, I can feel my guides move in and turn the volume down when a murder is involved. Being sensitive by nature, I cannot watch movies with murder scenes because they impact me negatively long after the film is over. Because I see real murder victims when they come through for clients, or feel them tap me on the back in public places, I have absolutely no desire to view anything of the sort on the silver screen. The screen in my head is all I care to handle.

Whatever the situation, the mode of death is usually communicated in an abbreviated fashion. Cancer is shown as a dark spot on the body; a heart attack is a sharp pain in my heart; choking or strangling is indicated by a tight feeling on my neck; a stroke is a sudden lack of air and absence of thought, followed by silence; and drowning may be illustrated as a body of water. Death by gun is a loud noise in my ear or a pressure on my head. Other details are usually not necessary unless it is essential to my client's healing processes.

Ashley did not need me to see how he died, but Vara did. Rather, she wanted confirmation of my skill, and perhaps to see if I knew who had killed her brother. I told her that he had been hit over and over with a heavy object. He had left his physical body before it officially died. There likely was more than one victim, as I felt his terror at seeing someone else, a woman, in a fetal position, in pain. He wanted me to let his sister know that he was really okay and that the man who killed him would pay karmically. No matter what happened on this side, the other side was waiting.

Ashley was not coming through with an angry energy. Most spirits do not seem to harbor vengeful thoughts. In my experience, those on the other side are more concerned with what they themselves did to cause harm than what anyone else did to harm them. They are trying to right their wrongs by taking responsibility for their actions. It's rare that a spirit addresses karma; it's common that a spirit addresses love.

Vara confirmed that Ashley and another person, his girlfriend, had been murdered. They were tortured and killed by the girlfriend's jealous ex-husband. Vara said they had arrested the murderer. She wanted to know what the outcome of the trial would be.

A naturally loving woman, Vara had lost trust in life and in the Universe as a result of this event. The fact that her brother had died was made worse by the way he died. I sensed that she would not be wholly satisfied by the end result of the trial because only the murderer's freedom would be taken, not his life.

Ashley made reference to someone meaningful he had left behind. He referenced someone dear, who had humor similar to his own. This appeared to be Vara's son, who had a heart of pure honey like his Uncle Ashley. The two had a shared a level way of viewing life. He dropped a picture of himself smiling, standing next to his nephew, which meant that Ashley was around him often. Vara had suspected as much, and was pleased with the affirmation.

Ashley also helped guide Vara. He gave his sister advice about moving on and having fun. Words that encouraged her to allow her son to have the room to grow filled the reading. Ashley was one of the clearest spirits with whom I had ever communicated. He showed his sister a kindness and acceptance that elevated her soul as well as my own.

I continued to see Vara over the course of the next few years. She sometimes asked questions directly related to investment and finance. As a rule, that sort of information is met with silence by my guides, as it is not my place as a medium to engage with it. But my guides revealed answers to Vara's questions; this spoke volumes about her, and Vara never misused what she learned. Another unusual aspect of my work with her was that distinct information pertaining to her brother's murder was shared. Vara maintained her decorum, even in the courtroom just a few feet away from the murderer. Also, Ashley would occasionally visit me at my home and drop messages into my head when Vara needed direction; he used me to communicate with her in a more personal way. These things, along with Vara's own dynamic personality, made it hard to maintain the line between "client" and "friend."

During one of her readings, I had a dark feeling about Vara's health. I strongly sensed the possibility of a recurrence of cancer; her life force had dimmed. Vara asked if her cancer would come back. I had a sense that all was not well. Vara interrupted my prayerful thoughts, looked me in the eye, and said, "I do not want to know if it is bad." I shared what my guides said about taking care of herself: "Where her health is concerned, she needs to be extremely diligent and, as always, continue to act on every hunch." I knew that I had to honestly answer all her questions in a way that would also give her as much hope as possible; fear is cancer's best food. And there was a chance I was reading the message incorrectly.

On a Friday morning, Vara did not show up for the appointment she had recently set. My intuitive flags were waving red. When I zoned in on her energy, it seemed faint. When she did not return my call or email, I stepped out of my professional self and called the hospital, trying to discover what was happening. My intuition was telling me something I did not want to hear. I knew she had not crossed over, though I sensed it might not be long.

It was during the process of writing this book that I learned Vara had died. She was a truly brave and beautiful person who lived big and loved big, even as she struggled to maintain her own place on this side of the veil.

The feeling of overall admiration and respect I have toward those with whom I work is powerful, to say the least. While I care deeply for them, the relationship is professional to protect all parties. But Vara seemed to treat everyone, including me, with the same love and respect most people only show to close friends and family. She has given me, over the past years, some of the most validating, encouraging, and appreciative words about the work I do and how I do it that I have ever experienced. She was one the most life-affirming individuals I had ever met.

Vara faced her fears head-on, doing battle with darkness by finding the light in a frightening situation. A hero to me and to others, she was, and indeed still is, deeply loved. As she finds her place on the other side, all her acts of kindness become twins, finding a home both on this side of the veil and on the other.

Wounds, Compassion, and Grace

I've learned a great deal about grace and compassion from the intuitive slide shows my guides have shown me throughout the years. They illustrate where a client's psychic wounds initiate, and detail what the person is reacting to. Not only can I see the wound, but I can feel it and the tremors that followed. More often than not, my clients are responding to an "initial wound."

Initial wounds are those we placed in our lives before we arrived in our bodies. They hold one or more of our most powerful karmic lessons. For comparison, if you were occasionally teased because of the shape of your nose or your home, the painful impact of such wounds probably dissolved in time—they were not initial wounds. Meanwhile, having to change schools a number of times early in life is a more apparent injury. The pain of loss, and our reaction to it, most certainly could be described as an initial wound. But these emotional abrasions are not always easy to spot on the canvas of our lives. It is the fact that we are repeatedly reacting to them that holds vital karmic relevance.

We are more colored by our reaction to circumstances than the circumstances themselves. There is deep wisdom in allowing ourselves to be defined by the voice we give our soul rather than an experienced misfortune. Our soul's development is measured by how we respond to life's conditions and how well we hold on to our willingness to love.

Listening to the particulars my intuition offered was not always attractive to me. Repeatedly, I would overreact to something someone said or did in a way that did not totally fit with the circumstance. In this way, I was reacting to my own initial wound. Sometimes I found it impossible to feel anything except anger when I was hurt, because I was so afraid of being captive to my own wounds. As I mentioned, I can be outspoken. My angry words once carried quite a bite. At times they still do.

Initial wounds pack a punch by their very nature. Remember to approach with care anyone pretending to not be in pain when visibly they are. Everyone is governed by those emotions that belong to them, yet they refuse to claim.

I think of myself as a kind of a mystical thinker, though not everything that happens in my life is reflective of it. Oftentimes, fear smears my vision and I lose the wonderful, pervasive feeling of connectedness. Because I feel emotions at top speed, I need a variety of safety belts to help me retain balance. One is compassion. Compassion is a hand extended to others and to us. It reminds us of who we are and honors shared weakness. Compassion is feeling *with* someone, not feeling superior *to* someone out of fear. Compassion sits with the wounded and has no hierarchy.

My intuition has given me opportunity after opportunity to learn some of the most treasured lessons in life. For me, the one with the greatest value has been sympathy and acceptance without pity. It is from this understanding that the best part of me shines. In this space there is always love. Boundaries and compassion make a gracious team.

Intuition has served me well in teaching compassion to those around me. This includes those on this side of the veil and the other. When a friend, coworker, or family member makes a mistake that has a high emotional cost to me or mine, love and compassion are not usually the first emotions on the scene. But grace gently reminds me that we are all interconnected. To judge another harshly is simply another manner of not forgiving and loving myself.

Clearly everyone has lapses in judgment. Mine are often centered on my temper. When I am in a space of fury, I do my best to ride the sensation out and open up to understanding what it is I am so frightened of. The way I will feel in the future about whatever is occurring is important, and I try to see how my reaction could affect my life later on.

As a medium, I have been privy to the consequences of actions in the hereafter as well. As I have said before, visiting souls are not, in my experience, seeking vengeance. Depending on their individual heightened state of consciousness, they are seeking forgiveness.

A state of oneness or larger identity helps me to reconnect or reidentify with all that is. In this space, no feeling is foreign. I see myself in everyone. My sense of connection for all that is allows me to love and forgive, or at least accept. It may take some time to get there, yet get there I do.

Gratitude

One of the elements of intuitive work that I appreciate is the ability to profoundly connect with people. Most people feel alone and small, and fear being exposed. But I see the light in their souls. Most of all, I love and believe in people. Most are decent and kind. Connecting with and helping others is my passion. Like a marathon runner needing to run, I need to do readings. The energy I put forth to do this work backs up inside of me if unused. The feeling compares to drinking a tank of caffeine.

Helping my clients locate the areas within themselves where they are hung up brings me peace, because I understand the worth of such knowledge. Cleaning out the wounds of life is necessary to the healing process.

As the loneliness of not being understood falls away from a client's face, my heart is filled with gratitude for being given the opportunity to do this work. As my client finds their own strength, and tastes self-acceptance, I know the price of feeling odd and alone has just been lowered. Please know that in no way am I responsible for the consciousness raising that can and does go on in my office. The Universe sits alone on that throne. The brave person who comes to see me to learn what a higher part of their self has to say deserves the most honor!

Friends, Family, and Mediums

Family ties form a wordless connection between souls. We return to this earth, over and over, with the same souls in an effort to learn how to love. The drama and turmoil between family members is no accident, and the opportunity for spiritual growth is tremendous. Deceased parents, aunts, uncles, cousins, and great-great-grandparents frequent readings even of relatives whom they have never met, in an effort to provide validation and support. Family ties are that dynamic.

The bond we can feel with family members and friends holds a certain magic. As Eustache Deschamps said, "Friends are relatives you make for yourself." If in our lifetime we have one dear friend, we have much. They stand by us without question. They know what our hopes are and hold them for us when we have lost them or given them up. They lend a hand without being asked. They offer us a place in their hearts and take their own place in ours.

Sometimes, we are blessed with friends who are also family. The combination is a powerful one, enveloping our hearts from every side. Betrayal by a friend or close family member is bitter, since the wound bleeds from within. Betrayal does not kill love, but it arrests it, leaving our feelings for the one who betrayed us flat. Friendship cannot withstand one-dimensional love. Either the betrayal is dealt with openly, or it is the last exchange between friends.

Friendships are meant to be profoundly honored. They are a part of what makes life magical. There are those friends who disappear in the face of someone else's sorrow. Fearing their own pain, they take flight and act as if the a tragedy is contagious. These friends are not terrible people; they just allow their fear to govern their lives. Courage of the heart is rare. We know who our true friends are when we are knocked flat by something larger than ourselves.

Friendship is the dessert of life. As Kahlil Gibran wrote, "Friendship is always a sweet responsibility, never an opportunity." As a friend, I find it easy to love without question. As a medium, I have found it difficult to measure how much of my intuitive knowledge to share with those close to me. It is never a matter of not wanting to help. It is a matter of minding my own business and allowing those I love to do the work they came here to do. As a general rule, I do not do readings on friends or family. If something is psychically presented to me, I tap further into my intuition for guidance. If it feels right to share what I sense, I present the insight as casually and neutrally as possible. If not, I inwardly acknowledge the information and ask the Universe for further signs.

A key factor to consider for all psychics and mediums is, when close emotional involvement is present, complete objectivity is virtually impossible. Those developing intuitive skills are better able to offer strangers the neutrality necessary to act as a clear conduit. Objectivity is key. For much the same reasons, surgeons do not operate on family members.

If a family member is an occupational therapist, and he or she begins to notice a potential problem with your child, the appropriate action in most cases is to wait and see what evolves before alarming the family. The same is true with intuitive insights about friends and family. Emotional attachments can deepen the likelihood for insights to occur, but they also have potential to cloud the picture.

If my intuitive red flags alert me that a friend or family member is about to step into yet another drive-by relationship, I hold my tongue, as I hope the person would do for me. First of all, it is entirely possible that I am incorrect in my interpretation or that I am swayed by an inclination to protect the person I care about. I know that if I do step in with or without invitation, my loved one will be so resentful of having been given information that they were not ready to hear that, when ready, they will not want to think about it.

It is tricky to find the balance that makes a relationship sing. Being supportive and being a snoop are not related. Finding the happy medium in personal relationships is constructive. I weigh my words carefully. Emotional ties can play havoc with intuition, so it is important to check all motives at the door!

As my abilities and confidence have grown, so has my judgment on how or when to share messages from the other side. I do my best to remain respectful of every soul concerned. The motto I stand by is, essentially, "If they don't ask, don't tell, and even when they do ask, think twice!" There are few exceptions.

Innocent Insights

Innocent insights, drop-in insights, or drive-by insights are intuitive flashes that show up innocently and unexpectedly. They are uninvited and startling. Children are famous for these—and they tend to catch everyone by surprise. They ask their parents if everyone is going on the trip to Disney Land, the trip their parents have been secretly planning for months. Or they wake up crying about not wanting to go to the dentist. Later the same day, a dentist visit is necessary when a tooth is accidentally cracked.

Adults experience innocent insights less often than children because society insists that we maintain an inner control of the natural emotions that open the door to the intuitive process, and intuition is about letting go. Though it is certainly not appropriate to blurt out every emotional thought, it is healthy to acknowledge it as it passes through the mind.

Have you found yourself, seemingly out of nowhere, talking to a coworker about the unusual employment opportunities advertised in the newspaper, only to find out later that your coworker had recently been searching for a job? Given that everything, including thought, has a vibration, you were unconsciously responding to what was paramount on your coworker's mind. The vibration was hanging in the air and you innocently caught it!

There are moments when an intuitive thought catches me off guard. While visiting my friend Rebecca in Florida two years ago, I noticed a beautiful photo on the refrigerator of her brother, his wife, and his gorgeous son. Without thinking, I asked when her sister-in-law was due. She laughed and said she would let me know once they shared the news with her. Two months later, she emailed to let me know her brother's wife was ten weeks along.

Knowing her brother and his wife were expecting another child was, thankfully, safe news to share with my friend. She knows me well and is open to the intuitive process herself. I was relaxed and spoke without taking a moment to check the source of my insight. The pregnancy was as obvious to me as the color of her brother's red shirt. Innocent insights, or in my case, escaped insights, are only fitting to share if they bring no harm.

Had my comment been meant to wound or even prove a point, such as how perceptive I am, it wouldn't have been an authentic innocent insight. It would have been a psychic hit-and-run. Using the universal bank of information for anything except for good is, well, bad. It's wise to stay conscious so there are no casualties.

An Unexpected Visitor

Do you remember Ashley, Vara's brother, who would drop in and visit me in my home? Seven months after Vara's first reading, while folding the mounds of laundry that decorate the homes of babies and toddlers, I felt the sensation of someone in the room and had a flash of Ashley. His energy was warm and kind, easy to recognize. Of all the souls I have connected with over the years, his was the one I remembered best. I actually looked down at what I was wearing, hoping I looked presentable. Oh my God, I thought, am I flirting or am I simply surprised and self-conscious?

Whenever a family member or friend on this side of the veil drops in unannounced, I feel set off course momentarily—thank God for cell phones. If the unexpected guest is in spirit, humor helps ground me and brings me back to task. Those in spirit do not use appointments or cell phones to extend advanced warning of their arrival. Their visits are a part of life for us all. My deep respect for them has grown substantially over the years. Fear has been replaced by understanding. Death is an ending, yes, but not the end.

While Ashley's vibe was usually calm, this time was different. He was sending a foreboding message that something was happening to his sister Vara. I sensed his urgency; he wanted me to connect with her. It is not my policy to solicit or even contact clients unless I am doing marketing for a workshop. I told him this simply by thinking it in my head, and asked him to please have her contact me. That evening, she emailed a request for an appointment. While I would like to say that I was not at all surprised, the truth is, I was! I still marvel at this process.

The day of her appointment, as I sat down to meditate in my office in preparation for the day's readings, Ashley made an immediate entrance. He was sending messages about health and finances so rapidly that there was no way I could adequately remember the details and relay them to Vara. I jumped up, ran to the lobby, and asked her to follow me into my office.

Vara confirmed that she was in the process of signing onto a less-than-conservative financial investment. She had had second thoughts and was stalling on moving forward. After hearing what Ashley had to say, she decided to hold off until she could investigate other possibilities. The unease around her health, of course, was because her cancer had returned. Wise and resilient, she had found the most powerful course of action to take. Vara laughed at hearing about Ashley's visit to my house. He would do what it took!

Tact and Diplomacy

Every hour, thousands of songs are dancing over the radio waves. However, not every song is suitable for every set of ears. In the same way, not every psychic discovery is appropriate to share. In situations such as these, it takes tremendous composure and maturity to say nothing. Being blessed with insight is simply not enough. Knowing when, what, and if to express a thought takes time. It is a process, this finding a middle ground. Tact and diplomacy are gifts of time, and of trial and error.

Opportunities to find the middle ground will present themselves throughout your life. They will take the shape of secrets you should keep, and knowledge you wish profoundly you didn't have. Some life-altering insights you must face alone, at least initially. Life unfolds, as it will, with or without your consent. As long as balance is found and retained, the intuitive process is one that will bring joy.

There is no question about it—relationships, particularly friendships, offer a tremendous playground for personal and psychic growth. They add a certain sparkle to life. With genuine friends, we never have to apologize for living big, loving big, and mourning big, because they expect nothing less. Life is so full it is worth feeling it. Living it from the inside out is far more blissful with treasured friends around. And intuition is contagious! When we are around someone who taps into the universal bank of information on a consistent basis, we begin to do likewise. When we are near those with an abundance of energy to share, we naturally become more energized. Moods, attitudes, beliefs, and enthusiasm are all contagious.

We celebrate each other, standing by without judgment as we traverse the canyons life has to offer. My friendships are not based on my abilities as a medium. They are based on a respect and a connection of the heart and soul. When a friend is in the midst of dealing with any sort of pain, including loss due to death, my shoulder and I are unafraid. I am completely available to lean on. Yet despite being a medium, I am not always available as a conduit.

Maintaining your tact and diplomacy is, in short, a matter of maintaining healthy boundaries. Would you want to know when your father was going to die? The answer to this question is routinely "no." As long as there is nothing that can be done to change the outcome, it is better not to know. Tact and diplomacy count in life. So much so that they have scored a place in the universal code of ethics bylaws.

Though it is impossible to turn off my intuitive senses, it is possible to turn them down, and turn them down I do. I take my cue from other healthy professionals. A healthy psychologist is not constantly analyzing his or her friends and relatives. A sagacious professor is not forever in teaching mode.

Like most of you, those close to me have lost friends, spouses, babies, siblings, parents, or pets. I am infinitely sensitive to their sorrow and grief. I also recognize their lost loved one's spirit if they are hanging around. There are friends who wish to know and those wish not to know when this occurs. It isn't always appropriate for me to act as a medium. Sometimes, it is more important to just be a friend. When suitable, I am both.

Annabelle's Brother

When a dear friend's recently crossed-over brother blew smoke in my face for the third time in ten minutes, I realized I was being rude by not acknowledging him. I was in the middle of cleaning my living room. At first I felt unsure of who he was and did not want to call and interrupt my friend while she helped her children get ready for bed. I had met her brother Gary only once, over twenty years before. He had long ago found a home in a different state. Gary was a recovering addict who had made one last mistake. He'd gambled with drugs and lost the bet.

But I called my friend. "Hey Anne, who is Annabelle?" I asked. She replied, a slight irritation in her voice, that Annabelle was a long-forgotten nickname her brothers had called her when they were kids, and no, it was not a name she preferred now! "Annabelle," I asked, "did Gary wear a perpetually dirty-looking black leather jacket with some odd patches on it? Did he smoke clove cigarettes, and have a twinkle in his eye and a phenomenal skill with numbers?" She said yes—why?

After receiving her acquiescence to talking shop, I continued. "Well, he is here, you know, in my living room. He sees you in the car, crying over his loss and sitting in your living room surrounded by the pile of paperwork left in the wake of his unforeseen death. He is so grateful for all you have done, and are doing, for the family he left behind. He wants you to continue to pierce the silence, Anne, and stand up for yourself and those without voices. Gary is proud of the awareness you have spread about families and addiction. He loves you, Anne."

There was no sound on the other end of the phone. I waited patiently for Anne to find her words while I found my own space again. Her brother's presence had faded. He had said what he wanted to say, so he took his clove cigarettes and went home.

Assumptions

Do you remember the 1970s television comedy *The Odd Couple*, starring Tony Randall and Jack Klugman? Tony Randall's character, Felix Unger, uses a chalkboard to illustrate the folly of making assumptions. In large letters, he writes the word "assume." He then breaks the word apart and tells Klugman's character, Oscar Madison, something like, "Never make an assumption, or you will make an ass out of u and me." A statement that is both funny and true!

"What's in a name?" Shakespeare asks in Romeo and Juliet. Assumptions are made based on names, or more generally speaking, labels. In order to wrap our minds around the constant influx of information in our world, we categorize to simplify. Unfortunately, categories lull the mind. We become intellectually lethargic, and categories evolve into assumptive prejudgments, or prejudices. Statements such as "all blonds are stupid" and "all teenagers take drugs" are simply inaccurate.

Standing on either end of an assumption like this creates an obstruction in our energy flow. When we assume, our egos inflate while our intellect and spirit are diminished. As a result, our intuition naturally shuts down. If you reopen your mind, however, you are returned to a blissful neutral. The flow of psychic data is now liberated and able to reach the conscious mind at a more rapid speed.

Whether you are part of a hiring team for a new sales division or interviewing a potential physician, intuition can be at your side to deliver the missing piece that finalizes your decision. Staying in a space of non-judgment helps sustain your connection with the universal bank of information. You will then be privy to personal and at times idiosyncratic information about those around you. Remember the universal code of ethics—tread lightly and do not judge. Keep in mind that you are glimpsing only a simple frame of the movie. Don't be a critic. The information made available was meant to help you, not hurt others.

Dissolve obsolete assumptions about life after death and psychics by showing up for yourself intuitively! Be proud to speak openly about the success you have had due to your own instincts. Share your stories, and perhaps you will help clear up the fallacy and assumption that psychic phenomena are nonsense and only kooks believe in past lives.

Individuals with a great capacity for intuitive insight and even mediumistic abilities look like you and me—because they are you and me! People from all walks of life, with or without these trained abilities, can and do benefit from tapping into the universal bank of information. Access is unbiased.

As far as assumptions, please do not assume that because I am a medium, I levitate at the grocery store, channel the spirit of John Lennon, or can be spotted a mile away. As I see it, an integral part of mental health is to be able to mainstream fluently in society without losing a sense of self. I highly value my mental, spiritual, and physical health. Though there is nothing wrong with it, I do not wear a cape or carry a crystal ball. I have been known to dress in a tailored suit and look more conservative than my banker-type husband. I have my own style in both clothing and intuitive work. Over the years, I have become proficient in backing up my facts with intuitive insights and my insights with conventional facts. You may not be able to pick me out in a crowd. If you were lost, however, I would have an excellent chance of finding you.

A rose by any other name would smell as sweet.
—Shakespeare

Becoming a Medium

Do you wonder how people do psychic work? Not the nuts and bolts (or Clairs and quantum physics, in this case), but how, personally? Do you ever contemplate whether or not you can truly work as a healer, psychic, or medium? Have you wondered what qualifies a medium as a "professional" in the vocation? Or what qualities might separate a professional from a novice?

Perhaps the mediums you've encountered seemed to know and feel something you wish to be part of. Their work inspired you and pulled at something deep within you. Perhaps you have long aspired to restore people to well-being. Learning how to put your intuition to use is unique to each person. The one universal aspect is that motive matters.

There is more to it, of course, than meets the third eye (a little psychic humor there). The work of bringing through someone in spirit who was tortured to death or a child who died at three is not for the faint of heart. The medium must have a heart that can love beyond reason and stay open when it would be less complicated to close it. It is for a compassionate someone who is grounded enough to study carefully and become well-trained in something that at first glance does not seem reasonable at all.

Since everyone is born with some level of intuitive competency, nourishing the ability is all that is necessary, right? Not really. There are other important factors—such as ethics, morals, the ability to empathize, and your general character. I know first-hand how it feels to be manipulated by imbalanced people who misuse their intuition, breaking the rules and bending the truth. I also have known enough tenderhearted people with vast intuitive abilities who do not know how to protect themselves from darker energies. As a result, they have been left susceptible to emotional and physical ailments because they lack decent training and grounding.

If you have always wanted to ski, and the first time out try anything except the bunny hill, you may break something, or someone! Common sense dictates that you first take lessons from an experienced, qualified ski instructor before you head for the hills. Then, once you understand the ropes and have some decent experience yourself, let the snow fly! Without time and training, you could get hurt.

As you read these words, you may be wondering if I have switched gears and am now trying to discourage you from pursuing work in the intuitive healing arts. Perhaps I am. That is, if you are in it for the thrill of feeling that you have one up on others due to your superhuman abilities to see past lives and taste the future before it happens. If you are willing to look good at the cost of someone else feeling bad, and to replace integrity with fame and money, allow me to save you a few thousand years of karmic debt. Leave the psychic work alone and go for something else that toots your horn and strokes your ego.

There is a difference between feeling a powerful pull toward learning more about the metaphysical and feeling an intoxicating draw toward power. I wholly support people in their endeavors to follow the authenticity of their souls! If the higher soul calls you to more effectively and professionally tap into the universal bank of information, I am a sound and spirited advocate. I have long conducted workshops in support of such brave efforts.

More obviously, I have a deep desire to reach more people and write books (like this one!) that not only encourage the use of intuition but outline how to do it as well. Teaching and conducting workshops in this arena carries a high level of responsibility. Holding the hand, heart, and soul of another human being is a privilege, one to be taken seriously.

The chances are heightened that because you are reading *The Happy Medium*, you are interested in learning and growing and are light years away from wishing to use your intuitive insight simply for personal gain. It was as much for your own protection as it was for the protection of those with whom you may work that I wrote words of warning against misusing something so significant. The truth is, the temptation can be great, even for those who are great.

When I have an opportunity to conduct a workshop, I ask everyone who is on this wonderful journey of exploring the higher self to bring two things with them, and leave two behind. Besides bringing an open mind and a willingness to learn, attendees are asked to check their motives at the door and leave their egos behind.

To do this work justice, you must stay tuned to the higher self and give the ego, which can act as a loaded gun, time off. This is meaningful work. The people who are most amazing at it do it for one reason, and one reason only: to help.

Ask yourself if your drive to put what you know, intuitively speaking, to professional use is motivated by compassion and a desire to serve. If your answer is yes, you have a quality that is as professional. It is not about looking good, it is about doing good. Pedestals are for sculptures, not people. You have to appreciate the occurrence of having been laid low to experience and treasure the high of touching another soul, demonstrating to them that they are not alone.

When you work on an elevated intuitive level, your character radiates with lightning speed. The satisfaction of being a successful professional has something to do with knowing how to tune in to what the Universe has in mind, versus what you have in mind. It is all about being a tool for the greater good versus your own. A novice gives advice because they know it is correct; a professional imparts information only where appropriate and because it is accurate, was requested, and is for the good of all.

Especially in this area of your development, it's all about maintaining balance and finding the happy medium. In my experience, you have to trust and know yourself deeply to grow intuitively. It is a wonderful way to go through life. Maintaining balance not only helps you find your groove and promote your shine, but helps you sustain it. We are all here to shine—it is our natural state of being!

Now that being a medium is in vogue (or at least out of the leper category), I can, with less discretion, mention what I do for a living in polite company. As long as I am tactful, that is. In some circles, being tactful means not being quite truthful. (I find those circles to be square. You can call me weird, but you cannot call me square!)

Every portrait that is painted with feeling is a portrait
of the artist, not of the sitter.
—Oscar Wilde

Tools And Techniques:
Ethics

A Quick Fix

Like attracts like. When you are in a dark mood, darkness finds you. The valet loses your car, or your computer starts to smoke. Well, maybe not that dark, though perhaps close. If, for example, you are just about to walk into an important meeting and need to ditch that black cloud, a quick fix is in order. Here it is: say something genuinely kind to yourself, and then say something pleasant to someone else.

Too simple for you? Well, remember that you can change your life, moment by moment, with each thought. Why not make it a wondrous move? As discussed earlier, our thoughts offer a platform from which to view your world. So the next time you are around people, think a positive thought about each and every individual you see. Now take it a step further and say something positive to everyone with whom you interact.

No need to soak each word with syrup—you must be sincere. Let's say you are at a park on a Saturday morning. Do you like the color of someone's sweater? Is there a father holding his daughter's hand with tender affection? There is always something upbeat to think and say. When you do so, the mood-altering effects are astounding.

Everything flows with extra ease when positive energy is infused in it. Maintaining affirmative thoughts can shift dark energy to light. Opening up psychically occurs when your outlook remains light. Besides, it is irresponsible to stay in a dark place when you know better. Your energy, whether light or dark, bounces off of everyone else's and eventually links. When you are in an upbeat space, you beam, and good things and people find you.

Do you know how you feel and what energy you throw off at any given moment? Over the next three days, remain as conscious as you can about your emotional vibration. Replace every negative thought with a positive one. The climate you create for yourself through this process cannot help but to warm up. Remember, the more aware you are of your feelings, the more aware you are! When your consciousness is raised, so is your ability to receive spontaneous insights.

Mind Your Ethics

So now you are psychic... wait! You were psychic before you picked up this book. You were born with intuition, of course. While reading *The Happy Medium*, your level of awareness may naturally be raised due to the simple process of opening your mind. What you choose to do with the knowledge you gain is completely up to you. Since this chapter demonstrates how upholding principles translates into and affects action, I would like to offer a few words of encouragement, sprinkled with some questions.

Modeling ethical behavior is a powerful way to teach it and to live. If you found a hundred-dollar bill lying underneath someone's chair at the theater, would you ask if it belonged to the person seated there? Your vibration is raised if you do. The higher your vibration, the more perceptive you become.

There are a variety of ways to demonstrate your ability to mind your ethics. At times, it means minding your own business. The very next time you are blessed with some insight about another person, feel free to keep the goodies to yourself. In other words, don't toss it in your friend's face! Do ask your higher self if vocalizing your insightful thought would help or hinder. What feels right to you? Suitably exhibiting self-control is essential to growing your intuitive abilities. Saying nothing in certain instances is more powerful and loving than saying too much.

Chances are, you make daily decisions that are evidence of your honorable ethical standards. It might prove interesting to do a count. Over the next twenty-four hours, tally up these decisions and congratulate yourself on each and every principled choice you make.

7

Intuition and the Workplace

All life is an experiment.
—Ralph Waldo Emerson

Psychic in a Suit

Before I turned eighteen, I had been on my own for some time,
learning the ropes of adulthood. During my first year of college I lived in a dive apartment and fell in love with real estate.
I treasured helping people find homes and did well at it, most
likely because I'd lacked a home of my own for some time. This
was my introduction to business and those who reside in that
world. It is where I first learned to identify corporate barriers to
success.

As a medium, I want to reach as many people as possible.
My clientele range from the creative to the corporate. Whether

it's two or two thousand people, those who run businesses affect a myriad of others; they are in a position to help raise the energy vibrations for everybody. In conducting work as a corporate psychic, however, I tend to alter my language if doing so helps the process. Language is simply a communication tool. For example, I may not share with my CEO client that it was his deceased grandmother who just provided the crucial information about the land he was about to purchase (which was, as I learned later, at one time an unofficial dumping ground for waste).

Insight and expertise work in any climate, and differentiating between public and private roadblocks is a matter of semantics. Both stand in the way of success and act as a barrier to reaching the objective. My purpose as an intuitive coach for corporate clients is to illustrate and illuminate the core issue of a subject, and the path that will most effectively raise my clients' level of understanding and therefore their consciousness.

Business owners have been trained to think in a factual way, with spreadsheets and calculations. They are not inclined to rely on anything else, including other people, and certainly not their intuition or gut. The work I do helps people feel safe in trusting their intuitive signals. They feel enriched by, and not managed by, their work. And once they experience success with their intuition, they will be more inclined to trust it.

Intuitive Coaching

Wise business owners, driven to flourish, use whatever resources are available. If they've been successful in the past, chances are that their own hunches have been part of that winning chemistry. The work I do with my corporate clients helps validate and strengthen their insights.

As an intuitive coach, I am able to utilize both my background in business and my intuition to provide strategic planning advice that is specific to the goals and objectives of my clients. I am able to successfully help formulate solutions which enable them to create and attract opportunity, increase personal and professional effectiveness, train, develop, and manage staff, decrease employee conflict, and increase employee alignment. Business owners, seeking ways to incorporate personal insight to move to the next level, understand that my work as an intuitive coach facilitates those results.

Corporate CEOs often hire me to coach them on using their own intuition, as well. Though it may seem unconventional or unusual to allow intuition to be a guiding factor in a multi-million-dollar business venture, "unusual" is not necessarily "wrong." The unknown, or less-well-known, is sometimes a truth that just awaits understanding.

My goal has always been to elevate conscious energy by igniting positive energy. I have been witness to some incredible acts of brilliance, as well as kindness, in the world of business. In a work environment, success comes most naturally when positive energy, intuition, talent, and drive collaborate.

Over the years, I held a number of jobs as I obtained my college degree and developed my stripes as a medium. I have sold print media; managed, trained, and hired employees on a corporate level; cut and colored hair; painted apartments; and worked as a property and marketing analyst for some of the largest real estate companies in the Twin Cities. While the titles I've held have changed over time, the fact that I've been exceedingly careful not to exploit my intuitive knowledge has not changed. I strongly believe in playing fairly.

I do not seek to gain psychic knowledge that does not honorably serve everyone involved. Once again, the universal code of ethics is relevant. As I have said, to misuse insight is to show proof of missing the point of having it in the first place. The end result would be the loss of it—not an outcome I am willing or have ever been willing to bring forth.

I am often hired as an intuitive coach/corporate psychic to help identify a profitable location for my client's emerging business venture. I am also frequently retained to help identify which candidate would prove to be an unparalleled division manager. I move forward intuitively by detailing applicable strengths. My guides, in a format that resembles a resume, often present the person's assets to me.

It is not appropriate, of course, for me to share unrelated points about an applicant's personal life. For example, I would not disclose that the strongest candidate might be going through a divorce in the upcoming year. I may well say that his or her energy may be split for approximately twelve months due to an outside and unrelated matter, but then return full force. My intuitive eye is likely seeing this clearly. Ethically, I know there is no fitting place for the knowledge to rest safely.

Insights I do relay pertain to the job at hand, such as if I sense that a candidate has a serious issue with carrying projects through to the end. Or has an unethical vibration and might steal company funds or sell confidential information to a competitor. More often than not, I paint an accurate picture of what each candidate would bring to the table, and how.

By identifying a specific area of concern within minutes of meeting my client, the energy around the issue begins to transform. Validation is a powerful force. I help clients observe globally. In turn they learn to tap into their own intuition and help alter the energy around their businesses by igniting an elevated way in which to view everything. That elevated way of thinking holistically is highly contagious and increases consciousness. Make no mistake about it—given the right ingredients, an expanded awareness magnetizes the energy of success.

The greatest good you can do for another is not just to
share your riches, but to reveal to him his own.
—Benjamin Disraeli

EGO as CEO

Successful people want and need to be right. Accomplished successful people, however, are willing to be wrong! The ego wants to be right for the thrill, or high, of feeling of one-upsmanship. The soul, when it is aligned, moves forward for the good of all no matter the exterior outcome. Triumph is not the color of money or the false being superior. It is the ability to move in the direction of the soul's purpose despite greed and fear. As this is achieved, the beauties of this worldly plane display themselves, seemingly effortlessly.

If you are on a beach searching for shells and you happen upon a fifty-dollar bill, would you throw the money back onto the sand because it is not what you were searching for? If you were to listen to the voice of your ego, you would. The ego says "it will go my way or no way," ignoring even the obvious good offered by the Universe. The ego is a dictator and makes a poor CEO.

Over the years, my reputation as a skilled professional medium and intuitive coach has grown steadily. I have something significant invested in being accurate, as my business has been built on referrals. Achieving "hits" or being correct is paramount to this end. As my business increases, my abilities expand. Quality can and does attract quantity. A sign of an ego takeover is when quantity is allowed to supersede quality.

When I am working, the intuitively elevated part of myself wishes to tap into only the highest of sources and be a clear conduit so that I may deliver information that is for the good of all. My ego, on the other hand, wishes to continue to achieve. As I tune in, I must tune out the voice of my ego and release my stubborn desire to be right.

Personal wishes interfere with outcome, especially when such wishes are selfishly motivated and not for the good of all involved. This is one of the reasons I refrain from working with friends or family. The bank of information opens with a security code. Or rather, a "secure" code. I need to be secure enough to be wrong. Dead wrong, if you will pardon my pun. I must sincerely feel impartial in order to remain in tune.

Because I am able to feel the emotional responses of my client during a reading, I know when he or she is fearful or does not agree. I cannot allow my client's personal reaction or wishes to interfere with the flow of information I am tuning in to, however. For me, as well as my client, releasing desire for a particular outcome is key. Remaining neutral helps expand consciousness, which in turn magnetizes the energy of achievement.

If you authorize an "ego shut-down" and open up to your own self-assurance, you will be pleasantly surprised by the end product. Get out of the way of your own success by demonstrating confidence in your level of skill. This will help you tap into the intuitive process. Opening to it can be like the sensation of drafting when you are riding a bike! Go with the flow.

Life is a field of unlimited possibilities.
—Deepak Chopra

Office Drama

When economic margins narrow, companies undergo tangible as well as intangible pressure. Profit and loss is contingent on internal as well as external factors. In part, my job is to identify the intangible. As a corporate psychic, I am able to help change old, antiquated patterns. This is achieved in part by altering the emotional climate in an organization.

Thoughts are swirling, vibrating energy particles that have a power of their own. Your thoughts create much of your world. The ones you repeatedly think become a pattern that you swiftly become locked into. These patterns, in turn, generate circumstances that alight as personal drama.

Human drama seeks a canvas or stage from which to act out or perform. The stage may, for instance, take the form of a relationship between mother and child or between a supervisor and employee. The setting or stage is parenthetical—it is the opportunity for resolution that is essential to the soul's growth. The place of employment is a powerful stage because the majority of people need work to survive. As a result, those involved must return to the setting.

Step back and observe the challenges, both past and present, that you have had in a work environment. They likely mimic other challenges in your life. Be honest with yourself and observe the precedent. There are no coincidences. Keep in mind that the education of the soul takes time. If you find yourself inescapably making the same mistakes, congratulate yourself on identifying it! The first step in changing a pattern is recognizing it.

Drama and repeated scenarios unfold for your own personal growth. The setting is simply the venue. Are you habitually late for work? Do you have a history of disliking your supervisor? Have you never worked for any employer for longer than two years? Observe your patterns. When you begin to understand your own drama, you begin to be liberated from it!

Put yourself in neutral when you are in the midst of a familiar conflict. Is your reaction a level ten when the circumstance calls for a two? This is a sign that you are feeling and reacting to an old pain that has not been released. In recognizing this, you begin to feel released from it. In that moment, make a choice to change your view of your world, or else you will acquiesce to the same tired game. Choose to discern what is unfolding and be a person in bloom. When you recognize and value a deeper part of yourself, that part grows and brings with it the sweetest of life's gifts.

The trick is in what one emphasizes.
We either make ourselves miserable, or we make our-
selves happy. The amount of work is the same.
—Carlos Castaneda

Where's Your Focus?

The next time you walk into a work-related meeting to resolve a dilemma, consciously pick your point of inner focus. What concept or thought will your mind rest on during the meeting? Will it be resolution? Are you and your coworkers invested in solving a problem that will help make employee lives less stressful? Will it decrease debt and therefore bring a more positive light to every decision your employer makes?

Or will your thoughts and attitude be filled with dissension? Do you tell yourself that there is no answer because the problem is not solvable? Have you locked your creative self up in frustrated knots? Remember that you are entirely responsible for your thoughts and your actions. Why not be open to the possibilities, do the best with what you have to work with, and see where it leads? Retain an open frame of mind. This is the best you can do, so do it.

Place a positive spin on your focus by restructuring it. The ways in which your words and thoughts are shaped in turn shape the outcome. If what appears to be an unachievable goal has been set for you, choose to be proactive instead of reactive. You do not have all of the information, so can only surmise the reason for the goals.

By focusing on what can be accomplished, you increase the chance of achieving it. For example, if the goal revolves around sales, set your sights on the benefits of the product and reaching the highest objective attainable. Reject the internal negative banter your fear creates. This opens up your intuitive, creative self. When this higher self is employed, what can be achieved will be achieved. When focus is aligned with the intuitive process, outcomes far outreach rational expectations.

> *Nothing splendid has ever been achieved except by*
> *those who dared believe that something inside them*
> *was superior to circumstance.*
> —Bruce Barton

Office Bullies and Bandits

Everyone has worked with an office bully or bandit—the sort of person who sees nothing wrong with stealing a sale out from under a coworker or is consistently taking credit for projects others have completed. When confronted, the office bully denies or otherwise lies about his or her unfair antics and often assumes an accusatory stance toward those who are courageous enough to take a stand.

Office bullies and bandits are thieves in more than one way. They steal confidence and vivacity from the people around them. Their conduct is reminiscent of an energy vampire, with one core difference: energy vampires are not wholly conscious of their behavior, while office bullies and bandits are.

The broader picture does not hinge upon office bullies and bandits, however. They are merely acting out of their own fear and may otherwise be decent. What their behavior highlights is an environment that doesn't have appropriate safeguards in place to guard against such behavior.

Those in a supervisory position are at a disadvantage in identifying these brutes. At first glance, the bullies appear to be major players and producers. This is where the intuitive process, when offered the opportunity, delivers! When opened up intuitively, a supervisor will receive a heads-up or a psychic Post-It that addresses the situation in detail. It is a matter of seeing and reading the symbols.

As an intuitive coach, I help identify the issues and illuminate the signs that are displayed. Office bullies and bandits can be reformed. It is not uncommon for a deeper problem to be uncovered once the initial issues are exposed. Behind every thief there is a weakness in the system—which, as it turns out, is the bigger problem.

Ambition

Ambition is a spark sent from your soul. Your soul speaks to you through your passion and your peace. When you find your place in between the two, you have found balance. Balance stimulates insight, the use of which cuts down on the unnecessary work involved in the attainment of goals. It is a straight line versus a curvy one. Intuition streamlines.

Once, weeks before a milestone birthday, I temporarily flopped into a slight emotional trench. Counting my blessings had long been a personal birthday ritual, so this austere mood was a surprise. I asked myself if it was due to the physical effects of aging. My hair no longer came out of my head jet black, and my sons could now outrun me in a race. Thank God my daughter still has such short little legs—in her eyes I remain a jock.

One afternoon in May, while sitting at the park with my husband, children, and Baci Boychelk (our dog), I asked for some inner-eye guidance to understand my birthday blues. It appeared that my career—or where I was in it—was a player in the melancholy. Though I felt great about my work as a medium, there was something significant missing. The poems I'd published came to mind. Then, unexpectedly, a book plunged onto the screen in my head. That was it! I had always loved writing and had been sure that, by a certain age, I would be a published author of books about the intuitive process. I had yet to do so, and felt truly blue about it.

My children were chasing and racing with their father in the park. He was still faster than they were! I made a mental note to be jealous later. My mood lifted considerably that day. It never occurred to me that I might not get an opportunity to be published. All I knew is that I so wanted to add my contribution to that of the fabulous psychics and mediums out there who were telling the truth about the intuitive world.

Professionally as well as personally, people get in their own way. I vowed not to do so and kept my mind open and aligned with my intuition. The Universe is a superior navigator. I followed the signs and knew that in doing so, I was meeting my destiny no matter what the outcome.

As a first step in the book-writing process, I began submitting articles to magazines. Jason suggested a popular and well-written local magazine, *The Rake*, to go along with the metaphysical publications I had had my eye on. He also suggested a few other great publications, reminding me that it was a numbers game. However, I did not hear one word after he said "*The Rake.*"

My instincts were at it again. *The Rake* was where I must strive to be. I could feel this throughout my entire being. I wrote an article about the art of being a medium and submitted it to *The Rake* and only to *The Rake*. As it turned out, they were not interested in my article; they were interested in me and the work I do. The reporter who eventually wrote the article about my psychic work in the corporate world was an innovative writer who had an instinct for what topics are about to catch on with the public.

And apparently, he was right. As a result of the July 2007 *Rake* article, titled "Magical Thinker," my client base increased substantially because a new demographic of people was reached. Mainstream interest in metaphysics was significantly on the rise! Several months later, an editor at Llewellyn Worldwide contacted me after reading the *Rake* article. She wanted to know if I was interested in writing a book!

> *Work is love made visible.*
> —Kahlil Gibran

Tools and Techniques: The Workplace

The level of personal expectation we attach to our work is astounding. All of our endeavors, including the professional ones, illustrate who we are at the core. As I have said, the business you choose is simply a canvas. The loss of a vocation is the death of a dream and can throw us into mourning. Stress and fear partner with darkness to cloud our perspective. The best we can do is to be honest about how we are feeling. We can also pull out our tool boxes and put into motion the tools and techniques that will help raise our vibrations and make us magicians of language who know how to turn thought into form in our professional lives.

> *Let me have new energy. Let me have a new sense*
> *of purpose. Let me know that I am on this earth to*
> *serve. Let me not feel guilty about the expression of my*
> *power. Let me no longer play small, regardless of other*
> *people's reactions to me when I play big.*
> —Marianne Williamson

The Magic of Words

Human beings are magical creatures. Simply by combining specific letters to construct words that soothe, we are creators of magic. We can heal a broken heart or break a whole one with words that hold comfort and affection or anxiety and acrimony.

The words we say to ourselves are the most powerful of all. When good fortune is shining, it is imperative that we speak words of appreciation—out loud, in our head, to a friend, while in prayer, whatever and wherever it feels right. By showing gratitude for something, anything, beautiful in our lives, we attract more of it! Whatever we focus on grows. When there is turbulence, however, it is difficult to keep our thoughts positive, let alone our words.

Try these tricks of the trade from the toolbox of transformation. Allow words to help transform your state of mind. Here are some examples of ways to use the written word to your advantage. Remember, this exercise is just to help raise your vibration—you need not share or mail anything you write.

- Write yourself a glowing letter of recommendation.

- Compose a letter to your future self describing how you benefited from where you currently are in your life.

- Write a letter of appreciation, acknowledging everyone with whom you work or worked and their positive qualities.

- Write a letter filled with honest praise about the position you currently hold.

- Compose a letter of gratitude for your most recent supervisor.

- Write your own job description.

- When you magnetize something to yourself, it is the *feeling* you have when you imagine or create that matters, more than the details. For example, if your wish is to move to an office with a window, is it the window itself that you want? Or is it the sensation you have when you look outside? What feelings about work and life would having a window bring forth? Write a description of those feelings.

- Write about how you feel when doing your work. What are your feelings about your place of employment? How do you feel about yourself when you are there? A relationship exists between how you feel about your "working" self and the work you put forth. Cultivate it and you will thrive.

- Commit to taking two minutes out of your workday, each day, to clear your mind. When you have done so, jot down a positive, work-related thought.

- Create your own bin of inspiration. Find a shoe box or a container of a similar size. Fill the box or bin with positive, inspiring words. For example: formal letters or notes from managers that include remarks about something you did well, letters or emails from clients thanking you for a job well done, copies of work you have done that you feel especially proud of, name tags and paycheck stubs from your favored places of employment, photos of those you have worked with and enjoyed, and letters offering employment.

When you are in the midst of a job search or an employment slump in general, light some sage, open the box, and allow the positive energy to envelop you. It tempers your mood ... which alters your thoughts ... which modulates outcome. When you change your thoughts, you change your life.

> *All that is mine by Divine Right is now released*
> *and reaches me in a perfect way under Grace.*
> —Florence Scovel Shinn

8

Death and Grieving

While I thought that I was learning how to live,
I have been learning how to die.
—Leonardo da Vinci

Exit Stage Left

In a work environment, an exit interview is typically a final meeting between a representative from a company's human resource department and a departing employee. The interview is designed to provide a safe place to evaluate and find resolution and solutions to any matter that had posed a problem for the exiting employee and the department in which he or she worked. It is an admirable way for all parties to develop and evolve even as they part.

When I was a young girl pondering heaven, the potential of a similar exit interview crossed my mind. I used to imagine one or more of my recently deceased aunts or uncles sitting in front of a movie screen watching the film of their lives, noting the impact their actions had on everyone they touched. As time and my development as a medium continued, further possibilities emerged. They would be taking notes, finding understanding, crying, and laughing. During the movie, every joy experienced or delivered during the previous life was undergone in full color. Each sorrow brought to another was felt from the perspective of the other person—meaning that they experienced the pain they'd caused as if they were the one to whom they dealt it. As it turns out, I might not have been imagining at all; time will tell.

Eventually, I came to regard this idea of heaven's television show as a "life movie." The sole responsibility for every act belonged to the one viewing his or her life on screen. There are advanced souls present during the show, including our own guides to whom we may ask questions. The purpose of the life movie is much like that of an exit interview, where no pretense or politics are involved. An exit interview provides a powerful learning environment in which the goal is to learn and move forward.

At some point following the life movie, the spirit has an opportunity to meet with a gathering of highly advanced souls. Our guides are guided in part by these revered beings. It is here that the spirit has an opportunity to show off its shine. There are no secrets. How well the soul followed its path toward enlightenment, how loved and loving it was in the last incarnation, is all part of the theme and the reason for the assembly.

Loving thoughts and prayers from the ones who loved and were loved by the spirit are present. The soul's guides are in attendance as well. The advancement of the soul, past, present, and most significantly future, is measured and considered. The gathering is reminiscent of an entrance or re-entrance interview. It is another step toward the expansion of the soul.

These are simply some of the possibilities for life after death. As I have said, none of us will know for certain precisely what awaits until our own time arrives. It is comforting to know that the spirits of those who allow me to touch them as a medium by and large radiate a sensation of peace about the other side.

Firsts

There is no age discrimination when it comes to grief. No matter what our age, when we lose someone dear to us it is a heartbreaking experience. Who we are and where in our lives we are when the loss occurs has much to do with our view of it from that moment forward. Death now has a face—and it is one that we have known and perhaps have loved. In learning about life after the release of the soul, or at least in considering the possibilities, it's helpful to recall our first impressions of it. What face does it wear in our minds?

There is a certain impact that "firsts" have in our lives. When you think of your first love, what feelings arise? How do you feel when you think about your first kiss, car, or house? What about your earliest break-up, or loss due to death? They all leave a lasting imprint.

What transpires following death is mystifying. If we do believe in past lives, we still have little or no memory of them. We don't recall an exit interview or singing angels following our passing from this world.

What we do believe is that death should be fought against at all costs. But the unfamiliar becomes powerful because it is laden with fear. So it is empowering for us to do our homework, so to speak. Learning about life after death sheds a light on what has long been considered a dark subject.

Inevitably, someone we love will eventually die. Our emotional response is likely foreign to us in nature. It is difficult, if not impossible, to imagine that someone with whom we recently shared a candy bar and conversation had just disappeared. Those around us refer to our loved one as "gone." If we are able to feel our loved one's presence in any way, however, it is hard to believe that they are truly "gone," and our relief wrestles with confusion as well as grief.

How does your family deal with death? Has it changed over the years? Was the word "death" only uttered in hushed tones? Speaking about someone who had crossed over seems to have been discouraged in most families. The idea itself was all very mysterious.

The REM Reconnection

We are slammed, mind and heart, when a loved one dies. The thought of never seeing the person again haunts us so much that we can become closed to the reassuring consolation our guides provide in times such as these. Our loved ones in spirit know our pain and wish to grant us comfort as well, which they often do through our dreams.

The pain of a loss can break open our hearts. It can also open our minds. In this case, however, our eyes need to be closed because dreams occur, after all, in our sleep. Most of them actually ensue in a stage of sleep referred to as REM, which stands for "rapid eye movement."

When a dream featuring a loved one in spirit is remarkably vivid, and we feel lucid and composed during and after, chances are that it was a visit. I fondly refer to this as the "REM reconnection." Soul-to-soul contact through dreams is one of the least intimidating modes of communication with those on the other side. These experiences are so powerful they can amend our beliefs about life after death.

My loss of Grandma Faye was the first of its kind in my life. It hit directly home for me in a way other deaths had not. Her love was the strongest and most significant in my young life; I was reliant on it and on her maternal protection. The night she had the stroke that would take her life, we had talked on the phone for hours. I noticed that she was more forgetful than usual. Still, she was funny, loving, and a joy. She told me, as she always did, to wear my curly black hair long instead of short. I told her to never ever change her forty-four-year-old beehive hairstyle unless she wanted to traumatize us all. Just one hour after our conversation, Faye suffered a stroke. She managed to call 911 before she collapsed on her bed.

As a child, I knew that life existed after the body died (even if I was afraid of it). Knowing what I did, I felt like a dazed-out, grief-filled hypocrite to be grieving like I was. But the mourning process moves in whatever direction it must. I followed the signs, reluctantly experiencing shock, denial, guilt, rage, bargaining, and acceptance. Not necessarily in that sequence, or for equal amounts of time!

It was horrendous to believe that a woman who had been filled with such a love for life no longer had one. For months I cried myself to sleep. Sleep brought dreams. One night I had one that proved to be a gift from Grandma Faye.

In my dream, it was early evening and I was running water for a bath. I turned and saw her standing in my living room wearing one of her favorite formal dresses. She was looking through me, and I wondered why she was not opening her arms to welcome me into one of her warm embraces. All at once her color went from pink to pale gray. She then appeared to be choking or gasping for air, and in great pain. Her body turned in on itself. She fell over and did not stir again. It was a vivid dream that moved in slow motion.

When I woke, I realized Faye had sent the dream. She knew I needed to see what had happened to her in her final moments and to feel myself with her one more time. My grieving process changed color that night.

There is no order to grief. It grabs hold of our collective breaths and shakes the life out of the living. Then, when there is finally quiet, we can feel the now-invisible embrace, here but not here. Through Faye's death, I learned to respect an element of life previously unknown to me. There are some circumstances that are just too difficult to "get over." The best we can hope for is to get through them. When the pieces are done falling and move into place, we find we are now even more together. It is a lesson that is sobering, honest, and true.

My trust in Faye ran so deep that it followed her to the other side and turned the lion's share of my fear about ghosts into curiosity. From such a stance, I could for the first time in my life face the steady onslaught of spirit activity around me. It was a matter of learning the language and understanding the intuitive code. Faye was my first interpreter, and instrumental in helping me translate the dialect into practical dialogue. This loving act positioned me firmly on my soul's intended path.

It is worth noting that when my grandma was alive, she did not have much faith in the afterlife. Rather, she focused on those she loved on this side of the veil and was an artist at forgiveness. And if I had to choose between two experts on the afterlife—one a metaphysical scholar and intuitive genius, and one who lived for and believed deeply in love—my answer would be indisputable. Nothing compares to the wisdom of love.

Faye still comes to me with words of encouragement and feelings of deep love. I routinely feel her identifiable presence at family celebrations. She helped me find my wedding dress and comforted me during a terrifying miscarriage. She popped in almost daily during all of my pregnancies, and commonly hovers around the room when close family members are seriously ill. Faye would always let me know when my dad, her son, needed me, or when one of my aunts could use a hand or a hug.

Perspective

Effectively navigating life's travails involves gaining and maintaining a healthy perspective. The process takes time. Death does not mean the end of the life of a soul, but it does mean an ending. As much as we may feel the presence of those on the other side, we know they cannot physically hold our hand, drive us to prom, walk us down the aisle, or lift our veil and help us kiss our new life hello.

The feeling of missing someone may never entirely dissolve, and our love for them certainly does not evaporate. We have just become accustomed to living with the loss. The sadness makes a hole in our hearts, leaving space—if we allow it—for something else to grow.

On the other hand, or other side as the case may be, the messages from those who have crossed over clearly indicate that they remain, in an altered way, somehow a part of our lives. When given a chance (through, for instance, a medium), our loved ones validate events that have taken place long after their deaths. Our own perception of life after death expands; as our souls develop, our perspective is forever altered. We see life and death as more than one-dimensional.

The goal of the soul is to work toward enlightenment.
—The Happy Medium

Long-Distance Calling

In the natural order of life, children outlive their parents. But those who have lost a mother or father know the grief their passing can bring, and the heaviness of bereavement is not necessarily diminished when family and friends have time to brace themselves, as in cases of terminal cancer. Time may, however, bestow something beneficial. Much depends on the circumstance.

My kind and lovely friend Shannon is exceptional in countless ways. Her father had been ill with an incurable cancer since she was a little girl. The threat of his death hung silently over her happy childhood. And happy it was. Her father and mother were alive with love and embraced every minute of life. Theirs is an unusual story.

Whenever possible, Shannon and her husband and children would visit her parents in the small town of her childhood. The sojourns were filled with recreation and mirth. A sense of foreboding did not exist until shortly before her dad's final hours. I never had an opportunity to meet her father before he died—not in person, anyway. But I knew his energy well even before he died. He was a discerning social worker and had the sweetest, most open and accepting vibration. He was a man everyone loved—in this case, sight unseen.

As I said, Shannon is exceptional. When news about her father's health taking a turn for the worse reached her, she instinctively reached for solace. At a certain point in her journey, my intuition provided me with some information. My gut told me it would be wise to tell Shannon what I knew only if she asked—which she did. Afterwards, I did not remember what I had told her.

When Shannon learned about this book and the inclusion of readings in it, she sent me an unsolicited email filled with the words I had shared with her during the end of her dad's life:

Here is what I remember when my dad was dying: You told me that he would pass on Saturday, February 23rd, but I told you that it was my mom's birthday and you stated, no, the next day. He passed on the 24th. You could see him in a recliner chair—sitting up, slack-jawed, looking out a picture window, and that is how he was for two weeks.

Also, after he passed, you told me he was smoking a pipe, rubbing his beard, and sitting in a wood-paneled room. This is the epitome of my dad. He loved smoking a pipe in his younger years and hadn't smoked a pipe for over forty years. He loved his den (a wood-paneled room) and spent many hours there. He wore a beard every winter and would always stroke it.

Also, you communicated that he was helped crossing over by my two aunts who are nuns. They are still alive, but they were with him. They celebrated with my mom afterwards. He mentioned, through you, how happy he was that they celebrated with a glass of wine. The celebration was because of how he died—he was coherent and himself until he died.

Hope this helps. You are amazing!!
Shannon

Shannon has the rare ability to live her life with emotion, wisdom, and heart simultaneously. Her father is a wonderful long-distance communicator. He stands behind her as she moves forward in life with the zest he so proudly handed down.

Louise's Unintentional Party

In 2005, Louise was referred to me by a well-respected health care professional. She was a tall, striking, reserved woman with natural poise. Though I learned later that circumstances were complex early in her life, when she lost her mother, Louise managed to carry herself with sophistication and dignity.

From the moment she sat down for her reading, however, I felt overcome with a heavy, constricted feeling. My client was in deep mourning, and my empathy knocked me off guard. I then felt the presence of three spirits from the other side, and experienced a clear vision of a large piece of furniture falling on a little boy. Each of Louise's guests wanted to have a word with her. They were not taking turns. For them to make the journey and try so intensely to communicate with her meant that their messages were important; I wanted to do my job well. I needed to listen to one spirit at a time, so I asked my guides for help.

A spirit voice came in clear as a bell. I heard her say her name: Rosie. She'd babysat for Louise's family when Louise was twelve. Over and over, Rosie showed me a cabinet falling. Louise vaguely remembered Rosie, but she did not remember the cabinet falling and was confused as to why Rosie would want to connect with her. I told her that Rosie had loved and favored her at a time when Louise really needed mothering. With a face devoid of emotion, Louise mentioned that her mother had disappeared one afternoon, leaving her seven children in tears.

Louise later confirmed the cabinet incident. Though she didn't remember it, her sister Sandy had. When Louise shared her notes from the reading with Sandy, she excitedly substantiated the information. Their little brother, Perry, liked to play in the cabinet located in the bathroom of the family home. One day it fell with Perry in it. No one was hurt. The spirit of Rosie had showed me this because it gave my client a reference point from which to recall a hurtful time with her mother, and to start healing from it.

The next spirit that day was rather aggressive. She wanted to be heard because she had a poignant message. I told Louise that the woman coming through was somehow in a mother role, though she was not her biological mom. She thought of herself as a peer—she could have been Louise's husband's mother, and had died over a year ago. Louise confirmed that the spirit sounded like her mother-in-law, Virginia. She argued with me when I said the woman loved and respected her. Louise said that her mother-in-law was a stubborn woman who did not respect many.

The spirit gave me a sense that she had tried to drive a wedge between her son and Louise. In the end, she was pleased that she did not succeed. Louise's remarkable eyes filled with tears as she nodded her head in agreement. Virginia told me that Louise and her son were her heroes. The way they loved moved her. I sensed that this spirit had not much believed in love when she was alive, and had had a sad contempt toward couples. Louise nodded her head in agreement.

Virginia gave me the feeling that she had deep respect for her daughter-in-law because Louise had done what Virginia could not. Louise had taken care of Virginia's son when he was dying of cancer. Louise confirmed the information with the steady stillness born of a lifetime of well-managed hurts. Virginia showed me a family picture with herself in the background, scowling. She had been exceedingly hard on her children and their spouses. Now she wanted to take responsibility for being rude, distant, and manipulative. Louise verified that Virginia had seemed to appreciate how well she cared for her husband in the end.

Another spirit then moved in. Louise looked up from her note taking as I described him as having dark hair with lots of gray. He had a rather large frame and sallow skin from a wasting disease. My lungs hurt, so I knew he might have died from lung cancer. He had looked very different from his usual self when he died because he had lost so much weight from the cancer. He definitely died at home. He had a "J" name—he was Louise's husband.

A picture of Louise sitting in the corner of a large living room, alone and in the dark, played in my head. Her heart was broken, and the vibration she wore was hard and closed. She was grieving and needed some emotional light. Her husband was sending her extraordinarily intense and loving vibes.

I wondered how much of his love she was registering. Her face during the reading was blank. I knew how she felt, because as much as I was tuned in to her husband's energy, I was also tuned in to hers. Her stomach was tight and she was trying not to cry. My goal in a reading is to help my clients open up to their intuitive voice, not to make them cry. And while tears often flow as pent-up emotions are validated and released, they do not change how I interpret the information I receive. Though I may pause for a moment to hand my client a tissue, my message from the crossed-over spirit does not change.

The man with the "J" name, Jack or Jay, was referencing a sofa he had lain on days before he died, and a big dog he had been particularly fond of. He wanted Louise to know that he still loved her and was not far away. He felt sad and guilty that he had to leave her, and knew she was angry with him for doing so. He was holding his hands to his chest. I smelled the scent of cigarettes, which meant they were related to his death. He knew he made some unwise choices when it came to his health.

Like scores of people, Louise's husband had not understood that his choices would have such a major impact. He wanted to know if Louise could forgive him for leaving. His spirit was so clearly taking responsibility for the choices made while in body. The love he felt for her traveled well. He took it with him and was sending evidence of it back to her.

Louise was visibly moved; at that moment, I felt like I was spying. The two had obviously been pretty private about their emotions. He put a bottle of fancy perfume in front of me, complete with the scent. He did this over and over. Just for the record, I am not a huge fan of most perfumes. Obviously, Louise was.

The man then showed me a picture of himself as a young child and said he had been exposed to something that predisposed him to cancer. He referenced something about wanting Louise to dance, and he wished for her to travel because she loved it. He also said something about yellow birds. He showed me a picture of himself offering Louise yellow birds as a hello gift, which is a sign denoting his presence in her life.

Louise confirmed that she'd had a husband named Jay, an avid smoker who had very recently died of lung cancer. Jay had been large-framed before he became ill. They had loved to travel together, and his favorite gift to her had always been perfume. They had two large dogs, one of which definitely favored Jay.

Louise said she had suspected that Jay was around because she could smell fresh-lit cigarettes in her house. Also, seemingly out of nowhere, one of her dogs would bark, wag his tail, and stare at what was once Jay's favorite chair. As far as the reference to the yellow birds, she and Jay used to see yellow finches outside their window years before he died. They spent many sweet moments quietly watching the birds together. At some point the birds disappeared. A few months after Jay's death, however, the yellow finches returned and sat outside the same window. Sometimes they would stay for fifteen minutes at a time.

When Louise traveled to Illinois with her sister, she encountered the yellow birds again. She and her sister were shopping and visiting museums, and in one such museum, quilts were being exhibited. Large, wonderful quilts. Louise walked into one room and gasped at what she saw: a quilt featuring a huge yellow bird, with a blue jay head, hung on the main wall of the room. The quilt featuring the yellow bird (a Blue Tit rather than a finch) was displayed in a place of great honor, and there was no way anyone could miss it when visiting the museum. But the bird was significant to Louise on this day even more than on others, because it was the twenty-first anniversary of her first date with Jay—a day they had celebrated together until he died.

Over the past decade, I have been honored to read Louise a number of times. She has told me how affirming and life changing the information from Jay has been. It has given her a sense of peace and cleared a place in her heart to move forward. Her love for him helped her find a way to make a new life.

One winter, Louise purchased a gift certificate for a reading with me for her friend Connie. Connie lives in Arizona, so her reading was conducted over the phone. More than a few special someones from the other side paid a visit during this appointment. One had a familiar vibration. I mentioned an object that Connie would see in the coming months during a vacation. It was a piece of art that could be worn. It was, however, not for her. It belonged to the person with whom she was to travel.

Her travel companion's loved one in spirit wanted to extend the art as a gift. At that point, I recognized Jay's energy and asked if Connie and Louise were scheduled to take a trip together. Connie confirmed this. I described the object and encouraged her to strongly suggest to Louise that she purchase it, if she showed authentic interest. The only caveat I added to the suggestion was that she not tell her friend anything about the reading unless the circumstances revealed themselves. Louise was not one for spending money on jewelry. Jay was, and he wanted his wife to have the art piece.

Six months later, Louise came in for an appointment radiating a changed energy. She had obviously been doing meaningful emotional work. She asked me if her necklace looked familiar. My arm tingled. My mind was blank. It did not look familiar, yet I felt as if I had seen it before. I remember next to nothing of the readings I conduct because the information is not mine, so I do not hold on to it unless somehow my clients' information resonates with something in my own life.

Louise reminded me about Connie's reading and Jay's long-distance jewelry purchase. It was a beautiful piece of art, worn as a necklace. Most of the husbands I know (including my own) who are alive and well on this side are not easily convinced to purchase jewels. Perhaps I shall start calling jewelry "art."

Soul Evolution in the Afterlife

Whatever level of awareness a soul has reached at the time of its most recent incarnation is the level they begin at when they cross over. Ultimately, however, most spirits blend back into a natural state, complete with the memories of all the lives their soul has lived. This is a blissful state of consciousness where the soul knows its sole purpose. This development appears to be an extensive process—it takes time for the soul to transform back into its natural grace.

Those of us on this side of the veil do not usually have a conscious memory of being on the other. Dreams or our guides may take us there for a blink of a visit and then gently drop us back onto our pillows at night. The wisps of information pertaining to what transpires following death are sweet gifts, a spiritual enticement to further consider the possibilities this vast and dazzling Universe has to offer. Life is to be lived, and death is simply another ring of life. It is as though those in spirit have the answers to protracted, lifelong riddles. There truly is no reason to fear death—so live!

An extraordinarily clear and conscious understanding of the answers to the secrets or riddles of life seem to belong to some of those on the other side. Overall, most spirits seem to be aware of how their actions on earth affected those they love.

This essential comprehension permeates a visit during a reading and never fails to raise an eyebrow or cause a tear.

Soul development continues long after the body that once housed it has faded into dust. It was from Faye's presence after she died that I learned this. At the time of her death, I knew her energy by heart, so to speak. In time, her vibration, though in spirit, became familiar once again.

The changes I have sensed in her over the past twenty-some years are significant. From my perspective, Faye has developed appreciably as a soul. She dropped her fear and gained a perception that is difficult for me to fathom. Simply put, it is as though there is less noise around her. When I feel such peace and quiet in a visiting spirit's vibration, I understand that much work has been done to achieve that end.

Personal relationships are also capable of developing on the other side. And not only does life go on after our body dies, but learning does too! Just as there are countless levels of consciousness on this side, there are differing levels of consciousness on the other side.

The images and sensations that have come across to me from the other side over the years began making so much more sense once I began to observe a pattern of patterns. As I have said, take note of them, as they are excellent teachers! When people on this side of the veil develop emotionally and spiritually, their ability to recognize the heart of life heightens, and their souls reflect the work they have done by shining brighter.

It is the same for those who have made the transitions to the other side. Their souls also shine more brightly. The change appears to me in dazzling colors. Although Faye's spirit was the first I perceived as altering from one visit to the next, it certainly has not been the last!

Souls on both sides of the veil continue to grow spiritually because to do so is, and has always been, the goal of the soul.

The speed of this evolution is set by the choices the soul made during its most recent incarnation. It is possible to atone for wrong actions on the other side. One way spirits do this is by providing a kind of reinforcement to those on this side as they move forward. Their presence in our lives is a way of showing support.

Those on the other side, as I have said, tap into the intuitive code of a medium to uncover the most effective method of communication. Since the spirit is referencing my life and beliefs, I am quick to understand their precise meanings.

Also, spirits illustrate how active they are in the life of a client by appearing in a particular location in the room. A spirit who is with their loved one on earth on a rather consistent basis materializes behind my client's chair. For example, a mother in spirit might indicate she is with her daughter by standing behind her chair or directly next to it. If a spirit appears up and to my right, the visits are less frequent yet remain noteworthy.

Your departed great-uncle, with whom your son shares personality traits, would appear up and to my right as of way of communicating that he has his eye on the boy and empathizes with his temperament. It does not matter if you or your son knew or even met the uncle. For love or karmic reasons, perhaps, your great-uncle is watching your son's back. Generally, spirits seem to be motivated to help those on this side of the veil to move forward and make productive life choices.

This is why people feel their own deceased loved ones nearby during times of deep sorrow and of sweet joy. They are there, extending their hand from the other side. Take it. If it makes you feel more confident, loved, seen, or less alone, take it. You honor yourself and those who have crossed over in doing so.

A Son's Goodbye

Death resulting from a tragic accident naturally carries a weight that takes years to lighten, and dealing with a sudden and unexpected death brings its own kind of mourning. The spirits who depart in this way are sometimes as surprised as their loved ones. Such was the case for my client Ronnie, whose reading I conducted over the phone. The energy of someone closely related to her made itself known right off the bat. The spirit had rather recently crossed over as the result of a peculiar accident. I saw a dirt road that gave me an eerie, lonely feeling. Someone or something was stuck on or near that road.

The next picture presented to me was of a tender-faced young man who must have been dearly loved by all. I heard the name "Jeff" and felt an agonizing tug at my heart. The tug meant that the soul coming through was a son, or like a son, to Ronnie. I asked her if she had a child named Jeff. She said yes. I inquired if he had rather recently crossed over. He had.

Soap opera casting agents love actors who look like Jeff. His face instantly evokes tender emotion. His vibration, however, hardly matched his face. It was erratic, sad, and sharp. He had a heavy or stuck feeling, along with a prominent sense of apprehension. He stepped back and the spirit of a woman with a large presence moved in. I described her face in detail to Ronnie, and said her name began with the letter "G." She was standing protectively near Jeff. Ronnie confirmed the "G" woman as her dear friend, Ginger, who had died just weeks before Jeff. Ginger was waiting to help Jeff move on, but he apparently wasn't ready.

According to Ronnie, Jeff was in the military, stationed in Spain, away from obvious danger for the first time in years. Tragically, he was fatally hit by a civilian bus in a bizarre accident. I felt that his energy was resisting the natural pull to move on to the next level. When a soul stays near or on this plane after their body dies, the reason is generally tied to some kind of fear. But it is not necessarily an anxiety related to death or dying.

Ronnie recalled recent events where she felt the unsettled presence of her son in her home. But lights turning on by themselves and the sounds of something stirring in an empty room didn't shake this bereaved mother—she knew the creaking and commotion she experienced was caused by her son. What did bother Ronnie was the turmoil she sensed that he felt. She asked if there was something she could do to help.

Jeff showed me a picture of his young family. I could feel his agony. He remained on this earth plane out of a sense of responsibility. I suggested that Ronnie assure him he did not let anyone down—not his children, and not her. He didn't need to be concerned for them. Though they love him and miss him, they would be all right.

At the close of her appointment, Ronnie had a notebook filled with information and said she felt a sense of validation. I didn't know until her next reading, one year later, that something significant had transpired as a result of our meeting. She told me she was able to help her son move on with the help of what she had learned in her reading.

In the privacy of her home, and with a heart filled with compassion and sorrow, Ronnie spoke to Jeff, addressing his fear of letting down those he loved and who depended on him. She assured him that his family would be cared for, and told him he would be forever missed and loved. Two days later, Ronnie walked into her bedroom around 10:30 p.m. and felt her son's presence. He was peaceful for the first time since he'd crossed over. She heard his voice, clear as a bell, say, "I'm leaving now, Mom." The feeling of his presence vanished. These days, when she senses him, which is rarely, she feels only peace.

Ronnie had experienced the death of a child—one of the most crushing losses imaginable. But she is brave and has a sparkle to her that even her son's death could not take away. It is not that her heart isn't broken or that her son's death did not render a permanent tear in her life. Who we are is defined by our reactions to the circumstances life brings our way. Ronnie is a believer in life, so she has more of it.

Crossing That Bridge

I wish I could tell you there was a pounding on the door before he broke in, but it doesn't work that way in the spirit world.

It was a Tuesday morning in October of 2007. My client, a bright thirty-something young man, was in the midst of a career change. He came to me in hopes of attaining a higher level of intuitive knowledge than he was able to gain on his own. He had absolutely no idea that his reading would be momentarily ambushed by a spirit who had just recently crossed over due to a tragedy here in Minneapolis.

A serious man, about the same age as my client, dropped in from the other side. Actually, he sort of crashed into the reading. I asked my client (let's call him Dave) if he knew anyone who'd died in the I-35W bridge collapse. He did not. As the reading continued, the 35W man stood next to me and sent images into my head. He kept talking, and I honestly did not know what to do. Ever the hostess, I want everyone to be happy.

Dave was in the process of taking notes about what I'd been saying regarding employment options. He looked bewildered when I asked again, "Are you sure you are not somehow connected to anyone who died in the 35W bridge collapse, or perhaps, know someone who is?" "Yes, I'm sure," he replied impatiently. But I suggested he take the information down in case it made sense later.

Usually, I hold steady with this kind of questioning when something comes through with such direct speed, because it usually holds profound meaning. It may take a few minutes for my client to let down their guard and receive it. This time, however, my guides told me to let it go. Playing detective psychic medium is not my favorite role—the people-pleaser in me wonders if I have failed those on both sides of the veil.

It turned out that the man who'd crashed Dave's reading that day was on a mission to connect with his wife. Somehow he had spotted me and knew I would respond. He wanted my help. Even though this scenario is not overly common for me, I knew better than to argue with it. Those on the other side have a bigger understanding than we do of what can be achieved over here.

When I was young and under-educated, disembodied spirits would follow me around, hoping I would meet their requests or just acknowledge their presence. When they spot me today, as a trained medium, they usually keep on moving. The same is true of drive-by spirits, ones who, for no apparent reason, just happen by. They appear and disappear fast, leaving energy debris in their wake. But the reading-crasher was on an entirely different level and mission. He was pleasant, sweet, and determined to reach someone he loved.

Hours later I was talking to my friend Chloe on the phone while waiting for my daughter in the preschool pick-up line. Out of nowhere, guess who popped in? You guessed it, the kind man who lost his life in the bridge collapse. His energy barreled through with powerful intent. I knew with an intuitive calm that this meant it was Chloe who could provide some answers and the link to this spirit's loved ones.

"Chloe, do you have any connection with someone who died in the 35W bridge collapse?" She said no, but the spirit stayed with me. This time, I was certain I should remain with the question. "Hey Chloe, will you be seeing someone soon who might have a connection? Like, this Friday night?"

Chloe said she was going to a wedding Friday night. I explained what was happening and described the man to her. He was a caring husband and also an adoring father of two children. His wife was a private person, highly energetic at home but shy in public. He had light brown hair and was inwardly serious in nature, though outwardly exceptionally funny. My inner eye flashed a picture of the man carrying a briefcase. He was really adamant about my communicating something about an anniversary and/or a birthday. He did not want me to ignore this central message. This was by far the most significant point for him.

Having been on the receiving end of my long-distance communication more than once, Chloe told me she would tuck the notes she had taken into her purse. It had been a long while since I'd experienced anything remotely like the visit from what I began to affectionately and respectfully refer to as "the 35W man." He obviously knew how to reach his wife. I was simply a conduit. An SUV-driving, suburban-living medium that would carry his message forward, no questions asked.

As it turns out, Chloe—a rather shy woman who is not prone to approaching folks at a wedding about their lost loved ones—did make a 35W connection through her old friend Terra, who was in from New York for the event. Long ago, Terra and Liz, the 35W man's wife, had been acquaintances. She'd heard from mutual friends that Liz had lost her husband in the horrendous bridge collapse. Terra promised she would pass on the information.

Weeks later, the 35W man paid me another visit. I put myself in neutral and opened up intuitively. His vibration or presence let me know that his wife had not been contacted. I felt a little awkward calling Chloe. She was expecting her third child and had much on her proverbial plate. Additionally, she and I both understood that approaching someone who has not opened the door to this particular subject matter is not easy for anyone, and in most cases is also not appropriate.

This time, though, I had a very committed soul from the other side pushing me onward. There was no question he wanted his message heard. I knew I needed to react calmly in order to find a happy medium. I measured my boundaries, scanned the entire situation, and knew with certainty that I was meant to move forward. This was not about me or Chloe or the New York friend, for that matter. This was about a man who'd lost his life and wanted an opportunity to reach his wife. Understandably, she felt dejected and alone, and he sought a chance to wish her a happy something. It was not at all clear if the celebratory date he wished mentioned was a birthday or an anniversary. Typically, I am able to differentiate between the two; the reason for my confusion became apparent much later.

After some awkward detective work, Chloe and I found that there had been no attempts to contact Liz. I was certain this was not the end of the story, because my client (peculiar as the word "client" may seems in this case) would not be asking for my help if there were not a way to reach his wife. It was, on the other hand, not appropriate for me to call Liz, nor ask my now nine-months-pregnant friend to do so. I waited for a sign from my guides, or from the spirit who so wished to convey to his wife a happy something.

When Chloe's water broke, her healthy baby arrived, bringing blessing after blessing. Her New York friend Terra called to congratulate her on her third beautiful girl. Chloe reminded her about the "weird story." The next day, Terra contacted Liz. Apparently, it was the day before what would have been Liz's first wedding anniversary.

As it turned out, Liz greatly appreciated receiving the information. She was highly surprised at how it had reached her and considerably grateful. Some of the details made her laugh, such as the description of her personality—which, according to her, was right on. Though most of the particulars about her husband, whose name was Sean, fit, there were also a few things that did not, such as the number of children they had. The happy anniversary and/or birthday message had the most significant impact—the reason I hadn't been able to tell if Sean was referencing a birthday or anniversary was because he was referring to both. He'd died days before his birthday, for which Liz had planned a special surprise. He wanted to thank her, as a way of acknowledging his love and continued presence in her life.

The circumstances around the visit from Sean, the 35W man, were unique and strange even to me, and I specialize in strange! Sean had something to communicate, and he chose me to help him do so. He was persistent, respectful, and filled with love. That is why I pursued passing on the details he so carefully communicated. And this experience would not have appeared in my book had Liz not extended her approval; in honoring her wishes and the wishes of Sean's family and friends, particular nonessential aspects in this account have been altered for privacy.

The monumental courage it takes to move forward when life takes such a backward turn is no small thing. Choosing to live and love instead of die in sorrow takes a brave heart and knowing soul. There are no real happy endings to tragic events—there is, however, hope. Hope that life goes on, on both sides of the veil.

Significant Someones

One Sunday afternoon, my husband and I were leaving a birthday party for a parent of a dear friend. It was a grand celebration with over forty guests and tons of food and laughter. The moment we were out of earshot, I exclaimed, "Our friends have such nice dead people!" Jason looked at me and started to laugh.

Having never before shared this term with him, I could see why he thought it was funny.

Nevertheless, I had not meant to be humorous. Well, not totally. I'd originally designed the term "dead people" to put something really major into terms I could wrap my arms around. I found that using terms such as other people's "dead people" helped make being a medium less intimidating overall. As I have said, I certainly mean no disrespect to those who have lost a loved one or who have died. Those on the other side fully understand this. Crossed-over spirits were all once someone's significant someone, and they still are. That's why I have worked diligently to understand their language, despite my fear and society's fear. The terms I create help me react with grace.

On their visits back, spirits bring with them the personality they wore when they were here. This is one major way mediums have of identifying who is who, and to whom. In other words, if your favorite cousin had died and was present during a reading, the particular personality traits identified by the medium help you connect with who that spirit is. If you and I were at a party and your cousin was present, I would feel it and consider him or her your "dead person."

Your psychic capabilities will flourish as the foundation of your understanding of the Universe expands. Employ humor as a learning tool, if it serves you well. Losing someone in any way, especially to the other side, may always be sad. However, the other side does not have to frighten you. Neither do your natural intuitive instincts.

In the End

The sweetness of acts born out of love accompanies us everywhere, even to the other side, as a reminder of our fine accomplishments. When making everyday decisions, think about how your choices will look and feel when you reflect on your life.

Will you feel proud or petty? Will your exit interview be one that leaves you with an overall sense of serenity because you expanded yourself, and therefore your soul, by moving toward further enlightenment and choosing love more often than fear?

Tools and Techniques: Death and Grieving

Doorpost of Consciousness

Make a mental list of your childhood impressions about death. Were there movies that influenced you? Did someone close to you or close to your parents die?

Have your impressions about death changed much over the years? How? Your feelings about death lie at the doorpost of your consciousness. Relinquishing fear around dying frees up your energy for living. When you think about someone you love who has died, can you still feel the love you shared? Love is the only gift with everlasting power. It does not die, nor does it change form. It remains flawless forever.

The Medium in You

Do you enjoy fishing? Would you consider yourself to be a professional fisherman or fisherwoman? Let's say you've never fished in your life, but you had the proper tools and surroundings, and the patience to wait as well. Wouldn't you agree that if you tried, most likely you would eventually get a nibble from a fish?

Most likely, you are not a trained medium or a medium at all. But remain open-minded and optimistic. With the appropriate background, loving intentions, decent boundaries, and patience, you will likely get a nibble, and perhaps much more.

Your connection to those who have crossed over is not over. If you wish to send a message or open up to the possibility of a visit from the other side, here are some techniques that can send you on your way to reaching that goal.

Carefully protect yourself from intrusive, unwholesome energy. Do some belly breathing, check your personal borders again, and relax. Remember, you are a divine, loved child of the Universe. You will open up to only the highest of sources and everything you learn will be for the good of all.

Clear your mind of all thought. In this space, you are open to receive. Close your eyes and envision someone you love who has crossed over. Think of how you felt when you were near the person. Allow the feelings that arise to be absorbed within you. Memorize the feelings.

Remember, this technique is related to your feelings, not your thoughts. Your ability to identify the sensations you have when you envision your loved one is related to your ability to recognize their energy. Then, when for no apparent reason feelings arise that you had when you were near your loved one, you will know that they may be paying you a visit.

Such an experience can be compared to times when your sister, for example, popped into your head out of the blue. Minutes later, she was at your door or on the phone. Acting on a knowing sense or gut feeling makes sense. There is nothing wrong with trusting your instincts, so go for it!

9

Mourning and the Other Side

Death can break our hearts,
not the bonds that connect our souls.
—The Happy Medium

A Twist of Fate

It took me far longer to complete the last several chapters of *The Happy Medium* than it did any of the others. I seemed to have become lost in the process. In hindsight, the reason for my being stumped is perfectly clear. As I was writing these chapters, a significant and heartbreaking event occurred in my life. Once again I have been given the opportunity to put my money where my mouth is, so to speak. I'll not know how well I did on this "life test" until my own exit interview, but in the meantime, I will do my best to stay on my path, meeting the goals my higher soul set before I began this incarnation.

If your goal is to grow your intuition, choosing love instead of fear is one sure way to do so. Another way is to appreciate the emotions you have been gifted with. Life is so full of emotion—it is worth feeling it! Take time to see what is in front of you. In living your life, you honor all those who have given you the love and courage to move forward.

> *Neither fire nor wind, birth nor death*
> *can erase our good deeds.*
> —Buddha

Daddy-O

If hindsight is 20/20, what is foresight? A lot of good it does to think in reverse, right? Yes, actually, it does do good. It's often in tracing an event back through time that you may notice how your guides illuminated future incidents by sending you clairvoyant experiences or drop-in insights days, months, or even years in advance. There is no such thing as an accident or a coincidence, and every sign has significance. The very existence of signs offers validation that you are not alone in your life—a higher power is watching out for you.

Case in point—while describing how I maintain healthy boundaries with those closest to me (in the Code of Ethics chapter), I actually wrote these words: "Would you want to know when your father was going to die? The answer to this question is routinely 'no.' As long as there is nothing that can be done to change the outcome, it is better not to know." I was not conscious of the poignancy of those words until days later, when my life exploded.

Understanding the relevance of a precognitive dream or drop-in insight is not essential to its usefulness. As we discussed earlier, a precognitive dream is not exclusively sent to alter future events. Rather, dreams and intuitive flashes are sometimes sent to help *prepare* the dreamer for what is to come. This may be their sole purpose.

Back in the spring of 2006, I had started feeling a steady and clear sense of dread regarding the health of my father, Marshall—also known as Daddy-O, or by my children as Bonka or Grandpa Marshmallow. I felt that his life force was waning, but medical assessments showed otherwise. Nevertheless, the calm and unfaltering intuitive voice I had relied on all of my life seemed to be warning me of an upcoming transition.

At the time, memories of events that had transpired a few years prior came to mind. About ten years ago, after decades away, my father had permanently moved back to the Twin Cities. His return was a dearly welcomed one. The rips in the fabric of our relationship were slowly and steadily mended. He seemed more together and happier than ever before.

He was genuine and sweet and I was over-the-top thrilled to have him back. Spending time with his family took precedence, and obviously brought him joy. He was emotionally and physically present in a way he had never been. The first time I saw his new phone number run across my caller ID, I seriously almost fell down, since it differed by only two digits from the one my family had before my parents split up. I knew, on some level, that he was working on his past and had already begun to make peace with it. The phone number coincidence served to confirm what I had suspected.

When people begin to do solid emotional work, it is cause to celebrate. No one wants loved ones to carry around extra baggage. These accomplishments denote that they are moving forward and doing what they came here to do! It doesn't automatically indicate that they are tying up loose ends and heading out … though sometimes it does.

A few of these coincidences, when combined with my steady sense of dread, appeared to be signs from my guides, helping me prepare for what was to come. Maintaining my composure was a challenge. I had to balance my insight with my intellect and my heart. My siblings and I made certain that every aspect of our father's health was watched carefully. Yet overall, the medical reports remained decent. I pressured myself to remain psychically tuned in. Not a pessimist by nature, I took note, shared my sense of dread with a few people close to me, said nothing about it to my dad, and did my best to move forward.

Everyday life has a way of wrapping its arms around us and making us forget both our hopes and our fears. My father remained busy with work, his love of politics, and, most of all, his grandchildren. Then, abruptly, life changed direction.

My dad was scheduled for emergency quadruple bypass surgery one cold day in March of 2008. Not wishing to be the cause of any worry, he argued with the word "emergency." He also argued with the word "surgery," preferring the less-scary term "procedure." After his angiogram, which was on a Monday, he asked me half-jokingly if I had any "psychic thingy" about what was happening. We were all gathered in his hospital room; he gave my brother-in-law a sly, boys-club smile.

I was just about to shoot him a not-so-girl-scout-like glare when I remembered that he was scheduled for the "non-emergency quadruple bypass procedure" on Wednesday. Feeling heavy-hearted because I could not offer further words of encouragement, I told him what I had told him before. Optimistically, I repeated what his physician had said about the surgery. He would feel considerably better than he had in a long while and it would add years to his life.

While my sister, her husband, and I were talking to the cardiologist, I did sense someone from the other side move in. I mentioned this to my dad. "Oh really," he said, with more than a little sarcasm this time. Fear was showing up in the shape of sarcasm. I knew he had reason to feel apprehensive, so I smiled at him and turned to hang up his robe. I did not want him to see the expression of fear on my face.

I suggested he close his eyes and asked if he recognized my voice without being able to physically see me. Was he sure that it was me talking? How did he feel when he heard my voice? "It is much the same," I continued, "when I sense someone from the other side around me, Dad." Hoping that perhaps the drugs for the angiogram had altered his consciousness, I continued, "Sometimes, I feel the presence of your mother, Faye, as strongly as if she were sitting next to me futzing with my hair like she always did. She loved us, Dad, and love never dies."

He was quiet, taking it all in. We had spoken of life after death on a number of occasions over the past months under the guise of my book. "It was Grandma Faye," I told him, "who popped in on us when we were talking to the cardiologist." "Oh, I don't believe that stuff," my dad said with a not-so-hidden interest, then quickly added, "What did she say!?" I told him the truth: "That she loves you, and she is here."

As I walked out, a picture of my father-in-law, Marv, riding up in the elevator five years ago on his way to have his own open-heart surgery materialized on the screen in my mind. It was a scene my guides had been sending me for over a week. I thought about how emotional we all were, and I could hear Marv, not at all a religious man, silently praying.

It was not until that day that I realized what the repeat scenes playing in my head meant. My precognitive hit-and-run thoughts now had a home. My guides were giving me a heads-up of what was to come, a sort of "save the date" invitation for emotions.

I wrote part of this chapter while sitting in the hospital waiting room the next day. My father had been having jaw and chest pain, so his bypass surgery was moved up to Tuesday morning. None of us were able to see him before he went in for surgery. He never came out.

A Story's End

My father had beaten three cancers in his seventy-three years. He was a fighter with a sensitive heart. A heart that had been through legions, emotionally and physically. The bypass surgery was thought to be remarkably low in risk. He was going to come out of it a new man, we were told. He went into surgery with an excellent attitude, we were told, and his children were waiting to hug him hello when he came out.

Because my dad's surgery had been moved up, the last conversation I had with him was on the phone. He sounded rushed and was not as patient with me as usual. He said he was taking care of some last-minute work-related documents so had little time to talk. Not wishing to distract him, I told him I loved him with all my heart and would see him after the surgery.

The last thing my dad ever said to me was, "I love you, Jodi. Thank you for all you have done for me." I thought his emotions were understandably raw, so did not think his comment strange. My response was gentle. "You do more for us than we do for you. And besides, helping you is a pure joy. I love you so much, Dad."

On Tuesday, my husband, sisters, brothers-in-law and I all waited patiently for the surgery to be over. (At my dad's insistence, my little brother, Jeff, had taken his family on vacation Monday morning as scheduled.) The bypass surgery was meant to add years to my dad's life. None of us were prepared for what was to come—we knew that, like everyone, some day our dad would die. We did not expect it to be that day.

When the nurse told us that things were not going well in surgery and to call our rabbi, everything became surreal. And though it was hours and hours later, it seemed like all at once we were standing around his dying body, saying good-bye to a man who was a knight in shining armor, an arm on which to lean during darkness and ill health, our carpool-backup and giver of gifts. His last gift to us would be his allowing us to say goodbye. He held on for a brief few minutes longer as we gulped back our shock and allowed our hearts to speak. Tearfully, words came tumbling out of the mouths of his children and children-in-law. We spoke words that were unplanned—words that broke our hearts, cracked our voices, and dried up hope.

My sisters shined, somehow, in that darkest of life's moments. Whispering things that are their own to tell. I held his hand, kissed his face, wept, and prayed. The machines were blinking and blaring red alert; my heart was crumbling.

I could feel his sweet spirit hovering in and around his body. In a flash I felt his confusion. Praying for the right words, I leaned close and told him that although it was not what any of us wished for and our hearts ached, it was his time to die. He would be forever safe and loved where he was going and did not have to be afraid. Dying, I whispered, was just like jumping into the water—all he needed to do was let go. I spoke the words I had always believed, ones that I had shared with my grieving clients and friends. Words I wished with all my heart there were no cause to speak.

"You won, Dad—you chose love instead of fear. And all the love you gave and all the love that was given you is yours to take and keep. That love turns into twins and one part stays here with us, as well. We will always have your love, and you ours."

I placed my face gently against his cheek and promised with all my heart that I believed he was headed for the most beautiful and peaceful of places. I told him he would soon see that Grandma Faye was waiting to welcome him. I thanked him for being my dad and a grandfather to my children, and whispered that I was proud to be his daughter.

Gulping back tears, I tried not to choke on the death-stained air and said again that it was okay to let go. I stood up, took his hand, and instinctively placed my other hand on the top of his head. In that moment I felt a burst of energy, sort of like a mild electrical shock, buzz through my fingers resting on his head. Looking up, I saw the doctor come closer, wearing a face devoid of hope. He said my dad's heart had stopped.

At that moment, I was not a grown woman or even a medium. I was Marshall Livon's little girl and his story had just ended. As I write this, it has been merely one week since we buried him. I have called his phone just to hear his voice, slept in his coat, and my eyes are swollen shut from weeping the tears of grief that are a testimony to how much I loved him and love him still.

My father, the most private of men, allowed his daughters to stand beside him as he made his final journey upward as Marshall Livon. He did not die alone, as I had long feared he would. He died with the loving sounds of his children's voices thanking him for being their father and bidding him farewell, while the Universe was waiting to hear him sing his own praises and ignite and elevate his own soul.

I am emotionally raw, as so many of you have been or are due to the loss of a loved one. My father was not the first person I knew to transition to the other side, but he was the closest to me. As a medium, I have lived and breathed proof that life exists after death—but still, as I have said throughout this book, it's not the same as having someone with you in body. This change, in our relationship with our loved one, is what the mourning process is all about.

My dad will not be at my children's bar and bat mitzvahs. He will not take my family members out for Chinese food, serenade us with his version of rap music with a Jewish twist, take our kids to Target to pick out a gift for their birthdays, or bless us with a smile of complete adoration ever again. That part of his story has ended. For that I grieve.

It is impossible to mourn without remembering what I have learned about death over my many lifetimes. As a daughter, I want only to feel however I feel. True to my word, I cry whenever the tears hit. If I refuse them, they choke me. Mourning takes time.

Now You Know

Clients have asked me if I feel my father's presence. My answer is a selfish one: "Not enough." I knew that he stood beside his body following his death and permeated the sanctuary at his funeral. The evening of the day his body was buried, he gave me a hello as I entered a room where his oldest and youngest granddaughters played. I felt as though I were breathing fresh air for the first time since he had died. I said, "Hello Dad, now you know." I held my head up and escaped to the bathroom, with the illusion that he would not see me cry there—clearly, my brain had leaked out along with my tears. Thirty years of work as a medium and, in that moment, so much of what I had learned lay dormant. I was Marshall Livon's daughter, and I felt lost in a sea of grief.

My father, I believe, followed the path that most who cross over do. The belief system he held while in this life colored the scene he was greeted with shortly after he left his body. The presence of his mother, Faye, was so prevalent in the room at the moment of his death I could almost smell her perfume. She was one of the spirits who helped him make his transition. Following the burial, his spirit continued its elevator ride up in consciousness. The level of awareness he achieved in this life, and in all those that went before, impacted his soul as he was reintroduced to the blissful state of knowing: knowing that the long and the short of life is all about love and moving bravely through fear.

I would like to tell you that before my father died, he was a believer in life after death. But he was not. When he had an audience, he would on occasion tease me about my views. Not, however, when we were alone. That is when he would share stories of his own insightful moments and ask me questions. I believe there are so many out there like my father—wishing that this life-after-death theory is true, yet fearing it is not.

Well, now my dad knows. It brings me enormous peace that he is safe. The fact that he died mere pages after I'd written that I would not want to know about his death in advance, unless there were something I could do to change it, is not lost on me. My old pal Irony, showing up for duty compliments of my guides. In the end, it did not matter much that he and I disagreed on matters of spirit and politics. He believed in me, and I believed in him.

The Bear Truth

Although usually a private experience, sometimes the process of mourning and connecting with the other side is played out quite publicly and dramatically. Such was the case with Jamie and her daughter, Sam, who were mourning the death of Sam's father.

In the summer of 2007, a few of my girlfriends and I dressed up and went for a musical walk down memory lane. In years past we frequented First Avenue, a bar in downtown Minneapolis. We used to listen to live bands there while in high school (on Sunday evenings, First Avenue allowed underage patrons in; we couldn't drink, but we could dance!). Some amazing talent has passed through our not-so-giant Midwestern locale—a few of the more nationally celebrated musicians who come from Minnesota include Sounds of Blackness, Soul Asylum, Prince, and Bob Dylan. It was while going to First Avenue as a teenager that my love for music expanded into an adoration for live bands.

On this particular night, I was expecting to relive old memories and run into old friends—what I was not expecting was to be asked to work. While the band was on break, one of my friends ran into her brother's recently widowed sister-in-law, Jamie. Although Jamie was deep in mourning over the loss of her husband, her eyes retained a light that exposed her soul's sparkle. While being introduced, I shook her hand and felt the presence of her husband, Thaddeus. He clearly wanted me to convey a message or two to his wife and their beautiful daughters. He was a little pushy, but I was not. Their loss was too new, and the venue was not right. I told him to send his wife to me at a more appropriate time, and I would do my best to relay what he had to say.

Eight months later, one of his darling daughters ended up in my home as a babysitting co-pilot on a Saturday night. Our incredible babysitters occasionally invite a friend to help out, and Samantha (Sam for short), who turned out to be Jamie's youngest daughter, was one such friend. She had heard of my work, so took the liberty of bringing a list of her top questions. Seconds into her inquiry, I noticed that she also had brought company. Two spirits from the other side were hovering in the room. One was Sam's father; the other had dodgy, ominous energy, and clearly was feeding off Sam's fear.

As a prevailing rule, I do not put myself in the position of talking about anything related to my ability as a medium with children unless one or both parents give me the go-ahead. As I have said, too much information is not a good thing for kids. Remembering my promise to this sensitive and aware girl's dad, I silently acknowledged the ominous presence, learned what it wanted, let it know I understood but would not allow it to drain Sam anymore, and blasted it away by filling the room with white light. This took some intense energy, as it was pretty locked in to Sam.

I asked Sam afterwards if she felt the negative presence; she said no. I explained about the benefits of white light and staying connected to her body. Sam was in her early teens, a time when hormones and psychic energy dance. She was more than open to her father's presence. Because she did not yet understand how to discriminate between his energy and any other spirit passing by, she was left vulnerable.

Sam's dad clearly wanted me to ask her a few questions and impart some of his paternal wisdom along the way. Toward the end of his visit, he sent loving words to his precious youngest daughter, who was at home asleep. The word "bear" kept popping into my head. When I asked Sam about the meaning behind it, she was quiet, and then remarked that it sounded familiar, yet she could not place it.

When Jamie arrived to pick up her daughter, I immediately reintroduced myself and told her about the conversation that had transpired between Sam and myself, hoping I had not overstepped my bounds. She was more than open to what I had to say. When her daughter asked her who "bear" was, Jamie turned a pinkish shade of red. "Bear" was her special nickname for her husband. Sensing that Thaddeus was at work once more, I mentioned the workshop I was conducting the following day, "Insights and Outasights." It was all about the process of communicating with those on the other side.

Thaddeus had managed to orchestrate the circumstances that would bring his daughter to me and his wife to a workshop about communicating with those who have crossed over. When "strange" things like this happen, it's powerful proof that there is more to life than meets the eye. Signs from the other side can bring such joy!

Early the following morning, Jamie and a friend arrived at the workshop, pen, paper, and curiosity at hand. I admit I was surprised at how the whole thing unfolded. Jamie's husband had something to say, and he ensured he was going to have a chance to do so.

Thaddeus came through like a bowling ball rolling hard to hit its mark. He butted in front of two other spirits waiting to connect with a workshop attendee as he sought a word with Jamie. He wanted her to know that he knew what she was doing with her life. The minute I repeated what I heard him say, Jamie bristled. When he said he was happy for her and apologized for not invariably acting patient or kind, especially in the end, she exhaled, as though she had been holding her breath.

Thaddeus relayed what had happened recently at home with his "girls": private, yet not overly personal, moments they had shared together. I believe he did this for the same reason other souls do—it is their way of demonstrating their presence in our lives. Jamie confirmed each scenario.

Everyone in the workshop was sitting up, listening intently as this man who'd lost his life spoke his heart to the woman who had been the love of his life. Thaddeus showed me a picture of Jamie sitting in a car with a handsome man who was obviously smitten (his word!) with her. She appeared to be much younger in the scene, which meant she was not as adept or sophisticated in traversing through new relationships as the man was. I asked her if she had not long ago become involved with a new man.

Jamie looked a bit embarrassed, and nodded. She had recently started dating someone who was becoming special to her. She was struggling with guilt as she grew to enjoy this new man. When she and Thaddeus had originally met, she was a shy, under-confident woman. Their relationship had changed her. Jamie was getting to know her new self and liked who she saw.

Thaddeus wanted Jamie to live and love. The feeling he sent to me was not of jealousy. Jealousy does not seem to be a common emotion experienced on the other side. In all the readings I have conducted, I do not remember once feeling it emanate from a visiting soul. He wanted her to move forward on her own path.

When he referenced his girls that day, the messages became blurred. His daughters were headed in dissimilar directions. Feelings of loss and mourning were imprinted in each girl's heart with differing impacts. The breadth of the impact was apparent to him. He wanted the message conveyed that he had an eye on his girls, and that their own wise choices in life would go a long way. Only the way in which his guidance was communicated had changed, not his love.

Ritual to the Rescue!

Judaism, like so many other religions, has its rituals and mourning processes. Mourning can be understood as an internal process with an external focus: the loss of a person's physical presence is external, and the internal component of loss needs a voice. For some people, religion can help the mourner find the voice their sorrow needs in order to be set free.

Personally, I find considerable comfort in familiar rituals. At a time when my life felt as though it was spinning out of control, the arms of ritual wrapped around my pain, and around me, and held me tight. Perhaps I am mature enough now to gratefully accept what fits, and leave the other elements in peace.

In Judaism, the body of the deceased is buried within three days of death. I find this noteworthy because the soul begins a new level of transition first at death, and then after three days. *Shiva*, which means "seven," is a period of formal mourning that begins on the evening of the day of the funeral. If the next day is Saturday, the Jewish sabbath, shiva begins on Sunday.

Family and friends gather to say *Kaddish* (Jewish prayer) for the deceased and to comfort the family. It is a time where loved ones testify to God in favor of the soul of the departed. The immediate family, including the spouse if there is one and the children of the departed, recite the Mourner's Kaddish together. Kaddish is comprised of words of faith. As I understand it, our willingness to praise God in times of deep sorrow is significant, which is recognized in the reciting of the Mourner's Kaddish. It is a way to show our hearts that we have faced death and have chosen life. In her book *Mourning & Mitzvah,* Anne Brener addresses the goal of the Kaddish: "to bring together the two worlds of olam hazeh (this world) and olam haba (the world to come)."

A part of me reverted to a younger, more vulnerable self during the first weeks following my dad's death. I was without his protection for the first time in my life—this would take some getting used to. I sat alone, curled up in a ball, recalling all that I knew about death, including what I had learned in religious school.

My father will live on in the good deeds he performed in this life, and also because his loved ones will continue to do good deeds in his memory. Reciting prayers in his name is also a blessing, which helps cleanse and raise his soul. So the little girl in me was comforted, while the adult in me smiled benevolently.

My ability to read Hebrew has gone south over the years (please don't tell my rabbi), so I read the English transliteration to prayers. One such prayer, called the *Amidah*, is recited three times each day and is a central prayer of the Jewish liturgy. It is considered a formal opportunity to approach God in private prayer. There is a part of the *Amidah* which has to do with the resurrection of the dead, which closes with the words *Mechayyei HaMeitim.* I love this part, because its meaning (my understanding) has to do with God, who gives life to the dead. Reciting the *Amidah* helps me feel less alone in my metaphysical beliefs, more alive, and part of the bigger picture.

Rituals, when laden with love, provide protection to those in mourning. When the heart is exposed in grief, vulnerability exists. It is not uncommon for computers to crash, autos to malfunction, and ordinary illnesses to manifest in the lives of those who mourn. When loved ones surround the one who grieves, the mere action provides protection. The practice of charitable acts of giving, lighting sage, prayer, laughter, and love, all act as armor during times of vulnerability and stress. Simple as it may be, a genuine loving thought for a loved one on either side of the veil raises their vibration.

If your religion offers a place of comfort, go to it if that is what your soul longs for. Go where peace and comfort may find you. The soul, when given a chance, will guide itself through the grief process. As with everything else in life, follow your heart, maintain reason, and let your spirit lead. When help is required, ask for it. Anything in life that retains its significance long after time has passed leaves the soul stronger and wiser. Times of trial build soul.

It was incredibly helpful to have people who loved my dad, and who love me and mine, close by during those first few days following his death. At a time when I wanted to hide under my covers, Jewish ritual held that I mourn with loved ones. And so I did.

Many of my Catholic friends have said that their community and church support mourners through the funeral mass and through non-religious services such as wakes. Surrounding those who need support is a great act of love. In Buddhism, it is believed that during the forty-nine-day funeral period, the prayers of the mourners assist the deceased during their post-death transition and help enlighten the spirit about the true nature of death.

I am blessed to have friends of different religions, races, genders, ages, and spiritual beliefs. When my father died, many came together in an act of support. During shiva one night, a few of them were talking about how they could further help my family. Their words held such love that my broken and closed heart opened slightly. As I walked past another group of eighty-year-old shiva attendees, I overheard a few of people talking. "How is Jodi?" one asked with genuine concern. "She has her good moments and her bad," replied another.

As a society, I think we are confused as to which is a good moment and which is bad. For me, when I need to cry and do so, I am doing well. Releasing emotion, in this case grief, is a relief. I find that carrying it around with me is far too heavy a load. The willingness to feel my feelings is, in large part, what has made me a successful psychic medium. For the lion's share of my life, I have known that if people do not allow themselves the emotion that is theirs, those emotions will rule them.

Life is like a wild tiger.
You can either lie down and let it lay its paw upon your head
Or sit on its back and ride it. Ride the wild tiger.
—Ruth Tearle

The Good, the Bad, and the Ugly Mourner

Each of us deals with grief in our own way. I dealt with it organically and candidly. While sitting in services at the synagogue one Saturday morning, two weeks after my dad had died, I could not stop my silent tears. I missed my dad and his love so much that my entire being ached. I felt like a semi-truck was parked on my chest. I told my brother that everywhere I went, I leaked tears. In keeping with his dry sense of humor, he said, "Well, at least you are consistent." We both laughed. The bravest laugh is the one that looks death in the face and smiles anyway.

While still in *Sh'loshim*, the thirty-day mourning period following the burial of the deceased, a parade of suggestions meant to help me marched out of the mouths of those who sincerely believed they knew how it felt to mend a broken heart. Though I am certain their advice was what they themselves had followed, or believed they would follow given similar circumstances, methods of dealing with grief do not come in "one size fits all" plans. "Pretend this is not happening" was the number-one suggestion I received. "Take ibuprofen, vitamin D, anti-anxiety medication, sleeping pills, and large quantities of food (especially chocolate)" were other suggestions. When people offered such advice, I'm embarrassed to admit that I did not always have kind thoughts about them, because I was tired and grief-stricken. (Thinking these mean thoughts made me a "bad" mourner.)

During those weeks, I found exercise, writing in a journal, and crying to be the most helpful. People seemed concerned because of my continual river of tears. While their love and regard for my well-being warmed my heart, I felt once again misunderstood.

Losing a loved one is obviously a heart-wrenching experience. It is an anguish that will forever resonate. On countless levels, we as a society insist people not feel their agony (or joy, for that matter!). If we are witness to a friend feeling his or her pain, we are made more aware that we have ignored our own, and have darkened our spirit as a result. Comments dressed to soothe, such as "he is in a better place, you have to let go, your tears hurt him," or "she is gone, now move on" are in reality not-so-well-hidden invitations to shush. "Keep it together" means keep it hidden—from yourself and everyone else. Otherwise everyone's pain is exposed, and we cannot have that! (That attitude, of course, might be construed as "ugly.")

I have long agreed with the prevailing viewpoint that what is, is. A loss needs be mourned, and a joy celebrated. The truth must be affirmed in order for us to move forward. In my work, I have encouraged and supported clients in finding their own processes and moving through them. As a new mourner, I felt exasperated when other people, who knew little about me, insisted that I not allow my emotions to breathe. In the face of their own bruised hearts and anxiety, their words felt stifling.

During this time, my compassion chip was chipped. In other words, my natural ability to cut people slack had gone to sleep. Most likely it took some sleeping pills! My intuitive abilities continued to function. When a well-meaning someone told me to put it all behind me, I saw a spirit standing behind them. The spirit had much to say about the pain hidden inside that well-meaning person, but I did not share what I perceived. (I believe I was a "good" mourner in that regard.)

People in the throes of high emotion can change moods with lightning speed! One of fear's faces is anger. It is painful to be around the one unable to shed the tears, and more painful, still, to be the one unable to do the releasing! The sounds of grief are never pretty. Even so, when any pure feelings are honestly liberated, the mere action offers tender relief.

I knew that releasing what was inside of me was my ticket to peace. Everyone deals with grief differently. The right way is the one that takes direction from the heart, head, and soul. I found myself, off and on, thinking with the mind of the child I once was. Wondering if, from my dad's new vantage point, he still thinks of me as his loving Mazik. Since he sees only the pure soul, does mine shine? Are my choices as loving as I work to make them? Is he still proud of me? Can he see me as I inwardly march up to the counsel of Beaming Beings who are in deliberation over his life, and sing his praises?

Dancing Across the Veil

A spirit was swooping around my client Rafaela's head with such unrelenting speed I almost laughed out loud. He was obviously having fun. Another spirit, with a much fainter light, seemed to fly in and out of the room a few times. I took a deep breath and asked my client for her full name. Rafaela's energy was heavy. I sensed that she was dealing with something monumental in her life that was related to health. Not her own, but that of someone close to her.

Have you ever inhaled helium? Or heard how doing so raises the sound of the voice a few octaves? During Rafaela's reading, I felt as though her people on the other side were pressing the fast-forward button. The result was that my inner voice sounded way too high-pitched and funny, as if I had inhaled a tank of helium. I heard my new and not-so-improved voice explaining the download process to Rafaela.

The swooshing spirit rather took over the first part of the reading. I described what was happening to my somewhat impatient client. The spirit had strong paternal-grandfather energy. Rafaela and the spirit had been extremely close and much alike in personality. He understood her well, and she him; the connection was a beautiful one. He had been a pivotal character in her life, and continued to be so.

Pictures of her parents dropped onto the screen in my mind. I saw her mother with her arms tightly crossed standing near a young Rafaela. This indicated to me that her mother had a stubborn streak that colored the way she loved. Her father sat expressionless in a chair. Rafaela confirmed what I described as fitting her parents' personalities.

The spirit moved to stand behind Rafaela, demonstrating that he was with her frequently and continued to support her from the other side. I described his appearance and personality. He had a gentle but commanding presence, a unique combination. He was leaning toward her with a warm smile, listening to her every word. When I see a scene such as this, I know that the two are closely tied, soul-to-soul. She confirmed that the spirit I described was her paternal grandfather. I added that her dad's energy seemed to almost be dancing with her grandfather's.

To me, this indicated that her dad was either in a coma or in an analogous altered state. Some souls love to fly around the room or building when their spirit has long been tied down to an inert body. She said he'd had Alzheimer's disease for some time. Apparently, father and son were connecting on a soul level and wanted Rafaela to know it.

I had hit on the issues that Rafaela was in the midst of dealing with—such as her father's severely declining health. Her grandfather, in full support of his granddaughter, indicated how problematic her mother could be in matters of the heart. Rafaela felt alone, as though she was the only one seeing with precision what lay ahead.

According to Rafaela, who was Brazilian born and bred, the work of psychics and mediums is far more accepted and prevalent in other parts of the world than it is in America. She indicated that she had visited a good number of them over the years. As Rafaela gathered her purse to leave at the end of the hour, I could see her tears. She became openly and beautifully expressive.

Looking me directly in the eye, she said that she had seen many psychics and mediums over the years, hoping to hear something, anything, from her grandfather. He had been her biggest support before he died. She had wanted to see a sign or hear from him all her life, and had prayed and prayed that he would come through, even if only once. Smiling gently, she said that she had been searching for someone like me. She believed only an evolved medium could bring her grandfather through. I must say I suspect it was really her grandfather, and his swooshing dance, that made the exchange possible.

As grateful as I am to hear such positive feedback—and believe me, it is fun to hear—the truth is that I am simply a conduit. There are a myriad of highly skilled mediums with good intentions. If I believed otherwise, my work would cease to hold meaning. Too much ego is a psychic buzzkill.

The fact that I have done the work necessary to be in a space to receive and deliver information in a neutral and professional manner is something of which I feel sincerely proud. Any other credit belongs to the Universe and those on the other side. My gratitude and respect is extended to those who believe in themselves enough to find legitimate mediums who can act as both a voice for the higher self and a link between worlds.

Unmistakably, the most poignant wounds in life revolve around love, loss, and loneliness. Life circles around love. Love is the basis for our stay here on earth—the learning how to allow it in and to let it go. In its raw truth, loneliness demonstrates that love never disappears. It only changes context. As Kahlil Gibran wrote, "Your joy is your sorrow unmasked. And the selfsame well from which your laughter rises was oftentimes filled with your tears."

People feel hurt and forsaken in their pain. No matter the source or how the loss presents itself, through a broken love or death, none of us is alone. Those who have loved us and love us still sit by our sides in memory and in spirit as we grieve, marry, give birth, love, and ourselves die. We are not alone and will never be.

How Do You Doodle?

I knew that my father would eventually come through to me in his new state of consciousness. The first time he did so, I felt like I had been dehydrated and then allowed only a sip of fresh, clear water. It was astonishing, and it was not enough.

The second time he came through was on what would have been his seventy-fourth birthday. My plan was to sit alone in the middle of his apartment and listen to the recording of his funeral, and allow myself whatever feelings needed to be released. I needed to get back some of my sparkle.

Jason phoned during my much-needed liberation of clogged emotions. The boys had left their baseball gear in my vehicle, and it was required for their six o'clock game. My family needed me within the next half hour—or at least, they needed their gear.

While I got my things together, I said, "Goodbye, I love you" to my dad, as I always did when I left his now-empty apartment. I then heard a voice in my head say, *I'll be back.* I was sure my memory was just trying to coax a smile out of me. But next I heard, *How do you doodle?* This was something humorously endearing my dad used to say to his young children and grandchildren. I began to understand that, possibly, it was not just my memory playing an old tape.

My meditation skills at work, I waited readily, carefully tuning in and clearing my mind of expectation and thought. When I heard the name *Jodell*, which was one of his nicknames for me, I was sure it was my dad! I could feel him with every fiber of my being. I said, "Dad, I can hear you! I feel you, and know you are here!" It was just like my father to give someone he loved a gift on *his* birthday.

As I stood there, glorying in his familiar vibration, I offered my sheer gratitude to the Universe that my father seemed entirely devoid of fear and pain. My sparkle brightened that day. My father had waited to come through until he was ready, and I had found some peace and began to make a life without him in it.

Tools and Techniques:
Mourning and the Other Side

Metaphysical FAQs

For the moment—or at least for the next few pages!—please consider me your "spirited" guide. I've compiled a short list of frequently asked metaphysical questions for your reading pleasure. The Happy Medium (aka your spirited guide) will take you through these questions and their possible answers. The answers are built on what I have learned from those who have crossed over, as well as from my guides.

- Does my deceased mother think of me—can she see me? Does my sister know I named my little girl after her? Does my son know how I mourn over the loss of him?

Yes. Spirits on the other side know whatever information will help them optimally develop as souls. Never have I witnessed a visiting spirit in shock over something that happened on this side of the veil. Perhaps their senses are more alive than our own!

It is my understanding that they sit beside you as you weep, even as they know your reaction is related to your process and your development. They are aware of your grief because they are aware of you. Those in spirit do know for whom you named your baby girl. Your loving loved ones are your biggest cheerleaders from either side of the veil, and stand with you as you stand up for yourself.

- Do those on the other side miss us?

My answer is one of experienced conjecture. How can they miss what is in front of them? You are present in their lives because souls who love are never wholly apart. Those on the other side speak the language of soul, so they understand this far better than anyone on this side of the veil.

Imagine that you have a twelve-year-old daughter. When she leaves for camp for the first time, there is a flood of tears. It will be a huge adjustment for you both. You will miss her presence deeply. Yet you understand that it is only a matter of weeks before she is home with you again, and she will have much to tell! In a similar way, your loved one in spirit knows that he or she will see you when your own incarnation ends. It isn't that you are not missed—it is that you are not gone. The connection between those who share love is forever.

Another example of how spirits might view missing us offers the same message, just with a different twist. Before you leave home for work each day, you kiss your beloved cat. It is difficult to leave that warm ball of purring fur. You know how much you love her, and you will think of her during the day. You also comprehend that you will see her in nine hours, when your work day is done. Those on the other side have a similar discernment. They know that life is over in a flash and they will see you again in the blink of an eye. They are able to be near you, though you may not recognize their presence. They know that soon enough, you both will be sharing the same dimension.

- Does my own deep grief keep my loved one from moving on?

Suffering a great loss does one of two things. It either makes your spirit stronger and more filled with life, or it breaks it in two. When you are broken, you are separate from your higher knowing and have a difficult time feeling any light at all. This state of consciousness, or unconsciousness as the case may be, can last for hours and even lifetimes.

No need to pour guilt on top of your grief. Mourning the loss of someone who has crossed over does not hurt them or keep them from moving on. It is a part of your process, not necessarily theirs. Missing someone is a component of loving them, as is letting go. That love has extensive power on either side of the veil.

- Are those in spirit sad when they cannot be a part of a family wedding or party?

Who said they cannot be part of a family party? It is at those gatherings that people feel the spirit of a loved one the strongest! True, it is not the same. Life is all about change. To feel someone you love beaming out from your heart is a different classification of joy.

- Is my loved one angry at me because I was not present at the time of death?

As a devoted friend or relative, you may have stayed near your loved one as their health began to seriously decay and their soul started its ascent. You stepped out of the hospital for a brief moment to take a walk or a shower or just a break. It was then that your loved one died. For years, you have regretted not being there.

Our higher selves choose our exact time of birth and death. The act of letting go and dying is a personal one. Much like giving birth, some people want and need loved ones near by. Others prefer to make their final journey alone. It is truly your loved one's choice. Please know that for whatever reason, whether you could or could not be present, it was all preordained.

- Years before my friend died, we had a huge argument and betrayed one another's trust. Is he still angry at me?

Those on the other side, overall, are able to make a connection with our souls and know from the ground up what is happening in our lives. They see the true colors in our feelings. What's more, they are wholly aware of how we experienced their actions. Forgiveness is a leading topic during readings. While the lesson may stay with the soul as it journeys to the other side, anger does not make it over. Only love does.

- Does my deceased father see me while I shower or as I spend "personal" time with my spouse?

No. And please excuse my blunt honesty here—yuck! Sex is not a spectator sport. Those who visit from the other side do so as a way of showing you they still exist and care about you. Not to intrude on your time with somebody!

- Where is the money buried?

Sometimes tears are expressed as angry words instead. The afterglow, or actually afterdull, of losing a loved one is lackluster at best. Familial issues fly high in the face of emotional lows. The dividing of the goods is an especially fun game (more sarcasm here). Popular family arguments I have heard from my clients begin with, "That toilet paper means so much to me, as does the sofa and home in Florida." Will the fun never end? The game of inheritance, otherwise known as "You can't have it, it's mine," is not generally a topic during the question-and-answer period of a reading. Rather, the pain in my client's heart as it pertains to inheritance is. Maintaining perspective is no easy task when sorrow has hold of the heart. Emotional wounds resulting from misplaced grief stamp the heart with darkness.

Our departed loved ones do not care who has what bauble. They do care how we feel about them. I have been the conduit for more than one apology from the astral lips of someone who has crossed over. As a way to heighten consciousness, remember that each moment of your life is being recorded. How will you feel about the outtakes?

Have you ever played a board game and become completely engrossed in it? When the game was over, did you find that you had been so thoroughly involved that your focus was not on food, work, or even the time? When this incarnation is over, you may feel much the same. You were so immersed in your task that you forgot it was just a game. Or a playground, or classroom for the enrichment of the soul. In the end, you may find that the meaning of life never had anything to do with the amount of wealth you obtained or stuff you gained. It had everything to do with the abundance of love you exchanged.

CONCLUSION

Wherever we may come alive,
that is the area in which we are spiritual.
—David Steindl-Rast

A True Act of Soul

Our soul's development is measured by our reaction to life circumstances and how well we hold on to our willingness to love. Taking the steps necessary to fulfill our spirit's goal is what makes us sparkle. Valuing emotions, our own and those of others, is a true act of soul that significantly enhances our intuition. It requires personal alignment and a sense of self. When used honorably, the intuitive process helps build relationships, businesses, self-confidence, and soul.

My goal in writing *The Happy Medium* has been to present the intuitive process in its elemental state, to validate your own psychic abilities, and to provide sound tools and techniques that help you hone them. Visits from the other side resemble long-distance hugs. If you feel the presence of a loved one who has crossed over, it does not mean you are unsound. It is the body that dies, not the soul, and certainly not the love shared. On some level, you are already aware of this. When you act on an intuitive impulse, you are celebrating one of the thoroughly joyful aspects of life on this planet. That calm, guiding inner voice is a natural part of you and deserves to be honored. What is *not* natural is ignoring it. Remember to trust your gut, follow your heart, and use your head. You hold, and have always held, your own means to a priceless piece of bliss: your inheritance, your birthright, your own intuition.

Tools and Techniques:
Final Exam

Once again, consider me your "spirited" guide for the final Tools and Techniques portion of *The Happy Medium*. Please choose the best answer or answers.

1. An exit interview is:

   A. Conducted prior to being assigned a seat in the emergency exit row on an airplane.

   B. A meeting between the soul and the soul's guides at the end of an incarnation to discuss how effectively the soul followed its own path.

   C. A meeting between the authorities and someone who witnessed a drive-by insight and is willing to testify in a court of law.

Answer is B.

2. A relationship junkie is:

    A. Someone who adores eating sweets with the love of his or her life.

    B. Someone who saves every memento from past love affairs.

    C. Someone who is addicted to the initial stages of love, who craves only the emotional buzz of a relationship.

Answer is C.

3. The term "check-in baggage" refers to:

    A. Any bag made by Ralph Lauren, such as Polo.

    B. Emotional baggage that places too much weight on our hearts, so that we cannot carry it without getting some qualified support. When we cannot bear the weight, we need to have it checked.

    C. Something only trance mediums are allowed to carry so they can sit in the emergency exit rows.

Answer is B.

4. You know you are psychic because:

    A. Everyone is born with some intuitive abilities.

    B. You have studied this phenomenon for years and can properly spell phenomenon.

    C. You have always looked good in a turban and watched a lot of *The Twilight Zone* as a child.

Answer is A.

5. What holds some of our most powerful karmic lessons?

    A. Our hands

    B. Karma baskets found at all discount stores

    C. Initial wounds

Answer is C.

6. Dead people are always:

   A. Grateful Dead fans.

   B. Crossed-over souls.

   C. Out on Halloween.

Answer is B.

7. None of us are ever alone because:

   A. We are all interconnected through our souls.

   B. Our guides are eternally nearby.

   C. Those who have loved us and love us still sit by our side in memory and in spirit as we grieve, marry, give birth, love, and die ourselves. We are not alone and never will be.

Answer is all of the above.

8. If you have reached this stage of your development and this page, you are:

   A. Ready for a beer.

   B. Able to spell the word metaphysics.

   C. Psychic and savvy.

Answer is C.

9. Decent boundaries are:

   A. The building blocks of intuitive work of any kind.

   B. Toy blocks for toddlers found at Ugoofed.com.

   C. Predominantly for women.

Answer is A.

10. Life after death pertains to:

   A. Life continuing after the body dies.

   B. A superior soap opera on channel 2 at 2:00.

   C. A radical new rock band.

Answer is A.

11. Intuitive insights ensue:

   A. After lunch if chocolate is consumed.

   B. Only during a full moon.

   C. Every day—we simply need to be aware of them.

Answer is C.

12. The essential components to happiness are:

   A. Great food, money, good looks, and a cat.

   B. Loving and accepting who you are, which enables you to stay on the path your soul intended you take before you were born.

   C. Plenty of fresh air, and fruit such as prunes.

Answer is B.

13. An outstandingly effective way to grow psychically is to:

   A. Gain an understanding of what you are feeling and why.

   B. Look spooky and offer everyone you know a reading, free of charge.

   C. Decipher your intuitive code.

Answer is A and C.

14. Kicking an uninvited disembodied spirit out of your space requires:

   A. A good sense of boundaries and a good sense of humor.

   B. Kickboxing lessons.

   C. Homemade chicken soup.

Answer is A.

15. You know your intuition is on the mark when:

    A. Folks at the Psychic Hotline call *you*!

    B. After making a decision with the help of your intuition, you continue to feel calm and balanced about your choice.

    C. You are having a good hair day.

Answer is B.

16. "Follow your heart, trust your gut, and use your head":

    A. Was a popular Beatles tune in the 1960s.

    B. When followed, helps align you and enables you to make balanced decisions. Only works if you use it!

    C. Is the national contact-sport tagline.

Answer is B.

Bonus Question

17. The fingerprint of the soul is:

    A. Love.

    B. Taken once you reach heaven. "They" want to make sure you are who you say you are. No funny business is permitted over there.

    C. A new Korean restaurant specializing in spiritual music and kimchi.

Answer is A.

Scores are based on your sense of humor rather than your intuitive senses. If you laughed even once during this exam, you passed!

Glossary of Terms

The following glossary of terms is meant to prepare you in advance, so you can psychically buckle up and not be victim to a precognitive hit-and-run or drive-by relationship. As a bonus, perhaps your instincts will be sharp enough to help you avoid getting sideswiped by the boomerang effect.

- Boomerang Effect: The law of cause and effect in fast-acting action.

- Carry-on or Check-in baggage: Emotional baggage or issues. The weight these difficulties place in our hearts and the way we carry them determines the size of the bag! If we cannot bear the weight, we need to have the bag checked—meaning, get counseling.

- Code of Ethics: The universal code demanding that all action is taken for the highest good of all.

- Dead People: Significant someones on the other side.

- Drive-by Insights: People who produce drive-by insights on regular basis usually have some boundary work to do. Typically, the boundary-lacking sensitive person blurts out highly personal yet insightful information about another person in close proximity.

- Drive-by Relationships: Relationships that begin and end quickly. They leave one person feeling as though they were a victim of a hit-and-run, and the other person with a fast, emotional high.

- Exit Interview: A meeting between the soul and the soul's guides at the end of an incarnation to discuss the soul's progress.

- Happy Medium: A medium who has and manages to maintain balance. Usually they know how to trust their gut, follow their heart, and use their head.

- Head Blind: People who have made a choice to turn away from their inner truth out of fear of facing their own demons. They are not at all connected with their higher selves and are exhausting to work with on an intuitive level.

- Initial Wounds: The wounds we placed in our paths before we arrived in body. They hold some of our most powerful karmic lessons.

- Inner Parents: Guides.

- Innocent Insights and Drop-in Insights: Insights that drop in unexpectedly. They appear as clear flashing thoughts or impromptu waking visions. They are spontaneous and lack a feeling of malevolence and tend to catch everyone by surprise. Children are famous for them.

- Intuitive Code: The language of intuition.

- Mediums: People who have a telepathic connection with souls of both worlds.

- Precognitive Hit-and-run: An animated and powerful inner-eye picture of a future event spontaneously described in detail.

- Retrocognition and Precognition: Knowledge of events of the past or future, respectively, which could not be known by ordinary means. Retrocognition is also known as post-cognition.

My final words of advice? Always remember, prior to having a reading, to maintain a healthy perspective, take information with a grain of salt, and find a happy medium.

Who we are is defined by our reaction
to the circumstances life brings our way.
—The Happy Medium

ACKNOWLEDGMENTS

My heartfelt love and immense gratitude goes out to my sweet and understanding husband Jason Rein, whose love and support has never once faded. My profound love and deep appreciation is forever extended to my wise and beautiful children, Cole, Aaron, and Sophia. Your love is inspiring and infinitely priceless, and I am blessed beyond words to have you in my life.

I also extend my love and appreciation to my Great-Aunt Ide Schertzer for her style and everlasting affection, my incredible, supportive, and loving in-laws Marv and Lois Rein (special mention to Lois for her wit and love of grammar!), my encouraging and enthusiastic Aunt Muriel and Uncle Leon, and my entire humor-filled family, especially my siblings Cindy, Marshall, Bob, Jeff, and Michelle and their families (including those who don't wish to be mentioned). My deep appreciation is extended to Ellyn and all of my phenomenal Wolfenson cousins for their never-ending support and consistent belief in my shine.

My profound gratitude goes out to the amazing, loving friends whose support of my work on *The Happy Medium* presents itself on these many pages: Dawn Hagelee, Wendy Lovell-Smith, Colleen Rossman, Liz Rockler, and Antoinette Ferdelman. Special thanks to the wise and sweet Michelle Bloom for forever supporting and believing. Thank you also to *all* of my many dear and marvelous friends, near and far. I could fill a book with your names, and truly love and appreciate you all!

My sincere appreciation and admiration is extended to the staff at Llewellyn Worldwide, including my publicist Courtney Kish, my innovative and supportive acquisitions editor Carrie Obry, and my remarkably talented and tactful production editor Sandy Sullivan.

I would also like to thank Ruth for being so extraordinaire! Much appreciation also to the Cannings and Aizmans for their loving encouragement. And to Jon Lurie, many thanks to you for thinking outside of the box. My profound respect and gratitude is extended to my clients on both sides of the veil—special thanks to the ones on this side who have so graciously extended permission to print their stories in *The Happy Medium*. And my sincere gratitude is extended to all of you who are reading this book; thank you for the opportunity to tap your soul and touch your heart.

Unquestionably, my highest of thanks to the Highest of Powers. Whenever I lovingly address you, Universe, you always answer. And my heart is full as I broadcast my appreciation once again to Faye Livon. Thank you for being my guiding light. I see this world, and the next, more clearly because of you. These words of appreciation are the last written in *The Happy Medium*. So as I type them and press the *send* button on my computer, they fly to my editor and, with gratitude, to you, Dad, where you are now—in my heart, and on the other side.

BIBLIOGRAPHY

Brener, Anne. *Mourning & Mitzvah: A Guided Journal for Walking the Mourner's Path*. Woodstock, VT: Jewish Lights Publishing, 1993.

Gibran, Kahlil. *The Prophet*. New York: Alfred A. Knopf, 1923.

Hay, Louise L. *You Can Heal Your Life*. Santa Monica, CA: Hay House, 1984.

Hayward, Susan. *A Guide for the Advanced Soul: A Book of Insight*. Camarillo, CA: DeVorss & Company, 2008.

Keyes, Ken, Jr. *Handbook to Higher Consciousness*. London: Eden Grove Editions, 1997.

Newton, Michael. *Destiny of Souls: New Case Studies of Life Between Lives*. St. Paul, MN: Llewellyn Publications, 2000.

————. *Journey of Souls: Case Studies of Life Between Lives.* St. Paul, MN: Llewellyn Publications, 1994.

————. *Life Between Lives: Hypnotherapy for Spiritual Regression.* St. Paul, MN: Llewellyn Publications, 2004.

Nichol, David, and Bill Birchard. *The One-Minute Meditator.* New York: Perseus Publishing, 2001.

Orloff, Judith. *Intuitive Healing.* New York: Three Rivers Press, 2000.

Shain, Merle. *Hearts That We Broke Long Ago.* New York: Bantam Press, 1983.

Targ, Russell, and Jane Katra. *Miracles of Mind: Exploring Nonlocal Consciousness and Spiritual Healing.* Novato, CA: New World Library, 1998.

Weiss, Brian L. *Many Lives, Many Masters.* New York: Fireside, 1988.

Williamson, Marianne. *Enchanted Love: The Mystical Power of Intimate Relationships.* New York: Simon & Shuster, 1999.

————. *Illuminata: A Return to Prayer.* New York: Riverhead, 1995.

————. *A Woman's Worth.* New York: Random House, 1993.

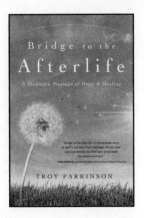

BRIDGE TO THE AFTERLIFE
A Medium's Message of Hope & Healing
TROY PARKINSON

What if you could talk to the other side? What would you say? And what messages would the spirits have for you?

Spiritual medium Troy Parkinson, a rising star in the paranormal world, shares fascinating first-hand stories of his communications with the spirit realm.

Channeling spirits was the last thing that Troy Parkinson ever thought he'd do. A North Dakota native and self-described "ordinary guy," he first attended a spiritualist meeting when he was a college student in Boston. After receiving a message that night from his grandmother's spirit, he decided to pursue mediumship training through the world-renowned First Spiritual Temple of Boston. Parkinson now travels around the country, doing readings for large audiences and presenting workshops that teach people how to develop their own spirit-communication abilities. Troy's moving story and amazing messages from spirit will touch your heart, inspire your soul, and remind you that your loved ones are always with you.

978-0-7387-1435-6
240 pp., 6 x 9 $15.95

You Are Psychic

Debra Lynne Katz

Learn to see inside yourself and others. Clairvoyance is the ability to see information—in the form of visions and images—through nonphysical means. According to Debra Lynne Katz, anyone who can visualize a simple shape, such as a circle, has clairvoyant ability.

In *You Are Psychic*, Katz shares her own experiences and methods for developing these clairvoyant skills. Her techniques and psychic tools are easy to follow and have been proven to work by long-time practitioners. Psychic readings, healing methods, vision interpretation, and spiritual counseling are all covered in this practical guide to clairvoyance.

978-0-7387-0592-7
336 pp., 6 x 9 $16.95

Spanish edition:
Tú eres psíquico
978-0-7387-0877-5 $14.95

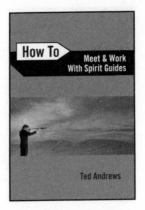

How to Meet & Work with Spirit Guides
Ted Andrews

We often experience spirit contact in our lives but fail to recognize it for what it is. Now you can learn to access and attune to beings such as guardian angels, nature spirits and elementals, spirit totems, archangels, gods and goddesses—as well as family and friends after their physical death.

Contact with higher soul energies strengthens the will and enlightens the mind. Through a series of simple exercises, you can safely and gradually increase your awareness of spirits and your ability to identify them. You will learn to develop an intentional and directed contact with any number of spirit beings. Discover meditations to open up your subconscious. Learn which acupressure points effectively stimulate your intuitive faculties. Find out how to form a group for spirit work, use crystal balls, perform automatic writing, attune your aura for spirit contact, use sigils to contact the great archangels, and much more! Read *How to Meet and Work with Spirit Guides* and take your first steps through the corridors of life beyond the physical.

978-0-7387-0812-6
216 pp., 5³⁄₁₆ x 8 $9.95

So You Want to Be a Medium?
A Down-to-Earth Guide
Rose Vanden Eynden

Are you fascinated by the spirit world? Wish you could communicate with loved ones on the Other Side? According to Spiritualist minister Rose Vanden Eynden, everyone possesses innate capabilities for spirit communication. Emphasizing the principles of modern Spiritualism, *So You Want to Be a Medium?* demonstrates how to enhance one's spiritual senses for working between worlds.

Through exercises involving meditation, breathing, dream work, symbols, and energy systems, the author teaches how to prepare one's mind and body for spiritual communication. Readers also learn about the many kinds of spirit guides and elemental energies, how to get in touch with them, and how to interpret their messages. Whether you're seeking to become a professional medium or simply interested in a closer connection to Creator, this fascinating guide to the spirit world can enrich your spiritual life—no matter what your religious background.

978-0-7387-0856-0
288 pp., 6 x 9 $14.95

Spanish edition:
¿Quieres ser médium?
978-0-7387-1045-7 $12.95

TO ORDER, CALL 1-877-NEW-WRLD
Prices subject to change without notice
Order at Llewellyn.com 24 hours a day, 7 days a week!

To Write to the Author

If you wish to contact the author or would like more information about this book, please write to the author in care of Llewellyn Worldwide and we will forward your request. Both the author and publisher appreciate hearing from you and learning of your enjoyment of this book and how it has helped you. Llewellyn Worldwide cannot guarantee that every letter written to the author can be answered, but all will be forwarded. Please write to:

Jodi Livon
⁒ Llewellyn Worldwide
2143 Wooddale Drive, Dept. 978-0-7387-1463-9
Woodbury, MN 55125-2989, U.S.A.

Please enclose a self-addressed stamped envelope for reply,
or $1.00 to cover costs. If outside U.S.A., enclose
international postal reply coupon.

Many of Llewellyn's authors have websites with additional information and resources. For more information, please visit our website at http://www.llewellyn.com.